THE NEW TESTAMENT SCOFIELD WORKBOOK

By C.I. Scofield, D.D.

ISBN: 9798379015367

This workbook is based on the 1907 Ninth edition of the *Course of Study: The Old Testament* originally that was originally published as part of a correspodence course by the Bible Institute of Los Angeles, California.

OUTLINE OF STUDY

SECTION I. THE SCRIPTURES

1. Inspiration: Its Nature and Extent.
   a. The testimony of Christ and of the writers.
   b. The proof from fulfilled prophecy.
2. The Divisions of the Scriptures
   (1) Structural or outward.
      a. Into Testaments.
      b. Into books (dates and writers).
      c. Into groups of books.
   (2) Spiritual—divisions by subject-matter.
      a. Dispensational divisions.
      b. Ethnic divisions (Jew, Gentile, etc.).
      c. Miscellaneous divisions (Saved and unsaved, salvation and rewards, standing and state, etc.).
3. The Interpretation of Scripture.
      a. Typical Scriptures.
      b Historical Scriptures.
      c. Prophetical Scriptures.

SECTION II. THE STUDY OF THE SCRIPTURES

1. How to study the Pentateuch and Historical Books.
   a. The types.
   b. Narratives.
   c. Prophetical portions.
2. How to study the Poetical Books.
   a. In general.
   b. Special books (Job, Canticles, etc.).
3. How to Study the Prophetical Books.

4, How To study the Gospels.
   a. Matthew.
   b. Mark.
   c.. Luke.
   d. John.
5. How To study the Acts and Epistles.
6. How To study the Revelation.

SECTION III. THE GREAT WORDS OF SCRIPTURE

1—Sin
2—-Sacrifice
3—Atonement
4—Redemption
5—Propitiation
6—Reconciliation
7—Righteousness;
8—Repentance;
9—Conversion;
10—Faith
11—Justification
12—Assurance
13 —Sanctification
14—Life;
15—Forgiveness;
16—Glory
17—Reward
18—Punishment
19—World
20—Church
21—Kingdom
22—Sonship
23-—Adoption, etc.

SECTION IV. GOD —FATHER, SON AND HOLY SPIRIT

The Father.

Old Testament names of God.

    b. The New Testament doctrine of the Fatherhood.

The Lord Jesus Christ.

His deity—Lord.

    b. His humanity—Jesus.

    c. His offices—Christ.

        (1) His prophetic office.

        (2) His priestly office.

Sacrificer.

Intercessor.

Advocate.

        (3) His kingly office.

The Holy Spirit.

    a. Personality.

    b. Deity.

    c. Offices.

SECTION V. THE SAINTS

1. What they were. The scriptural doctrine of man.

    a. By the new birth.

    b. By adoption.

    c. By appointment.

    d. By destiny.

SECTION VI. THE SERVICE OF SAINTS

1. The Enabling.

    a. Gifts of the Spirit. The guidance of the Lord.

2. The Conditions of Fruitful Service.

    a. Abiding.

    b. Cleansing.

    c. Filling.

    d. Prayer.

    e. Obedience.

3. The Ministry of the Word.

    a. The use of the Bible in personal work.

    b. What to preach.

    c. How to preach.

SECTION VII. THE FUTURE

1. Prophetical Epochs.

    a. The times of the Gentiles.

    b. The day of the Lord.

    c. The last days.

    d. The great tribulation.

    e. The millennium.

    f. The eternal state.

2. Prophetical Events.

    a. The fullness of the Gentiles.

    b. The parousia of Christ.

        (1) The first resurrection.

        (2) The rapture of the Church.

        (3) The bema of Christ.

        (4) The marriage of the Lamb.

    c. The glorious appearing.

    d. The judgment of the nations.

    e. The Millennium.

    f. The loosing of Satan and the revolt of the nations.

    g. The judgment of the great white throne.

INTRODUCTION

The New Testament Scofield Workbook is a project over a century in the making. The workbook is based on study material written by Dr. Cyrus I. Scofield and published as a correspondence course by the Bible Institute of Los Angeles, California. Dr. Scofield was one of the preeminent theologians and ministers of the early 1900s and a strong Futurist and Dispensationalist. The notes contained in this workbook were used as the basis of the Scofield Reference Bible in 1909. Updated by Scofield in 1917, the Scofield Reference Bible was one of the most popular study Bibles throughout the Twentieth Century, introducing many Christians to Scofield's dispensational views. The Reference Bible remains in print today.

The New Testament Scofield Workbook is the second of three books in the Scofield Workbooks series. The other two books cover the New Testament and a synthesis of the Bible. It is recommended that you start with the O.T. And N.T. books before engaging the Synthesis. It is our hope that this rigorous workbook will challenge you to dig deeply into God's Word. As it was a correspondence course, no answer key was published. This might be for the best as it will allow you to validate your findings through the guiding of the Holy Spirit. So, grab a highlighter and a pencil or pen and get ready to embark on a most satisfying spiritual journey.

SECTION II HOW TO STUDY THE SCRIPTURES

PART 5. THE GOSPELS AND ACTS

INTRODUCTION

1. The four Gospels record the birth of the Messiah foretold in Old Testament prophecy and prefigured in Old Testament type. They record also a selection from His works and sayings, and in full detail His death, resurrection and ascension. The Acts of the Apostles record the descent of the Holy Spirit, the formation of the church, and a selection of incidents and sayings connected with the extension of Christianity in the world. The five books, therefore, considered simply as history and biography, report the most important events in history.

2. The student is earnestly warned against the danger of beginning the study of the Gospels with a mind preoccupied by opinions, except as these may have been formed by preceding studies in the Old Testament. The Old Testament is the divinely given introduction to the New. Simply expect to find in the New Testament "Him of whom [loses in the law, and the prophets, did write, Jesus;" but expect to find Him infinitely more beautiful than any prophet's vision of Him. So far as possible read the Gospels as if for the first time you had closed the Old Testament and opened the New.

3. Another caution. Remember that primarily the mission of Jesus was to the Jews. He was "made under the law" (Gal. iv. 4), and "a minister of the circumcision for the truth of God, to confirm the promises made unto the fathers" (Rom. xv. 8). Expect, therefore, a strong Jewish and legal coloring up to the cross. Probation under the law lasted up to the cross. In the putting to death of Christ Jew and Gentile conspired, and the cross was the "judgment of this world" (John xii. 31-33). The death of Christ opened the way for grace to act, in the justification of the ungodly. The doctrines of grace are to be found developed in the Epistles. Foundationally those doctrines rest upon the Abrahamic covenant (Gen. xii. 1-4; xiii. 14-17; xv. 3-6; Gal. iii. 5-17); the gracious teachings of Christ; and, most of all, upon His sacrificial death.

4. Do not expect to find in the Gospels the doctrine of the church. In the Gospels the church is a subject of prediction, merely (Matt. xvi. 16-18). The great body of Christ's teaching has to do with the kingdom, not the church, and with His evangelistic labors for the salvation of the individuals to whom, in His earth-life, He spoke.

5. Do not expect to find in the Gospels a complete life of Christ. For some inscrutable reason it did not please God to cause to be made a record of all the sayings and doings of His Son (John xx. 30; xxi. 25). It may be questioned whether the efforts ceaselessly made to piece together the mosaic of recorded deeds and words into a continuous narrative have been greatly profitable. The combined effect of the Gospels is to set forth a unique Personality rather than the connected story of a life.

LESSON XLII

THE GOSPELS AND ACTS

MATTHEW

GENERAL REMARKS

Each of the Gospels has a distinct purpose, and that purpose gives the key to its structure and its interpretation. In the fulfillment of that purpose the writer, under the Holy Spirit, selected from the mass of the sayings and doings of Christ those words and incidents which develop and illustrate his distinctive purpose. As truth is many-sided, and as there is in the words and works of Christ a peculiar fullness of meaning, it often occurs that the same parable, or miracle, appears in two or three of the Gospels, while the great common testimony of all is that this unique four-fold Personage was made a sacrifice.

Matthew is "the book of the generation of Jesus Christ, the son of David, the son of Abraham" (Matt. i. 1). This connects Him at once with two of the Old Testament covenants; the Davidic covenant of royalty and the earlier Abrahamic covenant of redemption. There was to be a seed of Abraham, typified by Isaac, the son offered up, in whom all nations should be blessed; and there was to be a seed of David, typified by Solomon, to inherit Israel's throne. [See Section II., Parts 1,2, 4.] Of Jesus Christ in that two-fold character Matthew writes. Matthew, then, is the book of a certain King who died for the sins of His people. The key verses are i. 1, 21; ii. 2; the key-phrase, "the kingdom of heaven." This expression is peculiar to Matthew. The student will find the question of the various meanings of the biblical word "kingdom" fully discussed in Section III., "The Great Words of Scripture." Let it be said here that "kingdom of heaven," as used in Matthew, has three meanings.

1. It is used to indicate that earth-rule of Messiah, David's Son, described and predicted in the prophets. This is the kingdom "at hand" of John Baptist and of the earlier ministry of Christ. See Matt. iii. 2; iv.17; x. 5-7.

2. From (and including) Matt. xiii. the word is used of the mixed condition, tares and wheat—true children of the kingdom and children of the wicked one—growing together until the "harvest" at the end of this age.

3. In the prophetic portions of Matthew the expression is used in the first sense again. Those portions look beyond "the harvest," which is to be the end of the mixed state (Matt. xiii. 41-43, 47-50) now prevailing, and see the kingdom as covenanted to David and described in the prophets finally set up. To recapitulate:

From Matt. i. 1 to xii. 50 the "kingdom of heaven"' is identical with the Old Testament thought, plus the Sermon on the Mount, which is an amplification of the prophetic idea of "righteousness" as the special glory of the kingdom, e.g., Isa. xi. 4, 5; Jer. xxiii. 5, 6. The Sermon on the Mount describes the righteousness of which the prophets speak.

From Matt. xiii. 1 to xxiii. 39 it is the mixed state, though the true children of the kingdom are usually in the mind of the Lord in His instructions.

From Matt. xxiv. 1 to xxv. 46 the future is in view. This view includes "the harvest" of Matt. xiii., but goes no farther than the setting up of the perfected kingdom according to the prophetic description.

In other words, the whole present age, with the confusions brought in by the rejection of the King, was not in the vision of the Old Testament prophet. The revelation of it, as in Matt. xiii., was part of the prophetic ministry of Christ. See Matt. xiii. 11-17, where this is distinctly stated.

ANALYSIS OF THE BOOK

The book falls into three chief sections, and these again into divisions and subdivisions.

Section I. The Manifestation of Jesus Christ the Son of David. i. to xxv. inclusive.

Part 1. The official genealogy and birth of the King. i. The student will note how everything moves within prophetical lines; for the King's life had been written as prophecy before His advent turned prediction into history.

Part 2. The infancy and obscurity of the King. ii. Here again the fulfillment of prophecy is carefully noted. Messiah was born in Bethlehem because it was the city of David, and because the prophet Micah had said that Israel's future Governor should come out of Bethlehem.

Part 3. The kingdom "at hand." iii. to xii.

Note. "At hand" is a biblical term which is used in the sense of impending. It is never a positive affirmation that the person or thing said to be "at hand' will immediately appear, but only that no known or predicted event must intervene. When, for instance, Christ appeared to the Jewish people, the next thing, in the order of revelation as it then stood, should have been the setting up of the Davidic kingdom. In other words it was the next announced event. In the knowledge of God, not yet disclosed, lay the rejection of the kingdom (and King), the long period of the mystery form of the kingdom, the world-wide preaching of the cross, and the outcalling of the church. But this was as yet locked in the secret counsels of God. The, kingdom, as the next act in the mighty drama of God's purpose, was "at hand."

Part 3 falls into these subdivisions as follows:

(1) The King's herald, John Baptist, announces the kingdom as at hand, whereupon the King appears and is anointed. iii.

(2) The King withstands a three-fold testing of His humanity, His divinity and His royalty, and Himself announces the kingdom as at hand. iv.

(3) The King next declares the laws of the offered kingdom. v., vi., Vii.

Note. The Sermon on the Mount has a two-fold application.

(4) Literally, to the kingdom. In this sense it gives the divine constitution for the righteous government of the earth. Whenever the kingdom of heaven is established on earth it will be according to that constitution. In this sense the student will note that the Sermon on the Mount is pure law. It reenacts the decalogue (Matt. v. 17-19) with stringent additions (Matt. v. 21, 22, 27, 28). Here lies the deeper reason why the Jews rejected the kingdom. They had reduced "righteousness" to mere ceremonialism, and the Old Testament idea of the kingdom to a mere Solomonic affair of outward splendor and power. They were right in expecting a visible and powerful kingdom, but the glowing words of the prophets should have prepared them to expect also that only the poor in spirit and the meek could share in it (e.g., Isa. xi. 4). The seventy-second Psalm, which was universally received by them as a description of the kingdom, was full of this. For these reasons the Sermon on the Mount in its primary application gives neither the privilege nor the duty of the church. Under the law of the kingdom, for example, no one may hope for forgiveness who has not first forgiven (Matt. vi. 12, 14, 15). Under grace the Christian is exhorted to forgive lest he grieve the Holy Spirit of God whereby he is sealed unto the day of redemption, and is reminded 'that he himself is already forgiven (Eph. iv. 30-32).

(5 But there is a beautiful moral application to the Christian. It always remains true that the poor in spirit, rather than the proud, are blessed. And those who mourn because of their sins, and who are meek in the consciousness of them, will hunger and thirst after righteousness, and, hungering, will be filled. The merciful are "blessed" the pure in heart do "see God."

(6) The Anointed King, having announced the constitution of His kingdom, now authenticates' His divine power by mighty works. viii., ix. Twelve astonishing miracles are recorded in these two chapters. Through them

the King demonstrated His capacity to rule the earth. These group as:

a. Power over disease and hence to forgive sin, since divine authority is required for either.

b. Power over nature.

c. Power over evil spirits.

d. Power over death.

(7) The Anointed King, having announced the constitution of the kingdom, and demonstrated His power, sends heralds to announce to Israel the kingdom as "at hand." x.

(8) The King discloses the virtual rejection of the kingdom announced as "at hand." xi., xii.

Note. The student should note that, while the formal and official rejection comes later, and after the final offer of the King according to Zechariah (Matt. xxi. 1-5; Zech. ix. 9), it is in chapters xi. and xii. that our Lord points out how, really, His rejection is already apparent. That generation would have neither John Baptist nor Himself (xi. 16-19). The cities in which His mightiest works had been done had not been aroused to faith (xi. 20-24) and there remains for them a sorer judgment than that which had been sent upon Sodom. For a moment the course of kingdom testimony is suspended, and a magnificent gospel appeal is uttered (xi. 28-30). Returning to His place as Son of David, He conforms to the Davidic type, permitting an action which He defends by quoting what David did in the day of his rejection (xii. 1-4). Performing a gracious action, the Pharisees begin to plot His assassination (xii. 9-14). Then follows a quotation from Isaiah which brings into view blessing for the Gentiles, thus implying His rejection by Israel. See Rom. xi. 9-12. A sign being asked He declares that but one "sign" remains to be given, and speaks, not of ascending David's throne, but of death and resurrection. It was time, therefore, that His disciples should be told that what lay before them in the immediate future ~ was not the kingdom of the prophets, but the kingdom in a form never revealed to the prophets, viz.:

Part 4. The kingdom in mystery. xiii. to xxiii.

(1) The King describes in seven parables the state of the kingdom from its rejection by the Jewish people to the end of this present period. xiii.

a. The Sower. Genesis of the kingdom in mystery.

b. The Wheat and Tares. The kingdom in mystery to consist of true children of the kingdom and children of the wicked one, or mere nominal Christians, such as compose the majority of state churches, Romanism, etc.

c. The Mustard Seed. The rapid but unsubstantial growth of the kingdom in mystery.

d. The Leaven. The kingdom in mystery will be so defiled with evil, working subtly, that even the true children of the kingdom will become contaminated with Pharisaism, Sadduceeism, Herodianism (world-conformity), malice, and wickedness. See Matt. xvi. 12; xxiii- 23-33; Luke: xii. 1; Mark, viii. 15; 1 Cor. v. 6-8.

e. The Hid Treasure. Israel during the continuance of the kingdom in mystery.

f. The Pearl. The church of this age, composed of the children of the kingdom united together into "one body" (1 Cor.xii. 12, 13; x. 17; Eph. iv. 15, 16) "without spot or wrinkle or any such thing" (Eph. v. 25-27).

g. The Net. The mixed state of the mystery form of the kingdom, as in the wheat and tares.

(2) The "goodness and severity" of the rejected King. xiv. to xxiii. This division records works of goodness toward the blinded and unthinking; stern warning's to the self-righteous and willful; and tender counsels to the true children of the kingdom soon to be bereft of their Lord. Three passages call for special remark. (1) In chapter

xvi. our Lord declares definitely the purpose obscurely announced in the Parable of the Pearl, viz., that He is to build a church. This is the first mention in Scripture of the church. The student will observe that it is a prediction. He does not say, "have built," or "am building," but "will build." In His apostles and personal disciples our Lord had gathered material—living stones —toward the future edifice; but these must be built together by the Holy Spirit. See 1 Cor. xii, 12,13: Eph. i. 22, 23; ii. 19-22. (2) In chapter xvii. the King exhibits, upon the mount of transfiguration, a model, as it were, of the future form of the kingdom. This was the fulfillment of His promise (Matt. xvi. 28). The elements are:

a. The scene was on earth, not in heaven.

b. The King was in glory, not in weakness, rejection and humiliation.

c. Three classes of persons were present: Natural men (Peter, James, John), a glorified saint (Elijah), who had been translated without dying, and a glorified saint (Moses), who had passed through death. After this pattern the future kingdom will be modeled. It will contain the living nations upon the earth in their natural bodies; the translated church (1 Thess. iv. 14-18); and the saints both of the Old Testament and the New, who have passed through death and resurrection. Both the latter classes will be glorified.

(3) In chapter xxi. the King makes his final offer of Himself to Israel. There was some emotional response, but it did not even arrest the approaching' official rejection.

Part 5. Predictions concerning the course and end of this age, the return of the King, and the setting up of the kingdom in glory according to the Old Testament prophets. xxiv., xxv.

Note. This part should be read in connection with Luke xxi. in the following order:

Matt. xxiv. 1-3	The three-fold question.
Matt. xxiv. 4-14	Introductory: The path of
Luke xxi. 8-19	true discipleship in this age.
Luke xxi, 20-24	The first answer. Covers the question as to the destruction of Jerusalem.
Matt. xxiv. 15-26	The great tribulation, in which this mystery— age ends.
Matt. xxiv. 27-30	The return of the King glory.
Matt. xxiv. 31	The "harvest" of Matt. xiii. 41.
Matt. xxiv. 32 to Matt. Xxv, 30	Counsels to the children of the kingdom in anticipation of the King's return.
Matt. xxv. 31-46	The judgment of the nations at the beginning of the next, or kingdom, age

Section II. Tue Manifestation or Jesus Christ the Son and seed of Abraham. xxvi., xxvii. According to the Abrahamic covenant as illustrated by the offering of Isaac, and interpreted by Gal. iii., all nations were to be blessed in the promised Seed, through His offering by the Father, as an only and well-beloved Son, who should be raised from the dead after accomplishing His sacrifice. [See Section II., Part 1, Lesson. XV.] Gen. xxii. 1-8; Heb. xi. 17-19; Gal. i. 13-16.

Section III. The Resurrection of Jesus the Son of David, the Son of Abraham. xxviii. The sacrificed Son of Abraham was also the royal Son of David, and the eternal Son of God. For three reasons, therefore, His resurrection was imperative.

1. It was not possible that He should be holden of death, because He was in Himself the Lord and Author of life. He was declared to be the Son of

God by the resurrection from the dead. Rom. i. 4; Acts ii. 24.

2. David, being a prophet, and "knowing that God had sworn with an oath to him, that of the fruit of his loins according to the flesh, He would raise up Christ to sit on his throne; he, seeing this before, spoke of the resurrection of Christ." Acts ii. 25-31.

3. As Seed of Abraham He was "delivered for our offences, and was raised again for our justification." Rom. iv. 25.

The book of the generation of Jesus Christ, the Son of David, the Son of Abraham, would not, therefore, be complete without a declaration of His resurrection. That event was at once the proof of His deity; the seal upon His prophetic and redemptive work, and the first step in His royal progress to David's throne. The book closes, appropriately, with instructions for a world-wide seed-sowing pending His return.

LESSON XLIII

THE GOSPELS AND ACTS— CONTINUED

MARK

GENERAL REMARKS

Mark is the Gospel of Jesus Christ, the Son of God, "who, being in the form of God, counted it not a prize to be grasped to be on an equality with God, but emptied Himself, taking the form of a servant." Phil. ii. 5,6. This emptying was of the glory which He "had with the Father before the world was," not of power, nor of knowledge. He ceased to be "in the form of God." No part of the Scriptures witnesses more definitely to the divine power of Christ than Mark. It is the book of the servant, but that servant is the Son of God. The key-verse is x. 45. The characteristic word is "straightway," which is a servant's word, signifying punctuality and diligence in service. Accordingly, Mark is preeminently a book of deeds, rather than words. Miracles have in Mark the leading place, as parables have in Matthew. It would be out of character for a servant to teach.

In strict harmony, too, with this central purpose of Mark to accentuate the service of Christ, are the omissions. There is no account of His genealogy, His miraculous conception, the adorations of the shepherds, the Magi, and Simeon, as in Matthew and Luke, nor of His preexistence, as in John. Neither do we find in Mark any law-giving like the Sermon on the Mount, nor are judicial sentences pronounced upon the nation - and the city, as in Matthew, the Gospel of the King. In eleven brief introductory verses Mark brings us to the mature Jesus, baptized with water and with the Spirit, and in the full activity . of his appointed service.

The student should, therefore, seek in the study of Mark to hold his mind to the contemplation of Christ the Servant of Jehovah. The best possible introduction to this study is the prayerful reading of Isa. xlii, 1-21; 1. 4-11; lii. 13 to liii. 12; Zech. iii. 8; Phil. ii. 5-8.

ANALYSIS OF THE BOOK

Mark falls into the following sections:
• Section I. Introduction. i.1-11.
• Section II. The Servant tested as to his fidelity. i. 12, 13.
• Section III. The Servant at work. i. 14 to xiii. 37.
• Section IV. The Servant "obedient unto death." mV, 1. to xv. 47,
• Section V. The Risen Servant, exalted to authority (Phil. ii. 9, 10), commissions servants, but continues His own service, "working with them, and confirming the word with signs following." xvi. 1-20.

LESSON XLIV

THE GOSPELS AND ACTS—CONTINUED

LUKE

GENERAL REMARKS

Luke is the Gospel of the human life of the Son of God. His offices and His relation to the typical and prophetical Scriptures are not made prominent. The key-phrase is "Son of Man." The key-verse, xix. 10, "For the Son of Man is come to seek and to save that which was lost." In harmony with this central thought, the writer gathers into his account of Christ distinctively those actions and words which demonstrate how entirely human He was. His genealogy is traced back to Adam; the most detailed account is given of. His mother, of His kindred according to the flesh, and of His birth, infancy and boyhood. So marked is this that it doubtless gave rise to the ancient tradition that Luke received his information concerning all of these details from Mary herself. The student should note in this gospel the sweetly human accounts of the birth and infancy of Christ which are omitted in the other narratives.

But the significance of the humanity of the Son of God cannot be understood apart from Rom. v. 14-19 and 1 Cor. xv. 21, 22, 45, 47. It will be seen:

1. That Adam is a contrasting type of Christ. That is, the excellencies of Christ are not illustrated by similar things of Adam used typically for that purpose, but are brought into relief by contrast with something quite different in him.

2. That Adam sinned and drew the old creation into disaster and death, while the last Adam became its savior and the head of a new creation secure from disaster through union with its sinless and triumphant Head.

3. That but two men have ever stood in this peculiar responsibility; the first Adam and the Last

Adam, the first man and the Second Man. All living are either "in Adam" or "in Christ." All were born "in Adam;" only the born again are "in Christ."

The student, therefore, should; in the study of Luke, the story distinctively of the Second Man, bear constantly in mind His representative character. As He is the Last Adam all the hopes of the race center in Him. If Satan could have seduced Him in the temptation, or slain Him in Gethsemane, his victory would have been final and complete. «2422 |

But He is more than the champion Man, He is also the model Man; and hence to be studied in the Gospel of the humanity as the Pattern wholly pleasing to God.

But the Gospel according to Luke does not suffer us to forget either His deity or His royalty. In the first chapter three things concerning Him are brought into intimate connection; are, indeed, embodied in the salutation of Gabriel (i. 26-35).

1. The Coming One shall be truly human: "Thou shalt conceive in thy womb, and bring forth a son."

2. The Coming One shall be the fulfiller of the Davidic covenant: "The Lord God shall give unto Him the throne of His father David." The "throne of David" is a designation as specific and unequivocal as "throne of the Caesars," or "throne of the Hohenzollerns." David did not reign from heaven over a spiritual kingdom, but from Jerusalem over a temporal kingdom.

3. The Coming One shall be very God: "The Holy Ghost shall come upon thee, and the power of the Highest shall overshadow thee; therefore also that holy thing which shall be born of thee shall be called the Son of God."

We may say, therefore, that in a very real sense Luke, while bringing into greatest prominence the humanity of Christ, is a more complete presentation of His Person than either Matthew, Mark, or John, taken singly.

ANALYSIS OF THE BOOK

Luke falls naturally into seven sections:

Section I. Tue Evangelist's Introduction. i. 1-4. There is no reason to doubt, but every reason to believe, that Luke, "the beloved physician," the companion of Paul, was the penman of this book. His introduction, rightly understood, sets forth both the occasion and the sources of the narrative. Unfortunately, in the English version this is greatly obscured. He does not say, "having had perfect understanding of all things from the very first" (i. 3), but, "having been made acquainted from above with all things accurately." The word rendered "from the very first" is translated "from above" in John iii. 3, 7 (margin), 31; John xix. 11; Jamesi. 17; it. 17, where "from the very first" would be palpable nonsense. In other words, so far from being a mere compilation of traditions, the book was written precisely because many had taken in hand such a perpetuation of current sayings, and it was therefore needful that the certainty of those things should be established by one instructed, not by eye-witnesses, but "from above." The introduction is, therefore, an affirmation of the inspiration of the book.

Section II. The Human Relationships, Birth and Early Life of the Second Man. 1.5 to ii. 52. The student will note how simply the humanity of our Lord is presented. He is born of a woman, after true gestation. He is wrapped in swaddling clothes and laid in a manger. When eight days old He is circumcised and named. He is brought into the Temple like any other Jewish child. He grows in mind and body; and, as a true human being, accountable to God, increases in His favor. He is, therefore, sweetly and perfectly human. But interwoven with all this, and inseparable from it, are things which go with no other infancy and youth. As yet unborn, He was "that holy thing" (i. 35) free from the Adamic taint because generated by a creative act. The birth is announced by angels. He is declared by them and by the Holy Ghost to be the Christ, and as a lad of twelve years He is in the full consciousness of His divine paternity. ii. 11, 26-29, 49. His deity does not efface His humanity, but neither does His humanity restrain or impair His deity. He is the Second Man. The first man was of the earth, earthy. His body was formed of the dust of the earth, and he became a living soul by the inbreathing of God. The Second Man is the Lord from heaven, receiving an unfallen human spirit, soul and body by a creation, not in the garden of Eden, but in the womb of a virgin.

Section III. Tue Baptism, Genealogy and Temptation of the Second Man. iii. 1 to iv. 13. Eighteen years elapse between the close of the second and opening of the third chapters. They witnessed the testing of the second Man by obscurity, poverty, toil, and delay. They left Him neither stolid, impatient, nor discontented. At last the voice in the wilderness rings out its stern message, and the time has come.

Baptized in Jordan He receives the anointing of the Holy Spirit and becomes officially what by birthright He has been, the Christ of God. iii. 1-22. Then follows His genealogy traced back through David and Abraham to the first man. iii. 23-38. Then follows the supreme testing of the Last Adam.

Three scenes in our Lord's life have in them, with much that is obvious and simple, many elements of profound mystery—the temptation, the agony in the garden, the crucifixion.

Concerning the temptation, it is evident that Satan's effort was in the first and last to induce the Last Adam to deliver Himself by the exertion of His divine power, so ending the testing by omnipotence instead of bearing it as the obedient man. The second temptation was the effort to induce Christ to take the rulership of earth as the gift of the usurper instead of from the Father. Satan will find such a king when the beast is manifested. Rev. xiii. 1, 2.

Thus fully prepared and tested, the Son of Man enters upon His three-fold human ministry of Prophet, Priest, and King. As has been said, His kingship is more distinctively Matthew's subject, but Luke by no means omits His royalty.

Section IV. The Ministry of the Prophet-King in Galilee. iv. 14 to ix. 50. The key to this section is the quotation by our Lord at the very outset of His ministry from Isaiah lxi. 1: "The spirit of the Lord is upon me because He hath anointed meto preach...to preach the acceptable year of the Lord." Luke iv. 17, 18. The student should contrast the prophetic anointing in Isaiah lxi. 1 with that in Isaiah xi. 1, 2. The former — is a reference to Jesus the Prophet, the latter to Jesse's Rod, the King. In Luke the Prophet-Christ is prominent; in Matthew the Royal-Christ; in John the Priest Christ. Observe, in this same fourth chapter, how our Lord at once takes the prophetic character (verse 24). The miracles peculiar to Luke, found in this section, are the miraculous draught of fishes (v. 4-11) and the raising of the widow's son at Nain (vii. 11-18). The peculiar parable is the two debtors (vii. 41-43).

The student will note that chapter ix, marks a carne point in the history of Jesus. His mighty works and words have not won the people, but have only aroused a stupid or superstitious amazement. Herod thinks Him to be John Baptist come to life, but the general opinion is that He is Elias or one of the old prophets. The ninth and tenth of Luke resemble the eleventh and ~ twelfth of Matthew in that they mark our Lord's recognition of His rejection (Luke ix. 7, 8, 19, 20; x. 12-23 with Matt. xi. 16-26; xii. 23-50), and it is significant that, as the King and Prophet wane, the Priest and Sacrifice come more into view. Matt. xi. 28; xii. 39, 40; Luke ix. 22, 44, 45; John xii. 23-33.

Section V. The Journey from Galilee to Jerusalem. ix. 51 to xix. 44. The words and works of our Lord on this journey are in harmony with the fact of His practical rejection as Messiah.

1. As that rejection is not yet officially consummated. He continues the offer of Himself to the nation, sending forth the seventy (x. 1-24), and, finally, entering the city according to Zech. ix. 9 as King.

2. But far more prominent in His teaching during this journey are words foreshadowing the dispensation of pure grace which is to be ushered in by His cross, and to run its course of mercy before He shall assume His crown. The sweetest pictures of grace to be found in Scripture are in the words of this journey. They are to be found in His answer to James and John (ix. 53-56); the parable of the good Samaritan (x. 25-37); His answer to Martha (x. 38-42); the marvelous three-fold parable of the lost sheep, the lost coin, and the lost son (xv. 1-32); the parable of the Pharisee and publican (xviii. 9-14); the third and fourth announcements of His death (xii. 50; xviii. 31-43), the healing of Bartimeus (xviii. 35- 43), and the conversion of Zacchaeus (xix. 1-10). All these speak, not of the Son of Man about to take David's place, but of the Son of Abraham about to take Isaac's place.

3. The teaching concerning the kingdom now has to do with its postponement. It becomes evident that there is to be a season of rejection, cross bearing and witnessing for His disciples. The instructions to the seventy have a wider range and application than a mere temporary mission to the villages along the line of march to Jerusalem would require, and faithful warnings are given as to hardships and -self-denials. ix. 57-62; x. 1-16. Our Lord begins to instruct the disciples concerning their relations to the world (xii. 1-34); and they are plainly taught that the King is to go away, to leave them in' the world as His servants and trustees, and to come again to reckon with them as such. xii. 35-48; xvii. 22-36; xix. 11-27. He gives, also, such warnings and instructions as they would require in view of the postponement of the kingdom. xi. 1-13; xii. 3-10; xiii. 1-9, 22-30; xiv. 1-35; xvi. 1-13; xvii. 1-10; xviii. 1-8.

4. During this journey He uttered words of final rejection and judgment for the nation, the Pharisees, Jerusalem, and the cities where His chiefest works had been wrought, and lifted the veil of the underworld, showing that destiny is fixed in this life. xi. 37-54; xiii. 31-35; xvi. 19-31; xix, 39 to xx. 47.

Section VI. Events at Jerusalem from the Final Offer of the King to the Burial of the Lamb of God. xix. 28 to xxiii. 56. This is the central and culminating theme of all of the four evangelists. It falls into two parts:

Part 1. From the triumphal entry to the end of the Olivet discourse. xix. 28 to xxi. 38. Nothing here presents special difficulty except the prophetic Olivet discourse. The student should recur to Lesson XLII., Part 5 of Section II. of that lesson, where the discourse is harmonized.

Part 2. From the treachery of Judas to the entombment. xxii. to xxili. 56.

Section VII. The Resurrection and Ascension of the Son of Man. xxiv. Three things are especially significant:

1. The full authentication by the risen Lord of the Old Testament as inspired and authoritative. xxiv. 25-27, 44-46.

2. The Son of Man's authoritative declaration that notwithstanding His rejection as King the prophecies concerning Him must yet be fulfilled.

3. The promise of the descent of the Spirit uttered before His crucifixion confirmed in connection with a commission to preach—not the kingdom, but "repentance and remission of sins" among all nations.

Thus, the resurrection ministry of our Lord adds nothing new. He took up the predictive teaching of His mortal life only to confirm and renew it. And He expressly linked it all with the Old Testament teaching of Moses and the prophets. The sufferings of Messiah are past; the glories of Messiah predicted by the prophets and confirmed by the Christ await fulfillment when the kingdom shall be set up.

LESSON XLV

The Gospels and Acts— Continued

John

General Remarks

Happily, the critical battle over the authenticity and authorship of John has been fought and won. Forty years ago the same class of minds which now either disbelieve or doubt the authority and Mosaic authorship of the Pentateuch disbelieved or doubted the Johanine authorship of the fourth Gospel. Now, on critical grounds alone, no considerable number of persons deny that John the beloved disciple wrote the Gospel which bears his name.

1. The purpose of this Gospel is plainly declared by the writer himself. "But these ['signs,' evidences, see verse 30] are written, that ye might believe that Jesus is the Christ, the Son of God; and that, believing, ye might have life through his name." xx. 31. In other words the Spirit by John marshals in order the proof of two propositions:

(1) That Jesus, the Personage who was born in Bethlehem, who grew up at Nazareth, taught and wrought and was crucified in Palestine, was the Christ; that is, the Messiah predicted and prefigured in Old Testament type and prophecy.

(2) That He was the Son of God; that is, divine. And the object of the writer in demonstrating those propositions was that there might be a basis for belief— the faith which secures the gift of eternal life.

His theme, then, is the Messiahship and deity of Jesus, to the end that belief might be produced and eternal life received.

He does not tell all that Jesus did (xx. 30), but selects from His sayings and doings, and from testimony borne to Him, such evidences as should produce belief in Him as the divine Christ.

2. It will be remembered that Christ (Messiah, Anointed) is our Lord's official designation, as Jesus is His personal name; and that as an official title it means that He is the foretold Prophet, Priest and King. We should, therefore, expect in a book written to prove His Christhood a manifestation of Him in each of those characters. This, indeed, we shall find. In a book written to demonstrate His deity we should expect to find the manifestation of that deity; and so we shall. In the other three Gospels this is both a necessary inference and directly asserted, but in John it is directly and repeatedly demonstrated.

In a book written to furnish a basis re belief we should expect to find much about faith; and so it is. In. all Matthew, Mark and Luke the word believe, in its various forms, occurs less than forty times; in John alone it occurs more than one hundred times.

In a book written to the end that through belief in a divine Christ eternal life may be received we should expect life to be a prominent subject. The three synoptists all together have the word about twelve times, and that in repetition of the same teaching; John alone has the word about thirty-five times, without renstingn.

3. Another significant word in John is "true." It is used commonly as meaning "real" or "final." "I am the true Vine" (xv. 1). Israel was a vine (Isa. v. 2), but proved to be a mere wild or natural vine; Christ means to say that He is the real and final Vine through whom fruit will be produced. See also, e.g., John vi. 31, 32.

4. The Gospel, according to John follows more exactly the actual order of time than either of the others, though Mark is also closely chronological. This fact gives the primary analysis of the book.

II. Analysis of the Book

This is three-fold: viz., Historical, or the book analyzed in the order of the events, spiritual, or the book analyzed in the order of the manifestation of the Christ as Prophet, Priest and King, as having a structure based upon types and prophecies; doctrinal, in the order of the 'great teaching's.

1. The Student will first study the book as a Narrative History of the Earth Life of the Son of God, According to the Following Analysis:

(1) Introduction. i. 1-28.

  a. The Word (*Logos*) as deity, eternal, preexistent. Verses 1, 2.

  b. The creator of all things, and the fountain of all life. Verses 3, 4.

  c. He was always a light, but uncomprehended. Verses 5, 9.

  d. The ministry of John. Verses 6-8, 15.

  e. Before this, and from the creation, He was "in the world," but unrecognized. Verse 10.

  f. The apostle anticipates the fact of the incarnation, and states in verses 11-13 its history, purpose, and result.

  g. The incarnation; the Eternal becomes flesh. Verse 14.

  h. This incarnation prepares a new dispensation in contrast with the Mosaic. That was legal; this is to be gracious. Verse 17. [See Section I., Lessons IV., VII.]

  i. The Logos (now declared to be the Son) is the revealer of the Father.

Note. That the order of events may be clearly in mind, the student should here read Matt. i. 1 to iv. 11; Mark i. 1-12; Lukei. 1 to iv. 13.

(2) The beginning of His ministry in Galilee. i, 29 to 11, 12.

(3) His first Judean ministry. ii. 13 to iv. 3.

(4) His journey back to Galilee. iv. 4 toiv. 44.

(5) His second Galilean ministry. iv. 45-54.

(6) His second Judean ministry. v. 1-47.

(7) His third Galilean ministry. vi. to vii. 9.

  Note. Matt. xv. 1 to xvi. 12, and Mark vii. 31 to viii. 26.

(8) His third Judean ministry.

  Note. The student will here read Matt. xvi. 13 to xix..2; Mark viii. 27 to x. 1; Luke ix. 18 to xiii. 35.

(9) His fourth Judean ministry. x. 22-39

(10) His ministry beyond Jordan. x. 40 to xi. 16.

  Note. The student will here read Luke xiv. 1 to xvii. 10.

(11) His fifth Judean ministry. xi. 17-53.

(12) His seclusion at Ephraim and Bethany. xi. 54-57.

  Note. The student will here read Matt. xix. 3 to xx. 34; Mark x. 2-52; Luke xvii. 11 to xix. 28.

(13) His last ministry and death in Jerusalem. xii. 1 to xix. 42.

Note. The student will read the parallel accounts in the other Gospels, viz., Matt. xxi. 1 to xxvii. 66; Mark xi. 1 to xv. 47; Luke xix. 29 to xxiii. 56.

 (14) His resurrection ministry. xx. 1 to xxi. 25.

Note. The student will read the parallel accounts in Matt. xxviii. 1-20; Mark xvi. 1-20; Luke xxiv. 1-53.

The book properly ends with xx. 31. Chapter xxi. is an epilogue to the fourth Gospel, and the best possible introduction to the book of Acts. Init Jesus is seen in the relation to the disciples and their work which He is to maintain throughout the whole of this dispensation. The points are:

(1) He is invisible to the world.

(2) He is in direct personal communication with His servants.

(3) He is absolute master over their service and over their lives. Nothing is left to their wisdom or will. Indeed, the key-note of the chapter is found in the phrase, "If I will." It is no longer Jesus entreating, but Jesus commanding. As Master He:

  a. Directs where service shall be rendered. Verse 6.

Note. The student, remembering that this primary analysis of John is historic and chronological, should here read from the other Gospels in the following order, as the events therein narrated intervene between the second Judean and third Galilean ministries.

Matthew	Mark	Luke
iv. 12.	i 14, 15	iii. 19, 20.
-	-	iv. 14-30.
iv. 13-17.	-	iv. 31.
iv. 18-22.	i. 16-20.	v. 1-11.
-	i. 21-28.	iv. 32-37.
viii. 14-17.	i. 29-34.	iv. 38-41.
iv. 23, 24.	i. 35-39.	iv. 42-44.
viii. 2-4.	i. 40-45.	v. 12-16.
ix. 2-8.	ii. 13, 14.	v. 27, 28.
xii. 1-8.	ii. 23-28.	vi. 1-5.
xii. 9-14.	iii. 1-6.	vi. 6-11.
xii. 15-21.	iii. 7-12.	
-	iii. 13-19.	vi. 12-16.
iv. 25 to viii. 1.		vi. 47-49.
viii. 5-13.	iii. 20, 21.	vii. 1-10.
-		vii. 11-17.
xi. 2-19.		vii. 18 to viii. 3.
xii. 22-37.	iii. 22-30.	
xii. 38-45.		
xii. 46-50.	iii. 31-35.	viii. 19-21.
xiii. 1-23.	iv. 1-25.	viii. 4-18.
xiii. 24-52.	iv. 26-34.	
viii. 18-22.		ix. 57-60.
viii. 23-27.	iv. 35-41.	viii. 22-25.
viii. 28 to ix. 1.	v. 1-20.	viii. 26-36.
ix. 10-17.	ii. 15-22.	v. 29-39.
ix. 18-26.	v. 21-43.	viii. 40-56.
ix. 27-34.		
xiii. 53-58.	vi. 1-6.	
ix. 35 to xi. 1.	vi. 6-13.	ix. 1-6.
xiv. 1-12.	vi. 14-29.	ix. 7-9.
	vi. 30.	ix. 10.

b. Supplies the needs of His servants. Verses 9-13.

c. Commissions whom He will to serve. Verses 15-17.

d. Appoints the time and manner of the death of His servants. Verses 18, 19.

e. Teaches that service is a personal not corporate affair. Verse 22.

f. Shows that when service is directed by Him, divine power will accompany it. Verse 6.

These men were experienced fishermen and knew that water well, yet caught nothing until they came under the. Pine direction of the Master. -

Having thus followed the narrative of the human life of the Son of God, the student should recur to John's declared purpose, to show that Jesus is the Christ, the Son of God, and note the proof adduced. This is five-fold, as classified by our Lord Himself (John v. 33-47), viz.:

(1) The witness of Christ Himself. iii. 13, 17, 19; iv. 26;; v. 17-23; vi. 33, 57; vii. 28, 29, 33; viii, 42, 58; ix. 35-385 x. 30-34; ae xvii. 5; xx. 26-29.

(2) The witness of John the Baptist i. 15, 19-36; ili. 23-36. John was universally acknowledged to be a prophet. He had nothing to gain, but, as a mere religious leader, everything to lose, by the recognition of Jesus as the divine Christ. i. 36, 37; iii. 26, 30. He was of exalted character, unselfish, humble, consistent. His testimony, therefore, was of the highest value.

(3) The witness of the works. Seven "works" (out of thousands) are selected by the Spirit for record by John. The eighth miracle (the miraculous draught of fishes, xxi. 6) is in the epilogue, and, therefore, not referred to in xx. 31.

The seven evidential works are:
• The water made wine. ii. 1-11.

• The nobleman's son. iv. 46-51.
• The healing at Bethesda. v. 1-9.
• The five thousand fed. vi. 1-14.
• The walk upon the Sea. vi. 16-21.
• The blind man healed. ix. 1-7.
• The raising of Lazarus. x1. 40-44.

The two words used by John to designate these miracles are significant: "signs" and "works." Signs, because they were often illustrations of some central doctrine taught by Him. Works, because they were manifestations of His deity. These works group as follows:

a. Evidences of creative power.
The water made wine.
The five thousand fed.

b. Evidences of recreative power.
The healing of the nobleman's son.
The healing at the pool of Bethesda.
The healing of the man born blind.

c. Evidence of power over nature.
The walk upon the sea.
Evidence of power to give life.
The raising of Lazarus.

(4) The witness of the Father.

a. The sealing of the Spirit. vi. 27; 1. 33, 34.

b. The new and heavenly doctrine of Jesus. vii. 15, 16, 45, 46.

c. The powerlessness of His enemies until the time came for His sacrifice. vii. 28-30.

d. The audible voice of the Father speaking from heaven. xii. 28-30.

e. The resurrection of Jesus. xx. 1-9.

(5) The witness of the Scriptures.

This was Jesus' appeal to the Old Testament, whose types and predictions He was fulfilling. [See Lesson II., Section I.]

LESSON XLVI

The Gospel and Acts– Continued

John–Continued

2. Spiritual Analysis of the Book in the Order of the Manifestation of Jesus the Christ The Son of God, as Prophet, Priest, and King.

(1) The offer of Christ as Prophet. ii. 13 to iv. 54. [See, for.a definition of a prophet's function in Israel, Section II., Part 4]. It will be seen that Jesus here enters upon the proper office of a prophet, as a religious patriot and reformer. His words in ii. 16 suit His action in verses 14, 15. The student will observe the significant; quotation from Ps. lxix. That Psalm. should be read as expressive of the thoughts of Jesus at this time. He well knew that the nation would reject Him as Prophet and King and that His real ministry for them would be priestly and sacrificial.

After this introductory act, Christ continues His prophetic ministry in the precise order which He afterward enjoined for the missionary activities of the church,—Jerusalem, Judea, Samaria, and then on to "Galilee of the Gentiles."

(2) The Christ takes His place as Priest. v. 1, 2. This is a highly symbolic act. Going up to Jerusalem He enters by the sheep-gate, the priestly entrance, the place of inspection of sacrifices. It is not meant, of course, that Jesus asserted His priestly office—that would have been premature—but that in a book so highly symbolical such an entrance is full of beautiful significance.

Note. The prophetic office work of Christ does not cease with this priestly act, but He is now to be thought of as Israel's promised Prophet-Priest. He still speaks to Israel, but is drawing near the altar.

(3) The offer of Christ "as King. xii. 12-18. This is one of the incidents recorded by all of the evangelists, and therefore deemed of such a

moment as to demand a four-fold emphasis. But in John the kingship of Christ is far less prominent than His prophetic and priestly offices. It is the book of the divine Prophet-Priest. As Prophet He unfolds the profoundest truths; as Priest He offers Himself without spot to God.

From i. 1 to ii. 13 He is the Son of God come down to manifest God. From ii. 14 to iv. 54 He is the divine Prophet. From v. 2 to xii. 12 He is the divine Prophet-Priest. From xii. 12 to the end He is the divine and royal Prophet-Priest. It is not that each division of the Gospel under the spiritual analysis is limited to a manifestation of Him in one particular character, but rather that successively these characters accumulate upon Him, until, in the last nine chapters we have before us the august figure of deity, manifest as Jesus, the final Prophet, Priest and King, not of Israel only, but of all humanity.

Immediately, He enters upon a series of deeds and words conformed symbolically to the temple order. The student will remember that the temple was approached through three exterior courts, those of the Gentiles, of the women, and of Israel. These may be regarded as Galilee ("of the Gentiles," Matt. iv. 15), Samaria (where Christ's principal ministry was to a woman), and Judea. Figuratively, the kingly Prophet-Priest had passed through these courts in coming up to Jerusalem, and now, in chapter xii., He enters the temple proper. Here, also, it will be remembered, there was a three-fold arrangement: the court, where were the brazen altar of sacrifice and then the laver; the holy place, where the priests ate the sin-offering (Lev. vi. 26), an act of fellowship or communion; and the holy of holies, into which the High Priest entered alone. If the student will hold in mind this arrangement, the beautiful structure of chapters xii. to xvii. will be at once evident.

a. In chapter xii. our Lord approaches the brazen altar of sacrifice. xii. 23-33.

b. In chapter xiii. He comes to the laver. Ex. xxx. 17-21. [See Section 1I, Part I.]

c. In chapters xiv. to xvi. He passes on toward the holy place in intimate fellowship with the disciples, His attendant priests (Rev. i. 6), discoursing of heavenly things, and of priestly privilege and service.

d. In chapter xvii. our High Priest enters, in spirit, the holy place to offer the great high-priestly prayer of intercession. Thus, in figure, the whole of redemption is unfolded. All begins with: the sacrifice. There is no union with the race by the incarnation of the Son of God, as unbiblical theology asserts. Christ's humanity was real, but not racial. He was the unfallen 'fast Adam." Hence He distinctly says: "Except a corn of wheat fall into the ground and die it abideth alone" (xii: 24). The cross is the true judgment (xii. 31-33). There is where destiny is fixed. The judgments of Matt. xxv. and Rev. xx. are merely declarative.

But those saved by the lifted-up Son of Man contract, alas, defilements, and these must be cleansed if they are to have part (literally, partnership, fellowship) with Him. This is dealt with in the laver chapter (xiii). Salvation is not in question; the point is that He cannot have fellowship with uncleanness. As Jesus only could save, so He only can cleanse those whom He has saved (xiii. 8). But this is not all. These saved and cleansed ones are in the world. This means for them danger on the one hand and opportunity on the other. This engages our Lord in chapters xiv. to xvi. They are to have no fears as to their eternal welfare (xiv. 1-3); their weakness and ignorance will be met by the coming of the Holy Spirit; and they will be the continual objects of the prevailing intercessions of their High Priest in the holy of holies. Thus are the marvels of the love of God told out. The sacrificial death of Christ secures for the believer perfect safety and assurance of the heavenly mansions. The Holy Spirit will come to be his Comforter, Guide, Teacher, and the power of his service. His rule of life is, simply, to abide in Christ. As to his dangers and necessities, these will

be the subject of the prayers of his Melchizedek High Priest, who ever liveth to make intercession for him. Could grace go farther?

Note. The student is affectionately exhorted to make chapters xii. to xvii. his meditation; asking with humbleness of heart that the Spirit may so take of these things of Christ and show them to him as that they shall become precious realities.

T<small>HE</small> G<small>REAT</small> D<small>OCTRINES OF THE</small> G<small>OSPEL</small> A<small>CCORDING TO</small> J<small>OHN</small>.

It will be observed that, as the fourth Gospel is less occupied with details than the other three, so it is surpassingly rich in truth. Of these, three receive especial emphasis, viz., the deity of Christ, regeneration, and resurrection.

Note. The student will find his attention drawn to the doctrines of fohn by the Examination. It is desired that the student shall find these by personal search—the purpose of the lessons being to guide the student to the fountain so that he may drink for himself.

1. C<small>HRIST'S</small> <small>TEACHING CONCERNING</small> G<small>OD</small>.

(1) The essential Being of God.

(2) The Father.

    a. What He is.

    b. What He does.

(3) The Son.

    His Deity

a. Direct assertion.

    By the Apostle.

    By John Baptist.

    By Nathanael.

    By our Lord Himself.

    By the Father.

    By Peter.

    By Thomas.

b. Indirect testimony.

    By the works.

    He received human worship.

He displayed omniscience.
By His resurrection.
By His ascension.
His Humanity.

a. Direct testimony.
By the Apostle.
By Himself.
By His enemies.

b. Indirect testimony.
By purely human actions.
By tests tangible.
By death.

(4) The Holy Spirit.
a. His personality.
b. His work.

2. The doctrine of the new birth.

(1) The necessity of regeneration.

(2) The method of regeneration.

(3) The human side of regeneration: what man must do.

(4) Where faith must see Christ to secure regeneration.

(5) The results of regeneration.

3. The doctrine of eternal life.

(1) What eternal life is.

Note. This subject is greatly developed in the first epistle of John, and by Paul in Colossians and Galatians. Briefly: Eternal life is the life of Christ Himself imparted to the believer by the Holy Spirit through the new birth, but not detached from Him. The best definition is Gal. ii. 20; the simplest passages, 1 John, i..1, 2; v. 11; 12; Col. iii. 3, 4:

(2) Christ's personal relation to the doctrine.

(3) Who may have eternal life.

(4) How eternal life is received.

(5) When eternal life is received.

(6) What Christ teaches as to the permanency of the gift.

Note. The sides should read the Gospel carefully through, making a note of every passage where eternal life is mentioned, and then classify the passages under the six divisions here indicated.

4. Christ's doctrine of the resurrection.

(1) As concerned Himself.

(2) As concerns believers.

(3) As concerns unbelievers.

5. Christ's doctrine of the future state.

(1) As concerned Himself.

(2) As concerns believers.

(3) As concerns unbelievers.

LESSON XLVI

THE GOSPEL AND ACTS—CONTINUED

THE ACTS OF THE APOSTLES

GENERAL REMARKS

This book records the beginnings of church life, and the first missionary operations under the great commission, "Go ye into all the world and preach the gospel to every creature." It covers a period of about thirty years; and, if. we. include the four preceding years, the time covered, namely, from A.D. 26 to A.D. 65, and the events :recorded, constitute the most momentous epoch in human history. The right understanding of this book requires that the following facts be held in mind:

1. It records the advent of the third Person of the Trinity. Just as, in the Gospels, everything at once took color from the fact that the Son of God had come to earth, so the great distinctive fact in the Acts and Epistles is the presence on earth of the Holy Spirit. As has often been said, the fifth of the New Testament historical books ought to be called the Acts of the Holy Spirit. With the exception of Peter and Paul, the apostles are not more prominent in the Acts than in the Gospels. It is the Holy Spirit who fills and dominates the scene. This may be more clearly seen if the whole Bible is considered. In the Old Testament God—the Trinity Himself—is seen at work for man. The Persons are not clearly discriminated, though plurality is evident; it is the unity, the oneness, of God which is emphasized. In the four Gospels God, in the person of the Son, is seen at work with men. That brought to light the Trinity. In the Gospels the Trinity is asserted (Matt. xxviii. 19); inferred (John xiv. 13-17); and manifested (Luke ii. 21, 22). But it is the Son who fills the scene. As the time drew near for His departure He began to speak of another divine One who should come. Especially was His last discourse (John xiv. to xvi.) filled with talk of the impending advent of the Spirit. He was to be "another Comforter' (John xiv. 16, 17), the Teacher who should complete the revelation of truth left incomplete by the Lord Jesus (John xiv. 25, 26; xvi. 12-15); in moments of danger and difficulty they were to look to Him to give them words and wisdom (Luke xii. 11, 12), and the staggering task of convincing the world of its sin in rejecting Jesus, of righteousness only in and from Jesus, and of the judgment of sin in His cross—all this should be the alone work of the Holy Spirit.

After His resurrection our Lord resumed this testimony. He completed the instruction of His disciples concerning the personal relationships of the Holy Spirit. Before His death He indicated two of these: "He dwelleth with you, and shall be in you." John xiv. 17. Up to that time the work of the Spirit had been to reveal Christ to them as the Son of God, the true object of faith, and to regenerate them when they believed (Matt. xvi. 16; 1 John iv. 15; v. 1; 1 Cor. xii. 3); but the Spirit had not taken up His abode within them. This (in John xiv. 17) our Lord promised. On the evening of the resurrection this promise was fulfilled. John xx. 22. But our Lord bade them still tarry for another manifestation of the Spirit, and this He described by the word upon: "Ye shall receive the power of the Holy Ghost coming upon you." "Behold, I send the promise of my Father upon you." And so vital was this to their service that they were forbidden any exercise of their apostleship until that should be accomplished.

Note. The student will find the doctrine of the Person and Offices of the Spirit fully developed in Section IV. It is sufficient to say here that all the offices of the Spirit are included in the threefold personal relationship indicated by our Lord's words, "with," "within," and "upon."

The Holy Spirit with convicts, converts, regenerates.

The Holy Spirit within has to do with the believer's inner life, growth, worship, prayer, emotions, and experiences.

The Holy Spirit upon has to do with the believer's outward activities, imparting gifts for service, clothing the believer with Himself in power, guiding him in his service, and uniting him to the living body of Christ, which is the church. 1 Cor. xii. 12,13. It is the "upon" relationship which is prominent in Acts. The relationship is indicated in Acts by three words: "Baptized," "upon," "filled." The first describes how the relationship begins, the second its nature, namely, the Holy Spirit laying hold of a believer that He may use him; the third the renewal and perpetuation of the relationship. There is but one baptism; there are many fillings.

The point for the student to grasp clearly is that Pentecost was a true advent of a divine Person, and that He came to take up the work of forming the church by converting sinners and baptizing them into the one body.

2. But, while the Holy Spirit is thus everywhere prominent, so that this whole dispensation of grace which began from the cross has been not inappropriately called the dispensation of the Spirit, it should ever be borne in mind that He is not here on His own behalf, but solely and only on behalf of Christ. In a very real sense He takes the place, in the Acts and Epistles, of the infinite and holy Servant of Christ. In the Old Testament the Father serves the unspeakable need of humanity; in the Gospels Jesus is among men "as one that serveth;" in the Acts and Epistles the Holy Spirit takes the servant's place. See, especially, John xv. 26; xvi. 13-15. Note the marks of the servant: "I will send Him;" "He shall not speak of Himself; but whatsoever He shall hear, that shall He speak;" "He shall glorify me.'" The beautiful type of this service is found in Eleazar, the servant of Abraham. Gen. xxiv. He is sent to choose a bride for Isaac, the obedient son; and he does not "speak of himself," but of the riches of the father whose heir Isaac is. He takes of the things of Isaac with which to persuade the bride, and guides her at last to the bridegroom. It is lovely to see that the servant's

name is not mentioned once in the chapter. In fact, we do not know the Holy Spirit's name. The words Holy Spirit are not a name, but a description. "Jesus" is a name.

This bring us to the third general remark.

3. The dispensation is, then, still that of the Son. Luke, the writer of Acts, in his introduction tells us that his "former treatise" was "of all that Jesus began both to do and teach." The Acts find Him still in ministry, the characteristic difference being that now He usually works mediately, through the Spirit, and the Spirit in turn in and through believers. Even this veil is broken through by the enthroned Christ again and again. See, e.g., Acts vii. 55, 60; ix. 4-6; x. 13-15; xviii. 9,10; xxii. 17-21; 2 Tim. iv. 16-18.

In short, Jesus is Himself Master and Lord, working after the model of John xxi. The energy, capacity, intelligence and power of the believer's service is that of the Holy Spirit, but all is on behalf not of Himself but of Jesus. It is impossible to overstate the importance of being filled with the Spirit; but it is easily possible to become occupied with the Spirit instead of with Christ. Our service is always due to Christ; from Him comes our commission; He alone rewards our toil. But His representative on earth, through whom His will is communicated and made effective, is the Holy Spirit, who is, equally with the Father and the Son, God. These three principles find constant illustration in the Acts.

A word of explanation may be helpful concerning the imparting of the Spirit by the laying on of hands. Three such instances are mentioned in the Acts (viii. 14-17; ix. 10-18; xix. 1-6); and there is, beside, the case of. Timothy (1 Tim. iv. 14; 2 Tim.i.6). It will be observed that the power of thus communicating the Holy Spirit was not exclusively apostolical, since in one case Ananias was alone in the act, and in another the eldership was associated with Paul in the imposition of hands. The form itself runs through the whole of Scripture and may be said to be a natural symbol of communicating anything. It was used patriarchially in blessing; typically, in the laying of sins upon a sacrifice; and by our Lord in both healing and blessing. That it was not, even in the lifetime of the apostles, and in their very presence, essential to the communication of the Spirit is clear from the case of the household of Cornelius. Acts x. 44. The truth seems to be that it was in the divine purpose to authenticate the Gospel preached (at first exclusively to Israel). by this repeated fulfillment of the prophecy of Joel, as also to put needed emphasis upon the mighty fact that the Holy Spirit had come. The baptism with the Holy Spirit was, therefore, at first not always contemporaneous with conversion. From the opening of the kingdom to Gentiles (Acts x. 34-48), however, it seems clear that conversion and the indwelling and baptizing with the Spirit were contemporaneous. See Rom. viii. 9,15, 16; 1 Cor. xii. 13, R.V.; Gal. iii. 26 with iv. 6; Eph.i.13. But the student will remember that a believer may be baptized with the Spirit in the sense of union with the body of Christ, and of the impartation of gifts for service, and yet need the fullness, or filling, of the Spirit. Power and blessing come, not from mere position or privilege, however exalted, but from that yielding of the whole being unreservedly to Christ, which is, with faith, the condition of being filled with the Spirit.

4, The student is reminded of the distinction which always exists between the kingdom (in its various aspects) and the church. [See again Section I., Lesson V.] The Holy Spirit did not come at Pentecost to set up the kingdom. That will be the work of Christ when He returns. Nor does this imply inability on the part of the Holy Spirit. He will be the Power then as now. In Isaiah the anointing of Christ is twice spoken of—as King (Isa, xi. 2) and as Prophet (Isa. 1xi. 1). It was the latter passage which our Lord quoted as being fulfilled at His first advent. Not until the King takes the sceptre will the whole power of the seven-fold Spirit, as in Isa, xi. 2, be manifested. In this

age His power is constantly hindered by the imperfection of the instruments which He must use. The most powerful and accomplished swordsman could do but little to show his might and skill if armed with a fragile lath.

The church, it should always be remembered, is not a mere aggregation or voluntary assemblage of saved individuals; it is one living organism made up of believing units, united to each other and to the risen Christ by the baptism with the Holy Spirit. Study with care the following passages in order: Matt. xvi. 18, the first mention in Scripture of the church; Eph. i. 22, 23, what the church is; 1 Cor, xii. 12, 13, how and of whom the church is formed ("we all," see 1 Cor. i. 2); Acts ii. 1-4, 41, 47, when the prophecy of Matt. xvi. 18 began to be fulfilled.

This body is neither the kingdom of the prophets, nor the kingdom of Matt. xiii., nor the future millennial kingdom, nor the kingdom of God. It is in the kingdom of God, but the kingdom of God includes much beside the church. For the content of the kingdom of God see Heb. Xl. 22-24. The church is in the mystery kingdom of this present age, as (1) the children of the kingdom (Matt. xiii. 38), and (2) the pearl of great price (Matt. xiii. 46), It will be in the millennial kingdom as (1) bride of the King (Rev. xix. 6-9), and (2) co-ruler with Him (Luke xix. 15-19; Matt. xix. 27, 28).

5. It will be remembered that in Matt. xvi. 19, after announcing His purpose to build the church, our Lord declared that Peter should be given the keys of the kingdom of heaven. The student can scarcely need to be reminded that this is not a promise to put into Peter's hands the keys of the church, nor the keys of the kingdom of God. The "kingdom of heaven" in our Lord's mind here is that form of which He had been speaking in chapter xiii. It is, in effect, the sphere of profession. That profession might be the expression of true faith in Jesus Christ, in which case the believer was by the Holy Spirit baptized into the body, the

church. Such a believer was in the kingdom of heaven and also in the church. A mere professor, destitute of true faith, was in the kingdom of heaven, but not in the church. Simon Magus (Acts viii.) was an instance of the latter class, the Ethiopian (Acts viii.) of the former. Peter could open the door of profession, but only the Lord, by the Spirit, could "add to the church."'

Note. It must be needless to say to any student who has followed the Course up to this point, that the kingdom of heaven does not mean heaven. Nothing can be more unbiblical than the Roman Catholic claim that to Peter were given the keys of heaven, or of the church. Neither can it be necessary to say that by "the church" is meant not any local congregation, nor any sect or denomination, nor all of them put together, but the body of the saved from the descent of the Holy Spirit onward to the end of this age.

The student should also bear in mind the intense bigotry and arrogancy of the Jews toward all Gentiles, and the contempt and hatred with which they in turn were regarded by the Greeks and Romans. This mutual aversion and hostility is constantly manifested as the gospel spread, and it finally invaded the church itself. The Jewish converts brought in the leaven of the Pharisees—ceremonialism and religious pride; and the Greeks brought in Sadducean "philosophy and vain deceit," and "science falsely so-called." The strife is manifest in the Acts mainly on the Jewish side. In the Epistles both Jewish legality and Gentile philosophy are seen at work in the "three measures of meal." Against both Paul stood for the truth of the gospel. Galatians is his defense of the gospel against legality; Colossians against philosophy.

Analysis of the Book

The Acts falls naturally into two grand divisions, and these again into subdivisions.

Section I. From the Ascension of Christ to the Establishment of Christianity in Antioch—The Acts of peter. i. to xii.

The subdivisions are:

Part 1. From the ascension to Pentecost. i. The student will attentively note

(1) that the baptism with the Holy Spirit is an indispensable condition of ministry (verses 4, 5);

(2) that our Lord impliedly confirmed the expectation of a future restoration of the Davidic kingdom (verses 6, 7);

(3) that the baptism with the Holy Spirit is the source of power in service (verse 8);

(4) that Jesus went away visibly, corporeally, in a body having flesh and bones (verse 9);

(5) that the promise is unequivocal that He shall so return.

The action of the apostles in undertaking to establish apostolic succession by vote and lot was entirely ignored, and thus disowned, by the Lord. In the primary sense there could be but twelve apostles (Matt. xix. 28; Rev. xxi.14). When the time came our Lord Himself appointed Paul.

Part 2. The day of Pentecost. ii. The first use of the keys; the kingdom of heaven opened to the — Jews. This was the advent day of the Holy Spirit. The three results of the baptism with the Spirit were all manifested. 1. The individual believers were united into the church (1 Cor. xii. 12, 18; Actsii. 47). 2. There were gifts for service not previously possessed (Acts 11. 4, 6-8). 3. There was power in service (Acts ii. 37-41). Of these elements the first two are constant, the last variable. The believer is never unbaptized out of the body, and the gifts also remain, though they may need "stirring up" (2 Tim. i. 6) and assuredly suffer by "neglect" (1 Tim. iv. 14). But power is the outflow (John vii. 38, 39) and depends upon constant renewal. There are many "fillings," therefore; but one "baptism." The disciples were baptized with the Holy Spirit in Acts ii. and were also filled. In Acts iv. they were again filled.

The sermon of Peter demands notice, as also the general character of the preaching up to x. 37-48. Its distinctive character was the affirmation of the

Messiahship of Jesus, with a renewed appeal to the Jews to receive Him as such. In his sermon on the day of Pentecost Peter, as Professor Stifler has pointed out in his altogether admirable analysis of that discourse ("Introduction to the Book of Acts"), did not at once announce his theme. It is in verse 36. He had already covered every possible Jewish objection. The most forcible would have been the apparent failure of the Davidic covenant by the death of Him who was set forth as Messiah. It is noteworthy that Peter does not meet that objection by saying (with many Protestant commentators since Whitby) that the Davidic covenant had in view a purely spiritual kingdom ruled by an invisible King in heaven, but quotes from David himself to show that he foresaw the resurrection of Christ to sit on his throne. The answer then to the Jewish contention that Jesus could not have been the Messiah because a dead man could not be the fulfiller of the Davidic covenant, was that God had raised that Man from the dead that He might yet sit on David's throne. The sermon of Peter in Acts iii. is also entirely specific on that point. If the nation will repent, the times of refreshing, the restitution of all things according to all the prophets, will come, "and he shall send Jesus Christ who before was preached unto you." As our study of the prophets has taught us, the sign of the "times of restitution of all things" will be the repentance of Israel. Deut. xxx. 1-3; Matt. xxii. 37,39.

The student will, therefore, understand that the preaching on the day of Pentecost, and afterward so long as Israel alone was the object of the apostolic ministry, was the affirmation that the Jews had slain their Messiah, but that God had raised Him up, and that they should repent and believe on Him. Two promises were given in case of such repentance, the blotting out of their sins, and the return of their Messiah. The actual effect of the preaching fell short of moving the nation to repentance. As our Lord had predicted (Luke xix. 11-14) His citizens sent a message after Him, saying, "We will not have this man to reign over us." Individuals who believed were, therefore, added to the church" (Acts ii. 47; iv. 4).

Part 3. Events in Judea from Pentecost to the stoning of Stephen. iii. 1 to vii. 60.

Part 4. The Gospel breaking out of Judea. The second use of the keys; the kingdom of heaven opened to the Gentiles. viii. 1 to xii. 25. This part records four events of immense importance: The preaching of Philip; the conversion of Saul; the second use of the keys (opening the kingdom of heaven to the Gentiles); and the planting of the church at Antioch. Of these events the student will remark (1) that as soon as the gospel breaks its strictly Jewish limits the emphasis is put upon faith (as in the Gospel of John) rather than, as in Acts li. to Vit, upon repentance. The Jews were exhorted to a change of mind regarding Jesus, and to belief in Him as their Messiah. In the testimony to Samaria, to the Ethiopians, and to the household of Cornelius, faith in Him "led as a sheep to the slaughter" (viii. 32-37) and as "hanged on a tree," is what is sought.

It is not now a question of the King so much as of the Redeemer. (2) The church was dilatory, but, when finally scattered, took up the work of evangelization according to the divine plan of campaign in Acts i. 8; that is, no unevangelized territory was overlooked. When the regions beyond were reached Antioch became a new center of operations from which, in turn, the work was pushed in orderly progression. The preachers neither sought far off lands when those nearer were still unevangelized; nor, on the other hand, supposed it to be their work to linger in any land until all were converted. They "fully preached the gospel," and went on. They found, indeed, the gospel to be a savor of life unto life, but not to all. To some it was a savor of death unto death.

LESSON XLVII

THE GOSPELS AND ACTS.— CONTINUED

THE ACTS OF THE APOSTLES— CONTINUED

Section II. From the Establishment of Christianity in Antioch to the Close of Paul's Ministry —The Acts of Paul. xiii. to xxviii.

Note. In this section the ministry of Paul dominates the scene. Beyond question he occupies in the New Testament a place of interest and importance above that of any other man. Up to the beginning of Paul's full ministry Peter is the conspicuous man, both in the Gospels and in the Acts. In him is shown what Christ can do working for a man; in Paul the power of Christ working in a man. The personal history of Paul is gathered from what is said of him in the Acts and in the Epistles.

It is exceedingly important to see that he is a first-hand witness to Jesus Christ. He is converted and put into the apostolate by Christ Himself, owing nothing to those who were apostles before h'm. To him were given original and first-hand revelations of truth. It is either ignorance, or disbelief of Paul's repeated assertions, to speak of him as a mere theologian, reducing toa " Pauline" system the facts recorded in the Gospels. He may indeed have seen the Gospels according to Mark and Luke, but both these m n were mere helpers and adjuncts of his mighty ministry. He received his doctrine, as he repeatedly declares, by revelation. He never speaks of himself asa system maker, but asa trustee (Tim. i. 11). The truth he taught had been "delivered" to him (1 Cor. xv. 3). He "received it by revelation" (Gal. i. 11, 12); and they who were apostles before him "added nothing" to him (Gal. ii. 4, 5). What he received.he taught "not in the words which man's wisdom teacheth, but which the Holy Ghost teacheth." He was preeminently the witness of the

ascended and glorified Christ. Peter saw Him transfigured for a moment on a mountain in Palestine; Paul was caught up into Paradise itself. It was to him that Christ committed the doctrine of the church, as He had before committed to the witnesses of His death and resurrection the doctrine of the kingdom. Eph. iii. 3-11. It follows: (1) That the writings of Paul have absolute divine authority. They are not the conclusions of an able and spiritually minded man, but the addition to the body of revealed truth of the particular doctrine which appertains to the church. The member of Christ's body would search the Gospels in vain to find his position, duty, or destiny. As Exodus and Leviticus, reinforced by the mighty ministry of the prophets, gave instruction concerning worship, walk and work to the man under law, so the Epistles, with the discourses of Paul in Acts, give the distinctive teaching to the man under grace. His citizenship is in heaven, which is also his home (Phil. iii. 20; 2 Cor. v.8, R.V.). Down here he is a stranger, as Jesus was. He is occupied, not so much with the history of a Christ on earth as with a living Christ in heaven (2 Cor. v. 16, R. V.), to whom he is united, and of whom he is a part. Paul's doctrine, then, is Christ's Own post-ascension instruction to the church of this age. Acts xxvi. 16.

Note. At this point the student should review the history of Paul down to the beginning of Section II.

(1) His persecution of the church. Acts vii. 58 to viii. 3; xxvi. 9-11; 1 Tim. i. 12-16.

(2) His conversion. Acts ix. 1-18; xxii. 5-16; xxvi. 12-23.

(3) His first preaching. Acts ix. 10-25; Gal. i. 11-17.

(4) His first visit to Jerusalem. Acts ix. 26-30.

(5) His ministry at Antioch.. Acts xi. 25-30.

This section falls into the following parts:

Part 1. The first missionary journey of Paul. xiii. 1 to xiv. 28. The student will observe that, while the preaching is still "to the Jew first" (Rom. ii. 9,10; Acts xiii, 46), it is not a call to national repentance to the end that Messiah may be immediately sent back, as in Acts iii. 19-21, but is rather the glad tidings of salvation to the individual through personal faith in a crucified Redeemer, e.g., Acts xiii. 38, 39. The effect of this preaching was never, in any place, the conversion of all; but in every place some were saved.

Part 2. The council at Jerusalem. xy. 1-30. No chapter in the book is of greater significance than this. It marks the overthrow of the first formal attempt to mingle law with grace—Judaism with Christianity. The energy of the Spirit sufficed to overthrow the attempt. So far as circumcision and the grosser ritualism of Israel were concerned the defeat was final. But even inn the life-time of Paul the legalists largely succeeded in imposing the law upon believers as the ultimate standard of Christian living. Against this subtler form of legality rather than against mere ordinances, Paul afterwards wrote Galatians. The law of the Ten Commandments, like other preceptive parts of the Old Testament, was "written for our learning" (Rom. xv. 4) and, conceivably, for converts wholly uninstructed in divine things, "profitable . . . for instruction in righteousness." But Paul stood strenuously against shutting up the Christian to the law as a rule of life. [See Section I., Lesson VII.] The disputation, however, submitted to the council at Jerusalem concerned ordinances, especially circumcision. It was the first form of "the leaven of the Pharisee." Matt. xvi. 12; xii. 33.

The answer to the Jewish-Christian demand that something be added to simple faith as a means of salvation was three-fold:

(1) God had given the Holy Spirit to the Gentiles (and that, it will be remembered, without human interposition [Acts x. 44, 45), and

(2) He had purified their hearts by faith (xv. 7-10). Peter's conclusion was beautiful in its humility: "We believe that through the grace of the Lord Jesus Christ we shall be saved, even as they."'

(3) Paul and Barnabas added the third part of the answer; God had wrought miracles and wonders by them.

At this point James spoke. Professor Stifler ("Introduction to the Book of Acts") has here (as elsewhere in that remarkable book) furnished a most luminous interpretation. The legal party were silenced (verse 12), but honestly confused. Their prophets invariably connected blessing for the Gentiles with the exaltation and primacy of Israel. But now it seemed proven that God had been blessing Gentiles wholly apart from Judaism. What, then, became of the prophetic testimony? James completely answered that difficulty. As Professor Stifler says: "It is not the way of the New Testament to leave earnest, honest men in a state of perplexity. James proposes to show that all Scripture which the Pharisees might cite was relevant, but not relevant at this time."

He first interprets the state of things testified to by Peter, Paul and Barnabas. It. was not the Gentile blessing foretold by the prophets at all, but a new thing—God visiting the Gentiles to "take OUT of them a people." The prophets spoke of universal Gentile blessing; this was elective. Eighteen hundred years of Christian history have shown how perfectly James' words in verse 14 describe this dispensation. Wherever the Gospel has. been preached some have believed; nowhere, among Gentiles, have all believed. James then shows that this in nowise contradicts the prophets. After the out-taking from the Gentiles is complete Christ will return and take up the order of events foretold by the Jewish seers.

He quotes from Amos, who, more succinctly than others, sums up that order. It is as follows:

(1) "I will return"

(2) "and will build again the tabernacle of David which is fallen down; and I will build again the ruins thereof; and I will set it up"

(3) "that the residue of men [Israel] might seek after the Lord,"

(4) "and ALL the Gentiles, upon whom my name is called, saith the Lord who doeth all these things."

The fifteenth chapter of Acts is, then, one of the pivotal chapters in the Bible. The student will do well to master it thoroughly. It contains the authoritative declaration of the Holy Spirit (verse 28) which frees Christianity from ceremonialism; and it gives, in the declarative statement of James, the divine program for this age and the age which is to follow. The passage, therefore, is the key to unfulfilled prophecy. It will be found to fit all the wards of the lock. There is no unaccomplished prediction in the Old Testament or the New which it does not interpret.

(1) The church age is not in the Old Testament prophetic vision. The essence of it is the taking out of the Gentiles a people for His name. It is, therefore, not the age of universal conversion.

(2) It is to be followed by the fulfillment of the Old Testament predictions of universal blessing, in the order given by Amos, viz:

    a. The return.of the Lord.

    b. The reestablishment of the Davidic house.

    c. The ingathering of the residue of Israel.

    d. The conversion of the world.

This age is the age of the Ecclesia, the called-out assembly.

Part 3. The second missionary journey. xv. 36 to xviii. 22. The Examination will indicate the points of especial significance in Part 3. No part of the Bible is more instinct with life and vigor, none more suggestive in its bearing upon Christian service. The chief points are:

(1) Service is to be in absolute subjection to the Holy Spirit. Nothing is left to opinion or self-will. This superintendence extends to the smallest details.

(2) In the path of service the day of small things is never to be despised. The gospel had a very small beginning in Europe (xvi. 13-15).

Notre. The address of Paul at Athens may require a word of suggestion at verse 28. Paul's point is two-fold:

(1) The solidarity of the race, making absurd all racial distinctions as before God, and

(2) that we should see the absurdity of thinking that a dumb senseless idol could be like God, by the consideration that we ourselves, the offspring of God, as even the heathen poets perceived, are superior to such things.

The whole passage is an affirmation that the race springs from God as a special creation. The word Father is not used, for, in Scripture, "father" means more than creator, or begetter. The offspring of God are created in His image—triune, as having spirit, soul and body; moral, intelligent, rational; capable of knowing and trusting God. The children of God are partakers of the divine nature. 2 Pet. i. 4. By natural generation we are the offspring of God; by regeneration we become the children of God. John i. 12, 13; iii. 5, 6, John viii. 42; Gal. iii. 26, etc. Neither here nor elsewhere do the Scriptures teach the universal fatherhood of God.

Part 4. The third missionary journey. xviii. 23 to xix. 20. In this part also the student will find the Examination an induction as to the more noteworthy passages.

Note. The passage, xix. 1-6, may present difficulties. It has been used as ground for affirming that one may be a regenerate believer, and yet destitute of the indwelling Holy Spirit. The student will observe that (see Revised Version) Paul's question implied surprise that believers should seemingly be destitute of the Spirit: "Received ye the Holy Spirit when ye believed?" 'Their answer brought out the true state of the case. They were John's disciples; that is, they had been brought into expectancy of the coming of Messiah and into preparedness to believe on Him, but had not yet become such believers. Under Paul's instructions they took the forward step from John to Christ, as Andrew and the Apostle John had long ago done. Then they received the Spirit.

The passage does not contradict Rom. viii. 9,14; 1 Cor. vi. 19, etc.

Part 5. The lapse into self-will, and its consequences. xix. 21 to xxi. 40. The student comes now to a part of the book of the Acts which is at once painful and pathetic. The great apostle:to the Gentiles, in the very excess of his zeal, takes for a time the ordering of his own ways. Paul was a Jew. In the ninth, tenth and eleventh chapters of Romans the intensity of his love for Israel breaks forth into burning words. He was willing, if that would avail, to be anathema from Christ for his kinsmen according to the flesh. The sorest grief of the many griefs that wrung his great heart was the suspicion with which the Jewish-Christians treated him, and the opposition of many among them to the gospel which had been committed to him. He longed to preach to them, to win them from legalism, from that persistent lingering about Judaism which was dwarfing their growth in Christ. The Epistle to the Hebrews, in which, knowing the prejudice with which they would regard anything from his pen, he writes anonymously, is his effort to win them from the shadow to the substance. Now he has made, in the Gentile churches, a collection for the poor saints in Jerusalem, and he resolves himself to bear it to them. 1 Cor. xvi. 1-4;.2 Cor. viii. 1-24; ix. 1-5; Acts xxiv. 17; Rom. xv. 25-31. It was a beautiful service of charity, and clearly shows how completely the heart of the apostle had been kept from bitterness through all the malignant opposition of the Judaizing party, but it took him to a city which he had been expressly commanded to shun. It is to the honor of the apostle's noble sincerity that he himself tells us this. Acts xxii. 17-21.

The student will observe that we are expressly told that Paul went up to Jerusalem this time by his own determination. See xix. 21; xx. 22. The translators of the Authorized Version, as also the revisers, have correctly translated "spirit" as referring not to the Holy Spirit but to Paul's own mind, the word being printed without the capital.

Note. On xix. 21, Meyer remarks: "He determined in his spirit—he resolved." On xx. 22: "The words are neither to be taken as bound to the Holy Spirit, *i.e.,* dependent on Him; nor, constrained by the Holy Spirit; nor, I go at the instigation of the Holy Spirit; but, bound, *i.e.* compelled and urged in my spirit."

Instantly warnings began to accumulate in his path. xx. 23; xxi. 4, 10, 11. These, it as expressly said, came from the Holy Spirit. Paul could answer in all sincerity that he was unmoved by dangers or even by the fear of death, but we are permitted to see that burning and unselfish zeal led this noble soul against the express command of his Master and the faithful warnings of the Spirit. The consequences are apparent. There was at this time a strange indecision in the movements of the apostle; but it is what occurred at Jerusalem that is most sadly significant. Compare Paul's noble stand against the legalizing party on the occasion of a former visit with his weakness now. Gal. ii. 1-9 with Acts xxi. 18-26. It is painful to think of the writer of Rom. vi. 14; Gal. iv. 19-31; v.1; Heb. ix. and x., with a shaved head about to make an offering in a temple which his Lord had disowned and appointed to destruction. It is the most impressive lesson in all Scripture of the peril of acting in self-will, however exalted the motive may be.

But over against this humbling lesson the student will note the unfailing grace of Christ. He did not desert His dear servant. It should be noted, too, how instantly Paul recovered his integrity of conscience by frankly and publicly confessing that his presence in Jerusalem was an act of disobedience. xxx. 17-21. Two silent years of imprisonment followed (xxiv. 27), but the apostle's peace and power were never more manifest than in the trials before Felix, Festus and Agrippa; in the painful and dangerous journey to Rome, and in his powerful ministry there by tongue and pen. It must, however, always remain a subject of interesting speculation what ministry might have been his had he never taken his ways into his own hand.

Note. A word may be needful at this point. It seems to be considered by some writers that whatever an apostle did was right. This feeling, doubtless, arises out of confusing the infallibility of the man with the always infallibility of his writings. It is the Scriptures which are "God-breathed" and authoritative. The writers of the New Testament, equally with the writers of the Old Testament, are exempt neither from infirmity nor sin. Gal. ii. 11-14; Acts xxiii. 3-5; 2 Tim. i. 15.

Part 6. From Paul's arrest to the end of his ministry. xxii. 1 to xxviii. 31. In the study of this part the student will

(1) read it as a narrative; mastering the order of events, the places mentioned, and the chronology of this part of Paul's life.

(2) The student will make a special study of the great discourses.

The distinctive doctrines of Acts will be gathered by the student in answer to questions in the inductive Examination accompanying this section.

The Gospel and Acts.

1. Give seven references to show Christ's purpose in coming into the world.

_____

_____

_____

_____

_____

_____

_____

2. Give at least three references that show His personal ministry was to Israel.

_____

_____

_____

3. Give references to show the full deity of the Lord Jesus Christ.

_____

_____

_____

4, Give references to show that Jesus Christ was also truly human.

_____

_____

_____

5. Did Jesus Christ exist before His human birth?

_____

_____

6. What offices does Jesus hold by virtue of being "Christ?"

_____

_____

7. How many times is the church mentioned in the four Gospels, and where?

_____

_____

8. How many times is the kingdom mentioned in the four Gospels?

_____

9. How many times is the church mentioned in Acts?

_____

10. Do the Gospels present a complete life of Christ?.

_____

11. What aspect of our Lord's life and teaching is predominant in Matthew?

_____

_____

_____

12. What two characters of Christ are made prominent in Matthew?

_____

_____

_____

13. State from memory in your own words the three meanings of the phrase "kingdom of heaven" in Matthew. Note.—The student is earnestly advised to thoroughly master this.

_____

_____

_____

_____

_____

_____

_____

14. State from memory the three sections into which Matthew falls. Note.—This question does not refer to the sub-divisions, or "Parts," but the three grand divisions only. This must be memorized.

_____

_____

_____

15. What does the title "Son of David" mean?

_____

_____

_____

16. What rights descended to Jesus as heir of David?

_____

_____

_____

17. Are these rights which pertain to Him as divine or human?

_____

_____

18. What does the title "Son of Abraham" mean?

_____

_____

_____

19. What awful obligation rested upon Jesus as Son of Abraham?

_____

_____

_____

20. Did Jesus fulfill the obligation which He assumed as Son of Abraham?

_____

_____

_____

21. How did Jesus fulfill the obligation?

_____

_____

_____

22. Has He ever received His rightful place in the earth as Son of David?

_____

23. When the kingdom was preached as "at hand," did the preachers mean that the church was at hand?

_____

24. State in your own words the difference between the literal and the moral application of the Sermon on the Mount.

_____

_____

_____

_____

_____

25. Will the Sermon on the Mount ever become the fundamental law of human society?

_____

_____

26. How did Christ prove His power to restore and reign?

_____

_____

_____

27. State in your own words in what chapters of Matthew, and in what manner, Christ showed His rejection as king.

_____

_____

_____

_____

28. What is meant by "the mysteries of the kingdom?"

_____

_____

_____

_____

29. Where in the Old Testament are these mysteries found?

_____

_____

30. What period of time is covered by the parables of Matt. xiii.?

_____

31. Do those parables predict the conversion of the world during the period covered? Note.—"End of the world" in this chapter should be "end of the age." The word does not mean "world."

_____

_____

_____

32. Give in your own words the meaning of these parables.

_____

_____

_____

_____

_____

_____

_____

33. Why is not "leaven" in the fourth parable the Gospel?

_____

_____

34. Are the "children of the wicked one" (verse 38) to be converted during this age?

_____

_____

35. Did Christ build the church during His earth life?

_____

_____

36. State in your own words from memory how the Transfiguration symbolizes the kingdom.

_____

_____

_____

_____

37. The student will write out in his own words a sketch of the prophecies uttered by our Lord in Matt. xxiv., xxv., and Luke xxi. Note: This is one of the most important passages in Scripture. The student is urgently advised to master it. The following questions may aid him.

1. What questions did the disciples ask Jesus?

_____

_____

2. What does Jesus predict as to the character of this age till "the end come?"

_____

_____

3. What counsels were given as to the destruction of Jerusalem?

_____

_____

4. How does He describe the tribulation?

_____

_____

_____

5. Does the tribulation follow or precede the Lord's return?

_____

_____

6. How does Christ come?

_____

_____

_____

7. What does Matt. xxiv. 31 mean?

_____

_____

_____

8. What instructions and warnings are given to Christians concerning the Lord's return?

_____

_____

_____

_____

9. In these prophetic chapters is any Millennium described?

_____

_____

10. Who are judged in Matt. xxv. 31-46?

_____

_____

11. Who are the "brethren" there?

_____

_____

38. What bearing upon God's covenant with King David had Christ's resurrection?

_____

_____

_____

39. State the predominant character in which Mark presents the Lord Jesus Christ.

_____

_____

_____

40. Give from memory the proofs of Christ's character.

_____

_____

_____

_____

41. Show how as servant our Lord was tested as to fidelity.

_____

_____

_____

_____

42. What were leading characteristics of His work?

_____

_____

_____

43. Is He still serving?

_____

44. What is the predominant character of Jesus in Luke?

_____

_____

_____

45. What is the key-phrase?

_____

_____

46. Give from memory in your own words the leading proofs of your answer to question 44.

_____

_____

_____

47. State in your own words the bearing of Rom. v. 14-19, and 1 Cor. xv. 21, 22, 45,47 on the humanity of Jesus Christ. Note.—This is another detail which must be thoroughly mastered.

_____

_____

_____

_____

48. What three facts concerning Christ are prominent in the first chapter of Luke?

_____

_____

_____

49. Into what seven sections does Luke fall?

_____

_____

_____

_____

_____

_____

_____

50. How did Luke get his facts?

_____

_____

51. State in your own words entirely, the differences:

    1. Between Jesus and all other men born of women.

_____

_____

_____

    2. Between Jesus and Adam.

_____

_____

_____

52. State from memory the four ways in which the years of obscurity at Nazareth tested the character of Jesus.

_____

_____

_____

_____

53. What is the resemblance between chapter ix. of Luke and chapters xi. and xii. of Matthew?

_____

_____

54. What was the predominant character of Christ's ministry on the journey to Jerusalem?

_____

_____

55. Did the rejection and crucifixion of Christ nullify the Old Testament prophecies concerning His earthly glory?

_____

56. How did the risen Christ treat the Old Testament?

_____

_____

57. Who wrote the fourth Gospel?

_____

58. What is the central purpose of the Gospel according to John?

_____

_____

59. State separately the propositions of John xx. 30, 31.

_____

_____

_____

60. Why does John wish to prove that Jesus was the Christ, the Son of God?

_____

_____

_____

61. State carefully, from memory, in your own words, what offices Jesus has as "Christ."

_____

_____

62. Give from memory the three great characteristic words of John.

_____

_____

_____

63. Which of the four Gospels follows the order of time most closely?

_____

64. In what three ways may John be analyzed?

_____

_____

_____

65. State in your own words exclusively how John xxi. gives the character of Christ's ministry in resurrection.

_____

_____

_____

_____

66. State briefly, from memory, in what ways John proves that Jesus is the Christ, the Son of God.

_____

_____

_____

67. Into what four classes do the seven evidence-miracles reported by John fall?

_____

_____

_____

_____

68. Give, under each head, an instance from one of the other Gospels of a similar miracle.

_____

_____

_____

_____

69. In what five ways did the Father witness that Jesus was His Son?

_____

_____

_____

_____

_____

70. Explain in your own words how Christ offered Himself in His prophetic character.

_____

_____

_____

71. Explain in your own words how Christ offered Himself in His priestly character.

_____

_____

_____

72. Explain in your own words how Christ offered Himself in His kingly character.

_____

_____

_____

_____

73. What are the three great doctrines of John?

_____

_____

_____

_____

74, How does Christ teach what God is?

_____

_____

_____

75. How does He teach His own deity? Note.—Answer the doctrinal questions by references under each subhead of the lesson.

_____

_____

_____

_____

_____

76. How does Christ teach His humanity?

_____

_____

_____

77. State from memory how Christ teaches five things about regeneration.

_____

_____

_____

_____

_____

78. State (with references) the six teachings concerning eternal life.

_____

_____

_____

_____

_____

79. What does Christ teach as to the resurrections?

_____

_____

_____

80. What (giving references) does He teach as to a future state?

_____

_____

_____

81. What is the great subject of the Acts?

_____

_____

82. What is the most important event recorded in Acts?

_____

_____

83. Define the personal relationships of the Holy Spirit.

_____

_____

_____

84. Which of these relationships is most prominent in Acts?

_____

_____

85. Is Christ still at work in Acts?

_____

_____

86. What is His usual method of work in Acts?

_____

_____

87. Did the Holy Spirit come to set up the kingdom?

_____

88. What is the church?

_____

_____

_____

89. How is it related to the mysteries of the kingdom?

_____

_____

_____

90. Where did Christ give to Peter the keys of the church?

_____

_____

91. Who are the two most conspicuous personages in Acts?

_____

_____

92. The two next in importance?

_____

_____

93. When and in behalf of whom did Peter first use the "keys?"

_____

_____

94, What results to the disciples followed the baptism with the Holy Spirit?

_____

_____

95. What effect had the apostolic preaching upon unbelievers?

_____

_____

_____

96. State in your own words, from memory, the distinctive character of the apostolic preaching up to the conversion of Cornelius. Note.—The student will thoroughly master this.

_____

_____

_____

97. Give from memory the four most important events from the end of chapter vii. to the end of chapter viii.

_____

_____

_____

98. Define from memory the change of Cee in the preaching after the gospel reaches the Gentiles.

_____

_____

_____

99. Give illustrative passages showing the new emphasis.

_____

_____

_____

100. What is the divine plan of campaign in missions?

_____

_____

101. State from memory the reasons why Paul's writings have full divine authority.

_____

_____

102. Give a brief sketch of the life of Paul.

_____

_____

_____

_____

108. Give in your own words an account of the council at Jerusalem.

_____

_____

_____

_____

104. Give from memory the order of events for this age and the beginning of the next in Acts xv.

_____

_____

_____

_____

105. Where was Paul arrested?

_____

_____

106. Upon what charge?

_____

107. Write a synopsis of the life of Paul from his arrest to the end of Acts.

_____

_____

_____

_____

108. Answer each of the following questions by one or more references.
   1. Where is the doctrine of the resurrection taught? .

_____

_____

   2. Of Christ's deity?

_____

_____

   3. Of His prophetic office?

_____

_____

4. Of His kingly office?

_____

_____

5. Of His sacrificial death?

_____

_____

6. Of His second advent?

_____

_____

7. Of the Holy Spirit?

_____

_____

   a. Personality?

_____

_____

   b. Deity?

_____

_____

   c. Power?

_____

_____

8. Of angelic ministry?

_____

_____

9. Of miracles?

_____

_____

10. Of guidance in service?

_____

_____

109. How many parables are recorded i: in the Gospels?

_____

110. How many of these are parables of the kingdom?

_____

_____

111. How many are parables of service?

_____

_____

112. How many relate to the future state?

_____

_____

113. How many miracles are recorded in the Gospels?

_____

114. How many miracles are recorded in the Acts?

_____

115. How many of the miracles in the Gospels were wrought by Christ?

_____

_____

116. Give the names of persons in the Gospels and Acts other than Christ who performed miracles.

_____

_____

117. How many instances of resurrection are recorded in the Gospels and the Acts?

_____

_____

118. Give the names of all the persons mentioned in the Gospels and Acts.

_____

_____

_____

_____

_____

_____

_____

119. What Is the Holy Spirit represented as doing in Matthew?

_____

_____

120. What Is the Holy Spirit represented as doing in Mark?

_____

_____

121. What Is the Holy Spirit represented as doing in Luke?

_____

_____

122. What Is the Holy Spirit represented as doing in John?

_____

_____

123. What What Is the Holy Spirit represented as doing in Acts?

_____

_____

_____

PART VI. THE EPISTLES AND REVELATION

I. INTRODUCTION

The Epistles are, in three respects, a distinctive division of the Word of God: (1) their epistolary form; (2) their view backward toward the cross; and (3) that they have not primarily in view either Jews or Gentiles, but the new division of the human race, Christians.:

All Scripture up to the Acts (except the few brief chapters of the Gospels which record the resurrection and ascension of our Lord) looks forward to the cross, and has primarily in view the Jew. It might well have been anticipated that, just as the giving of the law was followed by an immense increase of the body of revealed truth intended to explain the law (namely, the entire Old Testament except Genesis), and the measure of blessing and of responsibility under it, so the uprearing of the cross would be followed by another addition to the Scriptures, explaining grace, and the blessings and responsibilities of man under grace. Surely the cross required interpretation.

But there is another reason for such a body of truth as the. Epistles disclose. Toward the close of His ministry our Lord briefly indicated His purpose to bring into being an institution of which the Old Testament had given no hint, namely, the church. Matt. xvi. 18. But there he left the matter, adding but one mention of this institution, and that incidentally, in giving instructions concerning brotherhood. Matt. xviii. 17. Not one word of description or explanation as to how, when, or of what materials He purposed to build His church did He vouchsafe. Neither did He disclose the relationships to Himself, to Israel, or to the world, of this mysterious structure. Obviously all this needed explanation. When,

now, we turn to the Epistles we find precisely these subjects dealt with. The Epistles explain and apply the work of Jesus Christ upon the cross, and they develop the doctrine of the church, supplying what our Lord had left unsaid in His own teachings. Doubtless, therefore, we have in these books, with the Acts and the Revelation, the "many things" of which our Lord said that the disciples were not able to bear them, but which He promised that the Spirit should teach them. John xvi. 12, 13. The Epistles and the Revelation have, then, for their great themes precisely. the truths made necessary by accomplished redemption, by the calling into being of the new body, the church, and by the reconciling of that new work with the covenants of God concerning Israel. A further purpose accomplished by the Revelation is to connect the present dispensation, which is parenthetical and not the subject of Old Testament prophecy, with the Davidic kingdom and with the eternal state.

To the Epistles, therefore, the Christian looks for instruction in the doctrines of grace, and in the principles which govern his life as a member of the church which is the body and bride of Christ. The Old Testament foreshadowed, in type, covenant, and prophecy, "the grace which should come unto us"; but attempted neither to define that grace, nor to fix its relations to law. The Gospels are a fourfold view of the person of Christ as the Seed of the Abrahamic and Davidic covenants, as the Servant of Jehovah, as the Son of Man, and as the Son of God. Doctrinally, as the student has seen, they are transitional between pure law and pure grace. In them the law receives its highest, most searching, and therefore most deathful application. No natural man can stand before the Sermon on the Mount. Besides this vindication and authentication of the law, the Gospels are necessarily largely Jewish in coloring, since Christ. was to the Jews a "minister of the circumcision." Rom. xv. 8. But also the cross was near, and the teaching of Christ concerning personal salvation looked always beyond the cross, and was based upon it as the consummation of a perfect redemption. The offer by him of eternal life upon the alone condition of faith was predicated upon His approaching sacrifice. But beyond laying the foundation of the doctrine of grace, and indicating His purpose to build His church, He did not go. The germ of everything which we shall find in the Epistles is in the teachings of Christ, but the growth and development of the plant was left to the ministry of the coming Comforter. John xiv. 26; xv. 26; xvi. 12-15.

Fittingly, Paul is the chief writer. His training in both Jewish and Greek learning, his birth outside Palestine, equally with his strict religious instruction within that land, made him a suited instrument of the risen Lord for the confirmation upon the one hand of the unfulfilled promises to the Jew, and of the revelation upon the other hand of the position in pure grace of the Gentile believer in Jesus.

To this wonderful ministry he was called by the risen and glorified Christ, so that the mind of the servant and witness was not preoccupied with memories of the day of his weakness, but was filled with an intense consciousness of His resurrection power and glory. Called in this way by the Lord's own voice from heaven, he was taken into the personal instruction of the Lord Himself. Gal. i. 15 toil. 6; Eph. iii. 2-4; 2 Cor. xii. 1-4. He was not suffered to learn truth from the other Apostles by hearsay and tradition, but was sent away into Arabia, Moses' school, where he received directly from the Lord the especial truths which form the subject of his distinctive ministry. Gal. i. 1, 11, 12, 16, 17; ii. 6-9; 1 Cor. xi. 23; 1 Thess. iv. 15; 1 Cor. xv. 3; Acts xxvi. 16, 17, etc.

The distinctive ministry of Paul, however, has relation to the new body, the church. And this particular ministry is very ample. Blot out the writings of Paul, and we should know almost nothing of the church. Through him alone we know that the church is a living organism, a vital body, as distinguished from an organization or association of persons—a body of which Christ is the Head and all regenerate persons since Pentecost the members. Through him chiefly we know that (in another sense) the church is the espoused bride of Christ. Through him alone we know the nature, purpose and organization of local churches, and the right conduct of such gatherings.

It would be wrong to exalt the writings of Paul above any other of the Holy Scriptures; but a peculiar distinction attaches to those writings, by reason (1) ef their volume, (2) of the variety of their contents, (3) of the immense importance of the subjects treated, and (4) of the exclusive revelations committed to him.

The great themes of the Epistles and the Revelation are:

1. Salvation by Christ, through faith alone; that is, upon the principle of grace, or undeserved favor.

2. The church as the living body of the risen and glorified Christ, and distinct, therefore, on the one hand from the saved of all past ages; and, on the other hand, from the saved of ages and epochs to come.

3. The Holy Spirit in His varied offices and relationship to this body and to local churches and individual saints.

4, The reconciling of this new dispensation with the promises to national Israel.

5. The walk, service, and future destiny of Christians; that is, of the saved of this dispensation.

6. Prophetic utterances covering the course and end of this age; the age to come; and the beginning of life in the new heavens and the new earth.

7. Incidentally this portion of the word contains much interesting, instructive, and touching biographical matter. Indeed, truth is often revealed in and through human experience rather than dogmatically.

II. HOW TO STUDY THE EPISTLES

1. GENERAL REMARKS

The student will bear in mind that these writings are letters not essays. He should, therefore:

First, read the Epistle continuously at one sitting, as if it were a letter written to him personally, or to his local church.

Secondly, read it again more slowly, noting the following distinctive peculiarities of the Epistle:

(1) The place of writing (if given).

(2) The occasion which called it forth.

(3) To whom written.

(4) The general theme of the Epistle. Note. In this second reading the student should note what places: or persons are referred to, and should carefully read all other New Testament references to the same. The only exception should be such places (*e.g.*, Jerusalem) or persons (e.g., Peter, James, et al.) as are already well known to the student.

Thirdly. The externalities of the Epistle being thus disposed of, the student should again read it, carefully listing the different subjects treated by the writer. It is at this point that the student should begin to use the Lesson Outlines and Examination Questions.

Fourthly. After any Epistle has been thoroughly studied, it should be compared with the other Epistles in the same group. (See Section I., Lesson III.)

Note. As the Epistles of Paul obey the great law of progressive growth (or development) of doctrine, they are best studied in chronological order, rather than in the order of their arrangement in our Bibles.

Above all, let the student be constantly mindful that these writings, so human in their form, reveal in that very way the emotions of Christ Himself toward churches and individuals, All this sorrow and joy, approbation and indignation, exhortation and rebuke, disclose the workings of the heart of Christ inwrought in the heart of Paul or Peter. or James or John. "I live; yet not I, but Christ liveth in me"—this is the key to the human side of these very human writings. The Head is not dwelling in a passionless calm while His members on earth are striving, suffering, sinning. "I am Jesus whom thou persecutest." Doubtless Paul is perfectly identified with Jesus in these emotions; doubtless the sufferings and joys are Paul's; but in a deeper sense they are the emotions of Jesus finding expression through the emotions of Paul. This gives an especially sacred and touching character to the Epistles.

LESSON XLVIII

First Thessalonians

General Remarks

Thessalonica, a city of commercial and political importance in the apostolic age, was visited by Paul on his second missionary journey in the year 52 or 53, that is twenty-two or twenty-three years after the crucifixion. At this point the student should read Acts xvi. and xvii. The stages of the thrillingly interesting journey are: Philippi, where a church was established and Paul was "shamefully entreated" (1 Thess. ii. 2); Amphipolis and Apollonia, where no halt was made, and then Thessalonica. | The entire distance from Philippi to Thessalonica was one hundred miles, and four days may have been consumed in travel. The pathetic aspect of Paul's condition after the outrage at Philippi must not be forgotten. His back must still have been lacerated when he entered Thessalonica. As the narrative shows, he was there not above four weeks. From the description of his labors in Acts xvi. and the references in the two Epistles (1 Thess. ii. 1-12; 2 Thess. iii. 7, 8) we gather that Paul and Silas at once sought employment for their support. From the words twice used of this employment it must have been exceedingly onerous. But beside this daily toil, the apostle preached in the synagogue on each of the three Sabbaths of his stay in the city, and also found time for a wonderfully rich teaching ministry to the young converts who had been gathered out. What amazing diligence!

The passage in Acts xvii. gives the result of the evangelistic part of his labors. A church was gathered composed of a few Jews and a relatively large number of Greek proselytes to Judaism, with many chief women of both these classes.

The usual result—Jewish persecution—followed; and Paul went on to Berea and to Athens. Immediately, the persecutors turned upon the church. 1 Thess. i. 6; 11. 14; 111. 3, 4. When the apostle, then in Athens, knew of this, all his solicitude was aroused in their behalf, and he sent Timothy to establish and comfort them. 1 Thess. ii. 1-3. It was the return of Timothy with good tidings (iii. 6) which led to the writing of the Epistle. The Epistle, therefore, was written soon after the apostle's departure from Thessalonica, to a church composed of young converts who were undergoing persecution because of their faith.

Accordingly, First Thessalonians has a threefold purpose: (1) To confirm the young disciples in the foundational things already taught them by the apostle (i. 1 to ii. 20); (2) to exhort them to go on to holiness (iii. 1 to iv. 12); (3) to comfort them concerning disciples who had already suffered death (iv. 1. to v. 28).

The apostle's method is to connect his teaching upon all the subjects developed in the epistle with the second coming of Christ. This, it will be remembered, was also our Lord's method in His later teaching, as in Matt. xxiv., xxv., where the ever impending second advent, the time of which remains unrevealed, is made the basis of His warnings and exhortations. The whole Christian life, according to His last teachings, is keyed to the expectation of the ever possible return of the Lord. The servant is to be diligent because a special blessing is promised to the one whom "his Lord when He cometh shall find so doing." It is the evil servant who says, "My Lord delayeth His coming." All are to watch for the Bridegroom and for the Master of the talents. This, then, is also Paul's method with his young converts in Thessalonica, and it is this which gives the primary.

Analysis of the Epistle

The second coming of Christ presented in five aspects.

Section I. The second coming of Christ and the believer's expectation, chapter i.

Section II. The second coming of Christ and the believer's reward, chapter i1.

Section III. The second coming of Christ and the believer's sanctification, chapter ili. 1 to iv. 12.

Section IV. The second coming of Christ and the believer's translation, chapter iv. 13-18.

Section V. The second coming of Christ and the unbelieving world, chapter v.

But the epistle presents also a Secondary Analysis.

Section I. The model church, chapter i.

Section II. The model servant, chapter ii.

Section III. The model brother, chapter iii.

Section IV. The model walk, chapter iv. to v.

Note. This, and the other lessons in Part VI., should be studied with constant reference to the examinations. It is desired that the student shall discover truth for himself, helped only by the general remarks, analysis, and inductive questions.

FIRST THESSALONIANS.

1. By whom was the church at Thessalonica founded?

_____

_____

2. Of what classes was the church at Thessalonica founded?

_____

_____

3. Under what circumstances was the church at Thessalonica founded?

_____

_____

4. How long was the founder at Thessalonica?

_____

_____

5. How long after his departure was the epistle written?

_____

_____

6. What circumstances caused it to be written?

_____

_____

7. Give from memory the primary analysis.

_____

_____

_____

_____

8. Give from memory the secondary analysis.

_____

_____

_____

9. State the names of God in this Epistle with the number of occurrences of each.

_____

_____

_____

10. In what relationship is God most prominently presented?

_____

_____

11. Enumerate the doctrines mentioned in the Epistle.

_____

_____

_____

_____

_____

_____

12. What three great elements of Christian character does Paul ascribe to the Thessalonians in chapter i.?

_____

_____

13. How are they said to have manifested these three graces?

_____

_____

14. What three things are said in chapter i. of the attitude of the Thessalonian saints?

_____

_____

_____

15. What three words in that chapter sum up the right position of a believer?

_____

_____

16. How did the Thessalonians know themselves to be the elect of God?

_____

_____

17. Is assurance a desirable or undesirable possession?

_____

_____

18. What seven elements characterize the model church in chapter 1.?

_____

_____

_____

_____

_____

_____

_____

19, Had the Thessalonian church, when Paul wrote the Epistle, any officers or even a pastor?

_____

_____

20. Who, then, "set them at work'?

_____

_____

21. What great work of Jesus is mentioned in chapter i.?

_____

_____

_____

22. Whence came the joy of the Thessalonian saints?

_____

_____

23. Find in chapter ii. seven chief characteristics of the model servant of Jesus Christ.

_____

_____

_____

_____

_____

_____

24. Add any other such characteristics as you may find in that chapter.

_____

_____

_____

25. What is said to be the reward of the faithful servant of Christ?

_____

_____

26. What is said of Satan?

_____

_____

_____

27. What is the difference between a pastor's work "as a nurse" and "as a father'?

_____

_____

28. Gather out of the entire Epistle the things which should characterize the believer's walk.

_____

_____

29. How many times in this Epistle are the Commandments mentioned in connection with the believer's walk?

_____

30. Give, from chapter iii., the characteristics of the model brother.

_____

_____

31. Why was it a hardship for Paul to be left at Athens alone?

_____

_____

32. Was Paul's chief solicitude about the good works of the Thessalonians?

_____

_____

33. How often is "faith" mentioned in chapter iii.?

_____

_____

34. How often is "faith' mentioned in the Epistle?

_____

_____

35. From what sources did Paul anticipate danger to the faith of the Thessalonians?

_____

_____

36. What blessing, beyond faith, does the apostle desire for them?

_____

_____

37. What is said in chapter iv. to be the "will of God" for the saints?

_____

_____

38. Gather up the teachings of the entire Epistle concerning the Holy Spirit.

_____

_____

_____

_____

39. How are believers taught to love?

_____

_____

40. What is said of manual labor?

_____

_____

41. By what name is death called in chapter iv.?

_____

_____

42. Upon what authority does Paul rest his doctrine concerning the return of the Lord?

_____

_____

43. What is the first event in connection with His coming?

_____

_____

44. What is the second event in connection with His coming?

_____

_____

45. What is the third event in connection with His coming?

_____

_____

46. Is this a general resurrection of believers and unbelievers?

_____

_____

47. What is said concerning the eternal condition of believers?

_____

_____

48. What prophetic epoch (see Part IV., Lesson XXX.) follows the resurrection and taking up of the church?

_____

_____

49. Does the apostle fix the date of the coming of the day of the Lord?

_____

_____

50. Will that day come in a time of general fear and expectation?

_____

_____

51. What will be the effect of that day upon the unbelieving world?

_____

_____

52. Are Christians to be overtaken by that day?

_____

53. Where will Christians be when that day comes?

_____

_____

54. What, therefore, should be our attitude and conduct now?

_____

_____

55. What sin against the Spirit is forbidden?

_____

_____

56. What great passage in chapter v. declares the threefold nature of man?

_____

57. Are "spirit" and "soul," then, the same?

_____

_____

58. Is sanctification a human or a divine work?

_____

_____

59. What does the apostle say as to the origin and authority of the truth ministered by him (chapter ii.)?

_____

_____

60. What is stated as the right attitude of a church toward its ministers and teachers?

_____

_____

61. Is this mere personal admiration and partisanship?

_____

LESSON XLIX

SECOND THESSALONIANS

GENERAL REMARKS

The present Epistle was evidently written almost immediately after the preceding one. The occasion of it may well have been the report of the bearer of the first letter. In any event information had reached the apostle that, in addition to the trials incident to fierce persecutions (i. 4-9), his Thessalonian converts were "shaken in mind" and "troubled'" by deceivers who asserted that they had already actually entered the day of the Lord. Let the student understand with perfect clearness the precise point of obscurity and difficulty to clear up which was the apostle's primary purpose in writing the Second Epistle. That difficulty is described in chapter ii. 1,2. The whole chapter should be read as in the Revised Version. Verses 1 and 2 are as follows: "Now we beseech you, brethren, touching the coming of our Lord Jesus Christ, and our gathering together unto Him (see 1 Thess. iv. 15-18); to the end that ye be not quickly shaken from your mind, nor yet be troubled, either by spirit or by word, or by Epistle as from us, as that the day of the Lord (see 1 Thess. v. 1-4) is now present."

The difficulty, then, was a fear which had come upon the Thessalonians that they had actually entered the day of the Lord, from which they had been taught to expect deliverance by the coming of the Lord Jesus Christ to take them up (together with the sleeping saints) to meet Himintheair. That expectation was doubtless founded upon the oral teachings of the apostle when in Thessalonica; and it certainly was the doctrine of his First Epistle, where the catching up of the church in chapter iv. precedes the day of the Lord in chapter v. The many erroneous teachings as to what constituted the real difficulty which called out Second Thessalonians, are thus set aside simply by translating two verses correctly. They were shaken in mind touching their gathering unto Christ before the day of the Lord, because false teachers were endeavoring to convince them that the day of the Lord was already present.

There is not the smallest warrant for such statements as that they were in a kind of Millerite excitement, supposing the Lord was coming immediately; or that in that expectation they had ceased earthly occupations, and fallen into grave disorders. So far from being in an unwholesome excitement over the expectation of our Lord's imminent return, they were "shaken" and "troubled" fearing that He had come and had passed over them and their beloved dead, leaving them to pass into the awful day of the Lord. It appears that the false teachers who were seeking to take away their "blessed hope" did not shrink even from forging a false letter as from Paul (ii. 2). This marks the working of "the father of lies." Undoubtedly, Satan has a peculiar hatred of the doctrines of 1 Thess. iv. 14-18. He either breeds disbelief of the whole doctrine; or (as with the Thessalonians) robs the "blessed hope" of all its joy and comfort by convincing saints that the horrors of the day of the Lord must precede the catching up of the church.

The great subject of Second Thessalonians, then, is the setting right of the relation of the day of the Lord to the two phases of our Lord's second advent; which two phases are, His coming into the air for His saints and His subsequent coming to the earth with His saints. In First Thessalonians the apostle had set forth the first phase of the return of the Lord; he now, in Second Thessalonians, occupies himself with the second phase.

ANALYSIS

Section I. Salutation. i. 1, 2.
Section II. Comfort. i. 3-12.
Section III. Instruction. ii. 1-12.
Section IV. Exhortation and apostolic commands. ii. 18 to iii. 15:

Section V. Benediction and authentication. iii. 16-18.

Note. Sections I., II., IV. and V. will be developed through the Inductive Examination. The real difficulty is in Section III. (Use the Revised Version.)

Section III. Here the apostle, first, discriminates the "coming of our Lord Jesus Christ and our gathering together unto Him" from "the day of the Lord." Verses 1, 2.

Secondly: He reminds them that when he was yet with them he gave them the signs which precede the day of the Lord, viz.

1. The falling away, or apostasy. Verse 3. 1 Tim. iv 1, 2; 2 Tim. iii. 1-5; iv. 3, 4.

2. The revelation of the man of. sin, or "lawless one." Verses 3, 4. Dan. vii. 8, 20, 21; viii. 9-25; 1x. 26, 27; xi. 21; Rev. xiii. 11-18; Matt. xxiv. 15.

Thirdly : Paul teaches that already, in the very apostolic age, there was a mystery of lawlessness at work; but. under a restraining One (the Holy Spirit at work in the church), who would restrain the full development of lawlessness and the revelation of the man of sin until He, the Restrainer, should be taken out of the way. 1 Thess. iv. 16-18. Verses 6, 7. This brings in the complete order of events.

1. The working of the mystery of iniquity from the apostolic period to the end of the age. The professing church becomes at the end largely apostate.

2. The coming of the Lord Jesus Christ and our gathering unto Him. This removes the Restrainer.

3. The tribulation. The nearness of the day of the Lord is indicated by:

   (a) Unrestrained apostasy from God.

   (b) The revelation of the man of sin. (Here occurs "the Great Tribulation" of Matt. xxiv. 15-22.) Verses 9-12 give the result of the lying wonders of the lawless one. The unbelieving world and the apostate church would not have God's Man; now they must have Satan's man.

4, The manifestation or glorious appearing of the Lord Jesus with saints and angels, and the overthrow of the man of sin and the false prophet, antichrist.

SECOND THESSALONIANS.

1. What brethren were with Paul when the Second Epistle was written?

_____

_____

2. What message did the Father and the Lord Jesus send to the troubled ones at Thessalonica?

_____

_____

3. For what did Paul give thanks?

_____

_____

4. Is trouble a hindrance to spirituality?

_____

_____

5. Is the coming of Christ described in chapter i. 7-10 identical with that described in 1 Thess. iv. 15-18?

_____

_____

6. For what did Paul pray in chapter i.?

_____

_____

7. State what is said in ii. 2 to have been troubling the Thessalonians.

_____

_____

8. Why should it have "shaken" and "troubled" them to suppose they had actually entered the day of the Lord?

_____

_____

9. What is the difference between the coming of the Lord as mentioned in ii. 1 and in ii. 8?

_____

_____

_____

10. What must be present to constitute the day of the Lord?

_____

_____

_____

11. What will the man of sin do?

_____

_____

_____

12. In what terms, and where, did Jesus refer to this man?

_____

_____

_____

13. What did Jesus say should follow the revelation of the man of sin?

_____

_____

_____

14. What was "working" when Second Thessalonians was written?

_____

_____

_____

15. Why did not the apostasy and the man of sin immediately appear?

_____

_____

_____

16. Does chapter ii. describe the conversion of the world before the return of the Lord?

_____

_____

_____

17. What happens to the true church when Jesus comes?

_____

_____

_____

18. What happens to the professing church when Jesus comes?

_____

_____

_____

19. What happens to the unbelieving world when Jesus comes?

_____

_____

_____

20. What happens to the man of sin when Jesus comes?

_____

_____

_____

21. What is the inevitable penalty of refusing to believe the truth?

_____

_____

22. What is said of Satan in Second Thessalonians?

_____

_____

_____

23. What is said in this Epistle of the work of the Spirit?

_____

_____

_____

24. What instrument does the Spirit use in that work?

_____

_____

_____

25. What were Thessalonian saints exhorted to "hold"?

_____

_____

_____

26. For what causes did Paul ask them to pray?

_____

_____

27. What two faults does Paul rebuke as being " disorderly"?

_____

_____

28. What should churches do with such?

_____

_____

29. Is there any intimation that the disorderly ones of iii. 7-11 were idle because expecting the near advent of Christ?

_____

_____

30. What is the right attitude of saints toward those who reject the teachings of this Epistle?

_____

_____

31. Give from memory the order of the prophetic events mentioned in First and Second Thessalonians.

_____

_____

_____

_____

_____

_____

_____

_____

32. Give a list of doctrines taught or referred to in Second Thessalonians.

_____

_____

_____

_____

_____

_____

_____

33. What truths are brought out which were not mentioned in First Thessalonians?

_____

_____

_____

_____

34. What truths brought to light in the First Epistle are added to or explained in the Second?

_____

_____

_____

_____

Note. The purpose of the last three questions is to fix the student's mind upon the progress of doctrine in the Epistles. It will be found, as we proceed, that the earliest Epistles are very elementary as compared with the later. The doctrines are developed gradually, progressively, harmoniously. "First the blade, then the ear, afterward the full corn in the ear."

LESSON L

FIRST CORINTHIANS

GENERAL REMARKS

The student should keep in mind the order of Paul's journeys and labors which he has already studied in Part V. of Section II. It will be remembered that from Thessalonica the apostle went to Berea, and from Berea to Athens. Acts xvii. Timothy and Silas remained at Berea for a brief period, until summoned to rejoin Paul at Athens. Here, news came of the afflictions of the Thessalonian converts, and Timothy was sent to comfort them and to bring tidings of their state. Silas also was sent into Macedonia. Both these brethren rejoined Paul at Corinth, whither he went after the notable events at Athens recorded in Acts xvii. 16-34. From Corinth Paul wrote the two Epistles to the Thessalonians. Corinth was an important, wealthy, and luxurious city, but with an evil eminence for licentiousness even in that shameless land and time. Here the apostle remained "a year and six months, teaching the Word of God among them." As was his custom, he supported himself by daily toil at tent making. At first he preached in the synagogue; but when the effect of his preaching had aroused the anger and opposition of the Jews, he moved his meetings to the house of a convert near the synagogue. The indifference of the Roman deputy Gallio frustrated an effort of the Jews to use Roman authority against Paul and his converts. After this, Paul departed from Corinth, going to Ephesus, Caesarea, Jerusalem and Antioch; and then entered upon a visitation of the churches in Galatia and Phrygia. After this he returned to Ephesus, where he stayed for three years.

It seems clear from 2 Cor. xii. 14, 21; xiii. 1 that the apostle had been a second time at Corinth at some time between his first visit and the writing of his two Epistles to that church. This visit is not mentioned in the narrative in Acts xviii. It appears also from Acts xviii. 27 and 1 Cor. i. 12 and iii, 4-6, that both Apollos and Peter had visited the church at Corinth. The carnality of the Corinthian saints was shown by the fact that instead of receiving these men as laborers together with Paul, watering what he had sown, they became divided into parties, each of which exalted a favorite teacher.

It appears also that in Corinth, as elsewhere upon the scene of Paul's labors, harm was wrought by the Judaizing teachers, who denied Paul's apostleship; and, by an unwarranted use of letters of commendation from Peter and James, affirmed themselves to be representatives of those apostles, for whom they claimed a higher authority than Paul's as having been with our Lord during His earthly ministry.

The brief visit above referred to having failed to set right the things in disorder at Corinth, the apostle wrote a letter (1 Cor. v. 9) which has not been preserved, rebuking the immorality of the Corinthian church. This seems to have drawn from that church a letter of inquiry concerning the relations of the sexes, (1 Cor. vii. 1) and apparently also submitting to the apostle questions at issue among them as to eating meat which had been exposed before the heathen idols.

This letter of inquiry from Corinth, together with reports from "the house of Chloe" of the deepening divisions and increasing contentions in the church gave occasion for writing the First Epistle.

Before entering upon the study of the Epistle the student should read it through, carefully noting what, in the Corinthian church, is commended, what rebuked, and concerning what the church seems to be merely in need of instruction. This will give the student a clear conception of the condition of the church. It will be seen that along with a low state of moral and spiritual life there was apparently great energy of faith. Their grievous errors were:

1. Sect Divisions

These were not due to heresies. The men whose names they assumed—Apollos, Cephas, Paul—were the foremost teachers of the faith, and in entire doctrinal accord. 2 Pet. iii. 15, 16; Gal. ii. 9; 1 Cor. xvi. 12. Neither were the divisions due to any desire for personal ascendancy and leadership on the part of these men. They were due solely to the carnality of the restless Corinthians. They had a truly Greek love for sophistical reasonings and_hairsplittings, and (like all unspiritual men) an undue admiration for " wisdom" and personal leaders. Apollos, a man of Alexandria, trained in the Greek schools of philosophy, eloquent and mighty in the Scriptures, inevitably gained admirers in such a church as Corinth. Peter—strong, humane, brotherly, fervent, and with the added distinction due to his long and intimate personal contact with Christ—would also attract many. To others Paul would be peculiarly dear as a spiritual father, and also for his exceptional gifts and graces.

2. Immorality

This was due to an upbringing and surroundings peculiarly depraved. Corinth was a center of the cultus of Venus. One temple on Acrocorinthus had 1,000 priestesses, who were simply prostitutes. Immorality was thus made an act of worship!

3. Disorders in Work and Worship

These were due to vanity, leading to a childish delight in "tongues" and other "sign" gifts; and also to the restless, lawless Greek spirit—sensuous, self-assertive, brawling, contentious.

4. Questions Concerning Paul's Apostleship

These were mooted by those persistent enemies of grace, the Judaizing teachers, who, claiming authority from Peter and James, exalted the apostleship of these men as superior to Paul's because they had been with the Lord in his earth-life. Paul magnified his office (not himself) against these contentions, because to him had been entrusted the revelation of the truth concerning the church. Apart from the writings of Paul we should know almost nothing of God's purpose in the outcalling of the church, of her relationships, her peculiar testimony, walk, worship and destiny. It was vital that the divine authority of these marvelous revelations should be put beyond question.

Analysis

A rigid analysis of this Epistle is not possible. It is not an epistolary treatise like Romans, Galatians or Ephesians. It is struck out of the apostle's solicitude, grief, and lofty indignation. Hence it does not calmly discuss one subject after another in a way of strict order and method, but returns again and again to something previously mentioned. See, for an illustration of this, i. 10-13; iii. 1-8; x. 16, 17; xii. 12, 18, where the apostle returns to the subject of their divisions.

Speaking broadly, however, and passing by recurrent passages of the nature just indicated, it may be said that the book falls into the following general divisions:

Section I. Salutation. i. 1-9. This would in no wise prepare us for what is to follow, for there are described wonderful endowments. Three reasons may be given for these endowments: First, Paul ascribes their spiritual riches to grace (verse 4); secondly, the Corinthians are never rebuked for lack of faith; thirdly, as a church, they are charged with no heresies.

Nort. The word "heresies" in xi. 19 should be "sects" as in the margin.

The rest of the Epistle, in startling contrast with this part, wonderfully illustrates the distinction between the believer's standing in grace and his possible state.

Section II. Divisions Rebuked. i. 10 to iv. 21. The apostle adopts a simple plan. First, he plainly states their sin (i. 10-12) and points out its absurdity (i. 13); secondly, he strikes at the root of all such divisions—intellectual vanity and pride in men. i. 14 to iv. 21. In this he begins by boldly asserting that the gospel is essentially "foolishness" to the wisdom of this world. It cannot be made anything else; and yet in that very gospel God has made foolish the wisdom of this world. The "world" is composed of unregenerate Jews and Greeks (or Gentiles). To the first the crucified Messiah isa stumbling block; to the second, foolishness. This sets aside Greek conceit. i. 17-25. Moreover, the apostle reminds these bumptious saints that even as Greeks they are not of the wise sort. i. 26-31. He reminds them, too, that when he came among them he determined not to use his ample Greek learning, nor his power of putting words prettily together (things which doubtless had bewitched them in Apollos), but to preach only Christ and Him crucified. Yet this plain preaching, "weak" in the estimation of rhetoricians and sophists, had in it the power of God—as they had experienced. ii. 1-8.

Proceeding, he strikes a yet more damaging blow at intellectual conceit in religion. The whole subject lies outside the reach of the natural powers of man. The things that God hath prepared for them that love Him are undiscoverable. He then traces the steps by which a religious truth reaches the heart of man from the mind of God. These are (1) revelation by the Holy Spirit; (2) utterance, in Spirit-given words, of the things revealed; (3) apprehension of the uttered words by Spiritual discernment. The natural man is completely set aside, whether learned or unlearned, wise or foolish; it is a supernatural matter from beginning to end. ii. 9-16. The apostle then shows the Corinthians how the great truth that only the spiritual can discern religious truth has affected his ministry to them. Their carnal state has debarred him from taking them on into God's deep things. Here is another blow at their conceit. They fancy themselves able to judge among their teachers,

when in point of fact they are mere babes in divine things. ii. 1-4.

It is necessary, therefore, to tell the Corinthians that he and Apollos are not rival founders of sects, but laborers together with God—farm servants. They, the Corinthians, are God's tilled land; Paul broke up the soil and planted; Apollos came after and watered—but God gave the increase. The result is that neither he nor Apollos is anything, but God is everything. Or, to change the figure, the Corinthians are God's building—God's house. God gave him grace to be the master-builder ("architectron") and he laid the foundation, Christ. Then Apollos came and carried on the work. iii. 5-9.

Now follows a warning to teachers who build upon Paul's foundation: a day of testing is coming. Wood, hay and stubble work will be destroyed, though if the builder be himself upon the foundation he shall be saved; gold, silver and precious stones work will abide and be paid for. But the church at Corinth is a temple of God, indwelt by the Spirit— not, therefore, to be destroyed by schisms and sects. iii. 11-17. The seeming wise are therefore to become fools (in the estimation of the world) and to give up foolish glorying in men. iii. 18-23. Then follows the touching illustration of these principles of lowliness of mind, humility and suffering in the lives of the apostles. iv. 1-13. And, besides, there is such a thing as apostolic authority, if need be. iv. 15-21.

Section III. Immorality Rebuked. v. 1 to vii. 40. As with their divisions, so with their immoralities, the apostle begins with a plain statement of the most glaring of their offenses (v. 1). It is the offense of one, but the indifference of the whole church makes them all guilty— Apollonians, Paulinians and Cephasites—all. What contempt this pours upon their divisions! The remedy is pointed out, and the responsibility put upon the church (v. 2-13). Litigation is sternly forbidden between saints (vi. 8); this is parenthetical. In verse 9 the apostle resumes his rebukes and exhortations concerning immorality, and brings in great principles—the body is for the Lord, not for fornication, and the Lord is for the body, to give victory over passion; the believer's body is a member of Christ—shall it be given to harlotry? It is a temple of the Holy Ghost, who already indwells it; we are bought with a price, and are to glorify (make manifest) God in our bodies (vi. 9-20).

This brings in the question concerning marriage and sex relationships about which the Corinthians had written Paul (vii. 1-40). Verse 40 does not imply a doubt in the apostle's mind as to his full inspiration. It is a claim to it rather (see Revised Version), as against the pretensions of his opposers. "I think that I also have the Spirit." The expression is Pauline, as, e.g., Phil. iii. 4—"If any other man thinketh that he hath : . I. more." But in this chapter Paul distinguishes between that which the Lord had said when on earth and that which He is now saying through Paul. It is a notable illustration of John xvi. 12, 13.

Section IV. The Limitations of Christian Liberty. viii. 1-13.

Section V. The Vindication of Paul's Apostleship, and the Rights and Obligations of True Ministry. ix. 1-27.

Section VI. Christian Conduct. x, 1, xi. 34.

Section VII. Christian Ministry and Worship. xii. 1 to xiv. 40.

This great passage should be most attentively studied. In xii. i. the rendering should be "things of the Spirit," rather than spiritual gifts. The latter word is supplied in the Authorized Version. The subject treated covers more than the doctrine of gifts, though that is mentioned first. A definition of "gift" is given in xil. 7; "the manifestation of the Spirit" in a believer's service. It is not intellect, as we say, "a gifted man; nor is it something added to the believer, as, e.g., new aptitude or talent. It is the Spirit Himself, manifesting Himself in a believer's service. These manifestations are diverse in different believers (xii. 4, 8-11, 14, 19, 20, 27, 29, 30); but all are for practical profit—not for display. xii. 7.

The enumeration of these manifestations (see also Eph. iv. 8, 11, 12) leads to the declaration of the tremendous and unspeakably exalted doctrine of the church as the body of Christ. xii. 12-27. This is no less than the affirmation that "we all" have been, by the baptism with the Spirit, formed into a living organism (not organization) like a human body of which we, severally, are members. This gives the fundamental basis of service, viz., the believer's service is already appointed, without consulting his wishes or preferences, by the sovereign will and power of God. xii. 11, 18, 24. Doubtless, it is done in perfect wisdom and perfect love. The danger is of insubordination; the foot saying, "Because I am not the hand, I am not of the body;" the ear saying, "Because I am not the eye, I am not of the body."

The student may, therefore, complete the definition of gift:

"Gift is the manifestation of the Spirit in the service of a believer who is obediently doing his appointed work."

Chapter xiii. gives the spring and motive of service; with great emphasis upon the truth that to be is more important than todo. The love character is better than the greatest gifts.

Chapter xiv. regulates the ministry of gift in the churches. Incidentally, there is a picture of a meeting of Christians in the early apostolic period. The leading thoughts are that all gifts may have expression, but within the limits of sobriety and order.

Section VIII. The Coming of the Lord in Relation to the Resurrection and Translation of Believers. xv.

Section IX. Special Directions and Greetings. xvi.

FIRST CORINTHIANS.

1. Describe in your own words the founding of the church at Corinth, and give the history of that church so far as it is found in Scripture.

_____

_____

_____

_____

_____

2. Give the passages which indicate the social position and moral state of the Corinthian saints before their conversion.

_____

_____

_____

3. Where was Paul when the First Epistle was written?

_____

_____

4. What eminent teachers had followed Paul in the ministry to that church?

_____

_____

5. How many times had Paul been at Corinth before the First Epistle was written?

_____

_____

6. What was the immediate occasion of the writing of First Corinthians?

_____

_____

_____

7. State in your own words what four chief evils in that church required correction, giving references to prove passages.

_____

_____

_____

_____

8. What is said in Scripture of Apollos?

_____

_____

_____

9. Were Peter and Apollos guilty of inciting divisions in the church?

_____

_____

10. To what, then, were the divisions due?

_____

_____

11. Give a reference to prove that Paul had full confidence in Apollos.

_____

_____

12. To whom is the Epistle addressed?

_____

_____

13. For what, in the Corinthian saints, does the apostle thank God?

_____

_____

14. In what, then, were the Corinthian saints enriched?

_____

_____

15. What does Paul point out as the source of the Corinthian saints riches?

_____

_____

16. For what were the Corinthains waiting?

_____

_____

17. In verse 8 does Paul warn them that, except they repent the evils he is about to point out, all these riches in grace will be lost?

_____

_____

18. To whose faithfulness does he look to free them from these evils and present them blameless in the day of Christ?

_____

_____

19. What does Paul plead in verse 13 against their divisions?

_____

_____

_____

20. How does the unconverted Jew regard the gospel?

_____

_____

_____

21. How does the unconverted Gentile regard the gospel?

_____

_____

_____

22. What is the special danger in trying to make the gospel intellectually attractive to the unsaved?

_____

_____

_____

23. What things has God chosen to overcome Gentile pride of intellect, and Jewish blindness and bigotry?

_____

_____

_____

24. Are (in your judgment) these "chosen"" things relied upon by the modern church?

_____

_____

25. What four wonderful things is Christ unto believers?

_____

_____

_____

_____

26. Is glorying in men a mark of spirituality?

_____

_____

27. What does Paul say, here and elsewhere in the Epistle of his preaching at Corinth?

_____

_____

_____

(a) As to his own state?

_____

_____

(b) As to his style?

_____

_____

(c) As to his power?

_____

_____

(d) As to his doctrines?

_____

_____

(e) As to the doctrines which he "first" delivered?

_____

_____

28. Were the inhabitants of Corinth a savage unlettered people?

_____

_____

29. Has Greek literature ever been surpassed for literary qualities?

_____

_____

30. What was the moral standard at Corinth?

_____

_____

_____

31. Was Paul familiar with Greek literature? Acts xvii. 28.

_____

_____

32. Does it not seem strange that such a man, speaking to a cultured people, should deliberately refuse to use the resources of culture?

_____

_____

33. Why, then, did he so "determine"?

_____

_____

34. Is it within the power of man to discover the truths of Christianity?

_____

_____

35. What is the first stage in the communication of these undiscoverable truths?

_____

_____

36. What the second stage?

_____

_____

37. Would that mean that the words of the various translations and versions of the Scriptures are given by the Spirit?

_____

_____

38. What is the third stage in the communication of revealed truth?

_____

_____

39. What two classes of men are mentioned in ii. 14?

_____

_____

40. Can the natural (or unregenerate) man understand the spiritual teachings of Scripture?

_____

_____

41. What, then, would be the value to a Christian of the writings upon Scripture subjects of even the most learned natural man?

_____

_____

_____

42. What is the marginal rendering of "judgeth" and "judged" in ii. 15?

_____

_____

43. Into what two classes are brethren (*i.e.*, Christians) divided in iii. 1?

_____

_____

44. Under what disability does the carnal (*i.e.*, fleshly) believer rest?

_____

_____

45. What, then, would be the value of a fleshly believer's judgment as to revealed truth?

_____

_____

46. What must we become if we are rightly to discern revealed truth? ,

_____

_____

_____

47. What is one proof of carnality in a believer?

_____

_____

48. What two illustrations are used of a local church in iii. 9?

_____

_____

_____

49. What is the relation of ministers to a local church?

_____

_____

_____

50. What are ministers in relation to God in verse 9?

_____

_____

51. What is the only foundation?

_____

_____

52. What two classes of work may we be doing?

_____

_____

53. Which of the judgments is referred to in iii. 13?

_____

_____

54. What is the result to the worker of work which stands the fire-test?

_____

_____

55. What is the result to the worker of the destruction of his works?

_____

_____

56. Are we then saved by works?

_____

_____

_____

57. What, notwithstanding their carnality, are the riches of the Corinthians in iii. 21-23?

_____

_____

58. What great principle is laid down in chapter iv. concerning the judgment of men?

_____

_____

_____

59. How in chapter iv. does the apostle rebuke the pride of the Corinthians?

_____

_____

60. How did the whole church of Corinth become blame-worthy for the sin of one?

_____

_____

_____

61. What ought they to have done?

_____

_____

62. What did the apostle now direct to be done?

_____

_____

_____

63. What is the principle as to the defilement of a whole church laid down in v. 6?

_____

_____

64. To what is leaven compared in v. 6?

_____

_____

65. To what is leaven compared in v. 8?

_____

_____

66. What event in Jewish history, and what sacrifice in Jewish ritual, are declared to be a type of Christ?

_____

_____

_____

67. What was the passover feast a memorial of?

_____

_____

68. What memorial feast do Christians keep?

_____

69. How should it be kept?

_____

_____

70. How are a believer's associations limited in v. 9-13?

_____

_____

71. Are lawsuits between Christians ever permissible?

_____

_____

72. Suppose a Christian must either suffer himself to be defrauded or go to law with a Christian, which must he choose?

_____

_____

73. What classes are excluded from the kingdom of God?

_____

_____

_____

74. How may one guilty of those sins nevertheless enter the kingdom?

_____

_____

_____

75. What motive is urged in vi. 15 for personal purity?

_____

_____

_____

76. What distinction is made between fornication and other sins?

_____

_____

_____

77. What motive is urged in vi. 19 for personal purity?

_____

_____

_____

78. Is it scriptural, then, to say that some Christians are not indwelt by the Holy Spirit?

_____

_____

_____

79. What motive for personal purity is urged in vi. 20?

_____

_____

_____

80. What restriction, in chapter vi., does Paul put upon himself in things lawful?

_____

_____

_____

81. Summarize in your own words the answers of Paul in chapter vii. to the questions (see verse 1) of the Corinthian church concerning marriage.

_____

_____

_____

_____

82. Summarize in your own words the answers of Paul to the questions concerning meats offered to idols.

_____

_____

_____

83. What great abiding principle, applicable in all ages, does Paul draw from this question?

_____

_____

_____

84. What three objections to his full apostolic authority does Paul meet by simple questions (as disdaining reply) in chapter ix.?

_____

_____

_____

_____

85. What do these questions imply as to the marks of true apostleship? [Note.—"Free" means free from human authority.

_____

_____

86. Did Paul's choice, to work with his own hands for his temporal support, imply that laborers in the gospel ought not to be supported by those to whom they minister?

_____

_____

87. What three illustrations to the contrary does Paul use in ix. 7.

_____

_____

_____

88. How does he prove from the Scriptures the right of laborers in the gospel to a support?

_____

_____

89. State in your own words the meaning of ix. 11.

_____

_____

90. State in your own words the meaning of ix. 14.

_____

_____

91. State in your own words, from ix. 16-27, the characteristics of a true minister of the gospel.

_____

_____

_____

92. In ix. 24-27 is the apostle speaking of salvation or reward?

_____

_____

Note. "Castaway" in ix. 27 would be better rendered "disapproved." It is the negative form of the word translated "approved" in 1 Cor. xi. 19; Rom. xvi. 10; 2 Cor. x. 18; 2 Tim. ii. 15. Conybeare and Howson render, "But I bruise my body and force it into bondage; lest, perchance, having called others to the contest I should myself fail shamefully of the prize." — Life of St. Paul, chapter xv.

93, In what five particulars were the children of Israel alike in the day of the Exodus?

_____

_____

94. Were they, therefore, equally well pleasing to the Lord?

_____

_____

95. What instances are given of the chastisement of a redeemed people?

_____

_____

_____

96. Why are these instances cited?

_____

_____

97. Why did those things happen to Israel?

_____

_____

98. What is the marginal rendering of "en samples'?

_____

_____

99. What Christians are in peculiar danger?

_____

_____

_____

100. What great principle is stated in x. 13?

_____

_____

_____

101. What great promise?

_____

_____

_____

102. What great reason is given in x. 14-21 explains why Corinthian saints should no longer eat in heathen temples?

_____

_____

_____

103. What two texts concerning "things lawful" does Paul impose in x. 23?

_____

_____

104. Is all social intercourse with unbelievers forbidden?

_____

_____

105. Give a modern illustration of the principle of x. 27.

_____

_____

_____

106. Give a modern illustration of the principle of x. 28.

_____

_____

_____

107. What great principle covering every act is stated next?

_____

_____

108. What threefold division of the race is given in chapter ix?

_____

_____

_____

109. What permanent principle is stated in xi. 3, and 7-12?

_____

_____

110. What application of that principle, having in view local customs, is made in xi. 4-6, 13-16?

_____

_____

111. What, in the public gatherings of the Corinthian church, is blamed in xi. 18, 19?

_____

_____

112. What, in the public gatherings of the Corinthian church, is blamed in xi. 20-22?

_____

_____

113. What is the true meaning of the Lord's Supper?

_____

_____

_____

114. What should precede coming to the table of the Lord?

_____

_____

_____

115. Which of the judgments is mentioned in xi. 30-32?

_____

_____

116. How may Christians escape chastisement?

_____

_____

_____

117. Give a revised rendering of xii. 2.

_____

_____

_____

118. What is the first law concerning spiritual gifts?

_____

_____

119. What is the second law concerning spiritual gifts?

_____

_____

120. What is the third law concerning spiritual gifts?

_____

_____

121. What is the fourth law concerning spiritual gifts?

_____

_____

122. What is a "gift?"

_____

_____

123. Enumerate the gifts in the Corinthians?

_____

_____

_____

_____

124. What is the fifth law?

_____

_____

125. State in your own words the doctrine of xii. 12.

_____

_____

_____

126. How is the believer made a member of Christ?

_____

_____

_____

127. Who are thus made members of Christ?

_____

_____

128. What is the bearing upon the service of the believer of this truth that he is baptized by the Spirit into the body of Christ?

_____

_____

129. What is the doctrine of xii. 11, 18?

_____

_____

130. What is the comfort of xii. 22-24 to Christians who have an obscure and little noticed service?

_____

_____

_____

131. What are "tongues" without love?

_____

_____

132. What are gifts without love?

_____

_____

133. What is zeal without love?

_____

_____

134. What are the evidences of love?

_____

_____

_____

135. What are the three chiefest graces?

_____

_____

_____

136. Which is the greatest of these?

_____

_____

137. Give the definition of "prophesying" as used in this Epistle.

_____

_____

138. What gifts should we chiefly desire?

_____

_____

_____

139. Give, in your own words, a description of a meeting of an apostolic church, as you gather it from chapter xiv.

_____

_____

_____

_____

140. What is said in xi. 5, 18, concerning the ministry of women?

_____

_____

_____

141. What kind of speaking is forbidden in xiv. 34, 35?

_____

_____

142. What is the authority of Paul's writings?

_____

_____

_____

_____

143. Give the revised rendering of xv. 1.

_____

_____

_____

144. What four things are said in xv. 1 of the gospel?

_____

_____

_____

_____

145. What did Paul deliver "first of all" when he went into cultured, corrupt Corinth?

_____

_____

146. What three facts in xv. 3, 4, constitute the essential substance of the gospel?

_____

_____

_____

147. State from memory how many appearances of the risen Christ are recorded in xv. 5-8.

_____

_____

_____

148. Was He seen more than once by the same persons?

_____

_____

149. Were they strangers or old friends and acquaintances of Christ?

_____

_____

150. Were they persons of good character?

_____

_____

151. What error concerning the resurrection was held by "some"' in Corinth?

_____

_____

152. Is the doctrine of the resurrection of the body an immaterial one?

_____

_____

153. Enumerate the consequences if it be true that Christ did not rise.

_____

_____

_____

_____

154, What is the meaning of "firstfruits" in the Bible?

_____

_____

_____

_____

155. In what sense is the resurrection of Christ a "firstfruits"?

_____

_____

_____

_____

156. Who was the "man" through whom came death?

_____

_____

157. Through whom comes the resurrection of the dead?

_____

_____

158. How far reaching are the consequences of Adam's sin?

_____

_____

_____

159. How far reaching the consequences of Christ's resurrection?

_____

_____

_____

_____

160. Are all the dead raised at the same time?

_____

_____

_____

161. When are the Christian dead to be raised?

_____

_____

_____

_____

_____

162. What must occur before "the end" of xv. 24?

_____

_____

_____

_____

_____

163. What three things, then, stand between this moment and "the end "?

_____

_____

_____

Note. The meaning of xv. 29 is that those who are being converted, and through baptism are openly stepping into the places in the ranks left vacant by the saints who have died, are indulging a vain hope if the dead rise not. The meaning is not that a custom existed when a convert died unbaptized to baptize someone else as a proxy.

164. To what is a buried body likened in xv. 36-38?

_____

_____

_____

165. What four things are said of the body which is sown?

_____

_____

_____

_____

166. What four things of the body which is raised?

_____

_____

_____

_____

167. Will all saints die?

_____

_____

168. When will be brought to pass the saying, "Death is swallowed up in victory"?

_____

_____

_____

169. What is the sting of death?

_____

_____

170. What three great principles concerning Christian giving are in xvi. 2.

_____

_____

_____

171. By what names is Deity called in First Corinthians?

_____

_____

_____

172. What is taught concerning the Father?

_____

_____

_____

173. What concerning the person and work of Jesus Christ?

_____

_____

_____

174. What is the doctrine of salvation in this Epistle?

_____

_____

175. What is taught concerning the inspiration and authority of Scripture?

_____

_____

176. What is taught concerning 'the baptism with the Holy Spirit?

_____

_____

177. What believers are baptized in the Holy Spirit?

_____

_____

178. What believers are indwelt by the Holy Spirit?

_____

_____

179. Enumerate the doctrines of First Corinthians.

_____

_____

_____

_____

_____

_____

180. What doctrines are taught in this Epistle which were not taught in First and Second Thessalonians?

_____

_____

_____

LESSON LI

SECOND CORINTHIANS

GENERAL REMARKS

After writing First Corinthians, which was sent to Corinth by Titus, Paul still abode in Ephesus. After the disturbances recorded in Acts xix. the apostle departed to go into Macedonia. From the brief account in Acts xx., supplemented by brief mention of persons and places in the Epistles, it appears that, departing from Ephesus to go into Macedonia, Paul came first to Troas. Here a "door" was opened for the gospel, and a church was gathered. But the apostle had no rest in his spirit " because Titus came not," and he departed into Macedonia. This almost certainly means that he went to Philippi, and there awaited the coming of Titus from Corinth. From Philippi, beyond doubt, Paul wrote the Second Epistle to the Corinthians.

That Epistle discloses in every line the touching state of the great apostle at this time. It was one of great physical weakness, weariness and pain; but this was as nothing to the spiritual burdens which were pressing upon him. These, broadly speaking, were of two kinds—solicitude for the maintenance of the infant churches in the pure faith of the gospel, and anguish of heart over the distrust and aversion felt toward him by his brethren according to the flesh, both Jews and Jewish Christians.

1. The causes of his solicitude for the churches we have seen in our study of First Corinthians. While it does not appear that other churches were afflicted with factional divisions, as at Corinth, it is clear that at this time the blight of legality was overspreading the scene of Paul's labors. We shall examine this grace-denying heresy more fully when we study the next of Paul's Epistles, that to the Galatians. It is sufficient for the understanding of the present Epistle to remember that the promulgation of the chilling doctrines of legalism among Paul's converts was accompanied by systematic depreciation of the apostle, and denial of his apostleship. The strenuous defense of his full apostolic authority, upon which Paul enters in the two letters to Corinth and in Galatians, is not due to lust of power. To him had been committed marvelous revelations of truth. In him, more than in all other New Testament writers combined, was fulfilled Christ's promise in John xvi. 12, 13: "I have yet many things to say unto you, but ye cannot bear them now. Howbeit, when He, the Spirit of truth, is come He will guide you into all truth." Strike out the communications of the Spirit by Paul and there would be left no doctrine of the church as the body and bride of Christ; no adequate definition of the great doctrines of grace; no clear teaching concerning the resurrections; no body of precept and exhortation as to distinctively Christian life and service. The apostle, therefore, could not retreat and still remain loyal to Christ. It cannot be too often repeated that there was no schism among the apostles themselves. Gal. ii. 1-9; 2 Pet. iii. 15, 16. Judaizing teachers claimed the authority of the Apostles James and Peter, but without warrant. Acts xv. 1, 24. Paul's defense of his full apostleship, therefore, was inseparably bound up with his defense of the precious truths revealed through him. And he knew that the very cause of Christ in this dispensation was inseparably connected with the prevalence of those distinctive truths.

It is evident from the particular line of defense adopted in Second Corinthians that Paul now perceived the especial danger of the Corinthians to come from those legalists who claimed to be especially "of Christ." 1 Cor. i.12. Doubtless the report of Titus had opened his eyes to see that here lay the subtlest danger. Those who were "of Apollos' probably had no distinctive doctrine; they admired the man; they "of Cephas" would be Judaising legalists, dangerous, indeed, but easily refuted. But what peculiar peril could come from teachers who were forming a sect upon the name of Christ? In his studies in the Gospels the student has seen how largely the teachings of our Lord were appropriate to His office (between His baptism and crucifixion) of "minister of the circumcision for the truth of God, to confirm the promises made unto the fathers," i.e., in relation to the kingdom; how largely, therefore, legal in spirit. Let it be remembered, also, that at this time the Gospel according to Matthew, in its first, or Jewish, form, was in possession of the church. It would be easy, therefore, for a teacher to say, "As against those who would put you back under Moses I am with Paul; but Paul errs in not declaring, for example, the Sermon on the Mount as the law of church life." In other words, they "of Christ" would avoid the grossness of the Judaizers, while failing to distinguish the Jewish, or kingdom coloring of our Lord's ministry to Israel. Such an error was then, and is now, exceedingly difficult to oppose. It seems harmless —even helpful—and yet is nothing less than the substitution of an external code for the law "written not with ink, but with the Spirit of the living God; not in tables of stone, but in fleshy tables of the heart" (2 Cor. iii. 3); and therefore to the church, the body and bride of Christ, untimely and injurious.

In the First Epistle, then, Paul had in mind (together with the immoralities of the Corinthians) the older legalism; in the Second Epistle the newer legalism, which was a misapplication in time of the precious and perfect kingdom teachings of Christ. As Dr, A. T: Pierson has well said, "They 'of Christ' [the newer legalists], met Paul's gospel of a Christ after the Spirit, the Son of God, with the kingdom gospel of Christ after the flesh, the Son of David." Protestant theology has devised a still more subtle legalism—the merging into one of these dispensationally distinct manifestations of Christ.

2. Paul was a converted Jew. He loved Israel, therefore, as a Jew and as a Christian. It was anguish to his heart to see Israel still going about to establish her own righteousness, instead of submitting to the righteousness of God; and it filled him with horror to think that Israel should remain in bitter rejection of her Messiah. There was in him, therefore, an unconquerable yearning to be heard in Jerusalem, and an unappeasable pain that prejudice closed the ears of his brethren according to the flesh against his voice. He was now contemplating a visit to Jerusalem, and was moving the Gentile churches to contribute to the relief of the poor saints of that church. These then were the causes of dejection and distress which at this period in the life of the apostle weighed down his spirit.

The occasion which called forth the Second Epistle to Corinth was the return and the report of Titus. Two things were clear —the First Epistle had wrought in the consciences of the Corinthians much which demanded commendation and encouragement; but much also remained to be set right. This Paul essayed in the Second Epistle.

ANALYSIS

The same facts which made a rigid, logical analysis of the First Epistle difficult are present here in even greater abundance. Second Corinthians is an outburst of mingled joy and sorrow—joy because of the evident working of the word in the consciences of the Corinthians; sorrow because the apostle clearly perceives that the deep tap-root of bitterness is not yet cut, viz., the utter failure of the saints at Corinth to see their position as heavenly beings, identified with a glorified Christ, and indwelt by the Spirit. The following divisions, however, are broadly accurate, and will be helpful :

Section I. The Solicitude of a True Minister of Jesus Christ. i., ii.

Section II. The Marks of a True Spiritual Ministry. iii. 1 to v. 10.

Section III. The Manward Side of Holy Living— Separation and Cleansing. vi. 11 to vii. 16.

Section IV. The Grace of Giving. viii., ix.

Section V. The Vindication of Paul's Apostleship. x. 1 to xiii. 14.

SECOND CORINTHIANS

1. Give an account, with Scripture proofs, of Paul's movements between the writing of First and Second Corinthians.

_____

_____

2. State in your own words his mental and physical state at this time, with Scripture proofs.

_____

_____

_____

3. Whom had Paul sent to Corinth with the first letter?

_____

_____

4. Where did that messenger rejoin the apostle?

_____

_____

5. State in your own words the distinction between the legalism of those who sought to put Gentile believers under the law of Moses, and those who were "of Christ."

_____

_____

_____

6. Give from memory the distinction between Christ's relation to the church and to the kingdom.

_____

_____

_____

7. Give Scripture to prove that Paul, in Second Corinthians, maintained this distinction.

_____

_____

8. Who is joined with Paul in greeting the Corinthians?

_____

_____

9. To whom is the Second Epistle addressed?

_____

10. What uses are we to make of the comfortings of God?

_____

_____

11. Who was suffering in Paul?

_____

_____

12. To what trouble does the apostle refer in i. 8?

_____

_____

13. Is the "anointing" of i. 21, identical with the "sealing" of sNaihir Payee

_____

_____

14, Explain the contrast in iii. 3 between the writing of God in the Mosaic dispensation and in the dispensation of Grace.

_____

_____

_____

15. How far does a true servant of Christ depend upon himself?

_____

_____

16. How far upon God?

_____

_____

17. Give the revised rendering of iii. 6.

_____

_____

_____

_____

18. Of what covenant is the servant of God in this dispensation a minister?

_____

_____

19. To what does Paul refer as "the letter' in iii. 6?

_____

_____

20. What is the effect of "the letter" upon sinful man?

_____

_____

21. What contrasting effect is wrought by the Spirit?

_____

_____

22. How does Paul continue the comparison in iii. 7, 8?

_____

_____

_____

23. Of what is the law a ministration?

_____

_____

24. Of what is the Spirit a minister?

_____

_____

25. Could the law give righteousness?

_____

_____

26. Was the law a full or a partial (veiled) revelation?

_____

_____

27. What becomes of the " veil" in Christ?

_____

_____

28. Does the "reading" (or knowledge of) the old covenant take away the veil?

_____

_____

29. What is the present condition of the children of Israel?

_____

_____

_____

30. When will the veil be taken away from the heart of Israel?

_____

_____

Note on III. 17. The apostle explains that the "Spirit" of whom he has been speaking in contrast with "the letter"—that is to say, "the ministration of death written and engraved in stones," is the Lord Himself; then he adds a word as to the Holy Spirit: "Where the Spirit of the Lord is, there is liberty." This does not mean unconstraint in preaching, but "free from the law." 'The Spirit makes actual in the believer's experience that liberty which he has in Christ.

31. By whom are we changed into the image of the Lord?

_____

_____

32. Is this effect wrought while we are beholding (or "reflecting"—see Revised Version) the Lord in humiliation, or the Lord in glory?

_____

_____

_____

33. What, in the light of chapter ii1., would you call the first mark of a true gospel ministry?

_____

_____

_____

34. What three evils in iv. 2 has the true servant put away?

_____

_____

_____

35. What commends the true servant?

_____

_____

36. Who is "the god of this world"?

_____

_____

37. To whom is the gospel "hid"?

_____

_____

38. Give the two marks of a true servant in iv. 5.

_____

_____

_____

39. What "treasure" have we in earthen vessels?

_____

_____

_____

40. What is meant by "earthen vessels"?

_____

_____

41. Why is the "treasure in earthen vessels"?

_____

_____

Note. The reference here is probably to the "lamps in the pitchers" of Gideon's three hundred (Judges vii. 16-20) and this thought—first, of the putting of the light within the "earthen vessels" and, secondly, that the light can only shine by the breaking of them—runs through the chapter. Verses 8, 9, 10 give the breaking and the result—"that the life also of Jesus might be made manifest in our body."

42. What is the distinction between "the outward man" and "the inward man?"

_____

_____

_____

43. Is the "glory" of all the saints in heaven equal?

_____

_____

_____

44, What makes a difference in the glory of one and of another?

_____

_____

45 How does the apostle, in chapter v., show that "we" may exist apart from our bodies?

_____

_____

46. What is the mortal body called in that chapter?

_____

_____

47. What is our condition in this body?

_____

_____

48. What should an instructed believer earnestly desire?

_____

_____

49. What is it which makes the believer "always confident "?

_____

_____

50. Give an illustration of walking by faith.

_____

_____

51. Give an illustration of walking by sight.

_____

_____

52. Where is a Christian who is "absent from the body"?

_____

_____

53. Give Revised Version rendering of v. 8.

_____

_____

_____

54. Of whom is the apostle speaking when: he says "we" must all appear before the judgment seat of Christ?

_____

_____

55. Which of the judgments is here spoken of?

_____

_____

56. What, in chapter v., does the apostle state to be his motive in service?

_____

_____

57. What effect upon the lives of believers should the death of Christ for them have?

_____

_____

58. What is it to know Christ "after the flesh'?

_____

_____

59. What is the "ministry" committed to the witnesses of Christ in this dispensation?

_____

_____

60. Upon what judgment of God does the ministry of reconciliation rest?

_____

_____

61. How does v. 21 interpret the first clause of v. 19?

_____

_____

62. Give illustrations of the unequal yoke of vi. 14.

_____

_____

_____

63. In what respects does the separation of 2 Cor. vi. 14-17 differ from that of 1 Cor. v. 9-11?

_____

_____

64. What was the effect upon the Corinthian church of Paul's First Epistle?

_____

_____

65. According to chapter vii., what is the relation of sorrow to repentance?

_____

_____

66. Was the repentance of that chapter that of the saved or unsaved?

_____

67. Give the passages which speak of sorrow in connection with the repentance of sinners.

_____

_____

68. State the principles governing Christian benevolence in chapters viii. and ix.

_____

_____

69. What is said in Second Corinthians of Satan?

_____

_____

70. Has Satan "ministers"?

_____

71. How do Satan's "minsters" make themselves acceptable?

_____

72. Why was Paul's "thorn in the flesh" given him?

_____

_____

73. What may that "thorn'" probably have been? See Gal. iv. 14, 15; 1 Cor. ii. 3, etc.

_____

_____

74. What effect had it upon his physical strength?

_____

_____

75. What reason did the Lord give His faithful servant for allowing the "thorn" to remain?

_____

_____

76. What was " sufficient?'

_____

_____

77. What are the "signs" of an apostle?

_____

_____

78. What names of Deity are given in this Epistle?

_____

_____

79. What is said as to the work of Christ?

_____

_____

80. What is said concerning the Holy Spirit?

_____

_____

81. Give a list of doctrines taught or referred to in Secord Corinthians?

_____

_____

_____

82. What truth is found in this Epistle not found in First or Second Thessalonians or First Corinthians?

_____

_____

LESSON LII

GALATIANS

GENERAL REMARKS

1. THE GALATIANS

Galatia was a province in the heart of the peninsula of Asia Minor, having Phrygia on the west, Bithynia and Paphlagonia: on the north, Pontus on the east, and Cappadocia and Lycaonia on the south. The people of this region were not of oriental origin, The Galatians, as the name indicates, were Gauls, "a stream from that torrent of barbarians which poured into Greece in the third century before Christ." Even in the time of Jerome (340-420 A. D.) "the language spoken at Ancyra was almost identical with that of Treves." 'This, however, is not to be taken as indicating that Greek was not also understood and spoken. In this respect Galatia might be compared to modern Wales, in which English is the language of law, literature and commerce, while the social intercourse of the people is still largely in the ancient tongue.

In the time of Paul Galatia was part of the all-conquering Roman empire. That many Jews of the dispersion also dwelt in Galatia is evident from the address of First Peter. 1 Pet. i. 1. The character of these oriental Gauls is sufficiently disclosed in the Epistle itself. All secular writers confirm that impression. "All writers, from Cesar to Thierry, have described them as susceptible of quick impressions and sudden changes, with a fickleness equal to their courage and enthusiasm."

The history of the work of the apostle in Galatia is of the briefest. Apart from the intimations of the Epistle itself, that story is contained in two short verses. As an incident of Paul's second missionary journey it is said (Acts xvi. 6): "Now when they had gone throughout Phrygia and the region of Galatia, and were forbidden of the Holy Ghost to preach the word in Asia," etc. (Acts xviii. 23.) "And

when he had landed at Cesarea, and gone up and saluted the church, he went down to Antioch. After he had spent some time there, he departed, and went over all the country of Galatia and Phrygia in order, strengthening all the disciples." From 1 Cor. xvi. 1, we know that the Galatians had part in the great offering to the poor saints in Jerusalem; and from Gal. i. 2 and 1 Peter i. 1, we learn that there were many "churches" in Galatia. Of the incidents of Paul's labors in that region, we know nothing. This very silence argues that the Jews were neither so numerous nor so influential as in other parts of the Greco-Roman regions evangelized by Paul.

2. THE OCCASION OF THE EPISTLE

After despatching Titus with his Second Epistle to the Corinthians (2 Cor. viii. 16-23) in which he announced to that church his own speedy coming "for the third time" (2 Cor. xiii. 1), the apostle departed from Philippi. 'The route and the details of the apostle's journey from Philippi to Corinth are not known. Even the place and time of the writing of Galatians are conjectural. It may be said, however, that the reasons for fixing the time as soon after Paul's arrival at Corinth on this third journey thither, and the place, therefore, as Corinth, seem to be ample.

The occasion of the writing of Galatians is sufficiently disclosed by the Epistle itself. In some way, it had come to the knowledge of the apostle that the fickle Galatians had become the prey of the legalists, the Judaizing missionaries from Palestine. The situation, by its very simplicity, presented an admirable occasion for striking straight at the heart of the error which, more surely than even sect divisions or immorality of conduct, poisons the gospel at its very source and makes of it of "another gospel." Gal. 1. 6.

What, then, was the Galatian heresy? The Epistle discloses it. It had two forms, the one fatal to the salvation of the sinner; the other, fatal to the sanctification of the believer.

The first form was the teaching that obedience to the law is mingled with faith as the ground of justification of the sinner. This Paul meets, first, by a flat denial (ii. 16; iii. 10-12), supported by a demonstration that salvation is through the gracious and unconditional covenant with Abraham, which the law, that was four hundred and thirty years after, can neither disannul nor make of none effect; and secondly, by vindicating the true purpose and intent of the law, which was condemnation and not justification.

The second form of the Galatian heresy was the teaching that the justified believer is "made perfect" by legal obedience. This Paul meets by a vindication of the office of the Holy Spirit as Sanctifier. .

In a word, legality always seeks to find in human obedience or goodness (even if it be no more than good intention) a reason for expecting blessing from God; while grace teaches that God finds that reason in Christ only.

The Epistle to the Galatian churches is the inspired answer to the constantly renewed attempt to mingle law and grace in the dealings of God. It is the subtlest and most pernicious of all the errors which have afflicted the churches of Christ. A thorough comprehension of Galatians is therefore essential to an established faith.

3. PAUL'S APOSTOLIC AUTHORITY

The student will remark in this Epistle an elaborate vindication by the apostle of his apostolic authority, and repeated and most solemn assertions that he received those distinctive doctrines of grace which he calls "my gospel" by direct revelation, and not by tradition from the apostles who were the companions of Christ in His humiliation. This cannot be too clearly conceived. Paul's message was not an echo, however faithfully repeated, of the earth teachings of His divine Master.

It was, in other words, of the precise nature of John's new ministry in the Revelation (Rev. i. 10-19). That is to say, Paul's gospel derives its authority from the risen Lord Himself—is the gospel of the risen Lord Himself.

The authentication to us of the divine origin of Paul's distinctive message is ample and indisputable.

(1) Paul asserts that he received his gospel by revelation. This assertion, therefore, has all the weight of his holy character.

(2) His gospel is in absolute accord with the teachings of Christ concerning sin and salvation.

(3) Paul's apostleship was fully recognized by the other apostles, one of whom (Peter) distinctly ranks his writings with "the other Scriptures." 2 Peter iii. 15, 16.

(4) His gospel is in entire harmony with the other apostolic writings and with the Old Testament.

(5) The blessing of God, both in the apostle's lifetime and continuously since, upon his distinctive testimony, is the abiding seal of the Almighty upon that testimony.

(6) The additional revelations given through Paul concerning the mystery of the church, are precisely such as the law of the progressive unfolding of truth demands. Beyond announcing His purpose to build His church (Matt. xvi. 18) our Lord did not go. To Paul was committed the revelation of the relationships, constitution, ministry and destiny of the church.

The sternness of Galatians, then, is not the sternness of an aroused controversialist, but the solemn judgment of Jesus Christ upon the perverters of His gospel—the only means for the salvation of the lost. Much error is, in divine forbearance, graciously borne with, but Galatianism is the destruction of the gospel, and therefore, intolerable to God. "Let him be anathema" is the necessary sentence of love upon whomsoever (even Paul or an angel) would dare preach "another" gospel.

ANALYSIS

Section I. Salutation. i. 1-5. The apostle at once asserts his apostolic commission as derived, not from man, nor through man, but directly from " Jesus Christ, and God the Father who raised Him from the dead." "Apostle" means sent one. Paul, therefore, affirms himself to be the sent one of the risen Lord. In verse 4 he states the true gospel— Christ in the twofold character of Sacrifice and Deliverer.

Section II, Theme. i. 6-9. Paul defines his controversy with the lapsed Galatian churches, and the controversy of Christ with gospel perverters. The Galatians are removed from grace. They have not deserted the churches, nor given up calling themselves Christians, nor fallen into gross immorality; but they have forsaken the gospel. The legalists call their doctrine a gospel, or "glad tidings" but there cannot be "another" gospel. The essence of the gospel is grace, or free favor to the undeserving. The moment human merit is brought in, grace is excluded and the gospel is destroyed. But the notion of human merit, as before a holy God, is a delusion and lie; to substitute goodness or law-keeping for grace is, therefore, to leave humanity helpless in its sins—" Christ is dead in vain" (ii. 21), and the holy wrath of God can but announce anathema upon false teachers who thus destroy the gospel.

Section III., The Vindication of the Divine Authority of Paul's Gospel. i. 10 to ii.14. First, the apostle appeals to their knowledge of him as to his character for sincerity. They know that the doctrines of free grace do not please men, who would fain have some credit for their morality and religiousness. None but a deeply sincere man would thus suffer the loss of popularity for conscience's sake.

Secondly, he certifies that the gospel which he had preached to them was neither "after man" (literally, "according to man") nor communicated to him through man, but only by direct revelation.

Thirdly, he reminds them that Judaism is no new thing to him. On the contrary, he had himself been a foremost Jew; and hence they might well conclude that he had maturely considered whether the law and the gospel could be united in the same system. His present position, hated and persecuted not only by Jews but by Judaized Christians, was wholly owing to the impossibility of uniting law and gospel. He had only to . mix legality with grace to be the most popular of Gpastane teachers. :

Fourthly, that they may see how completely independent of human authority his entire ministry had been, he rehearses his life from his conversion. This history makes it clear (1) that Paul had been preaching three years before he saw any of the other apostles. He then saw Peter and James. (2) Fourteen years later he went up to Jerusalem by divine direction, taking with him Barnabas and Titus—the latter an uncircumcised Gentile Christian. He communicated to them his gospel. Some difficulty was made by false brethren, who demanded the circumcision of Titus. That put the liberty of the gospel at stake, and Paul would not give way. But even that refusal did not hinder the fullest acknowledgment of Paul's apostleship. The "pillars,'" James, Cephas and John, gave to him and to Barnabas the right hand of fellowship that they should go to the Gentiles. (3) If the Judaizers were exalting Peter's authority (though falsely), his sufficient answer was that once at Antioch he, Paul, so far from conceding Peter's primacy, withstood him to the face. The apostle thus vindicates his authority to speak at first hand on behalf of the risen Christ.

Section IV. Justification is by Faith, without Law. ii. 15 to iii. 24. This marvelous vindication of the gospel of grace is in five parts.

Part 1. ii. 15-18. If any mortal might hope to find justification under law, it would be the Jew; but even the Jewish Christians, knowing that justification is not by the works of the law, but by the faith of Jesus Christ, have believed in Jesus Christ. Verses 15, 16. The student will note that

Paul here quotes from his words to Peter when he withstood him at Antioch! and the point is to show the Galatians that, whatever the legalists may have pretended, Peter and he were in perfect agreement doctrinally. The legalists must not, therefore, hide behind the pretended authority of Peter. It should be noted that verses 18, 19 are also quoted from Paul's rebuke of Peter. The point of the rebuke is that, by reverting to Jewish notions as to eating and drinking after "certain came from James" to Antioch, Peter was in effect denying the completeness of justification by faith alone. If a Jew's faith only put him upon Gentile ground, so that he had to perfect and round out his righteousness by obeying the dietary regulations of the law, then all Christ did was to make a Gentile sinner of him, and he had still to justify himself by obedience; the sum of the matter being that a sinner is wholly, completely, utterly justified by faith, leaving no place for law-work of any kind.

Part 2. ii. 19, 20. This is the second step in the apostle's demonstration. It meets the error that, though the sinner is not justified through the law, the saint must live under it as his rule of life.

The answer is that the law has so slain the sinner that he is forever dead to the law. He no more lives under the law than an executed criminal does. This statement Bengel calls the "summa ac medulla Christianismi"—sum and marrow of Christianity. It is the doctrine, fully developed in verse 20, that in the reckoning of God and of faith the believer was crucified with Christ, and that the new life which he has received is the very life of the risen Christ; in very deed Christ lives in him, so that neither the righteousness which justifies, nor righteousness of life are by the law. The effect of the demonstration down to this point is that the sinner is completely justified before God by faith in Christ without law-works; that he is dead to the law; and that Christ (against whom the law can say nothing) is now his life.

Part 3. ii. 21. Here the apostle takes the third step in his demonstration. The law does not

mingle with grace in the pure gospel, because if righteousness come by the law then Christ is dead in vain. This is the first use of the word righteousness in the present Epistle.

This word is used in Scripture in three senses:

(1) Self-righteousness, the result of legal obedience. Luke xviii. 9-12; Phil. ii. 4-6.

(2) That "righteousness without works' which God imputes to "him that worketh not, but believeth on Him that justifieth the ungodly." Rom. iv. 4-8, 22-25.

(3) The transformed character of the believer. Rom. viii. 4; vi. 17, 18. The first is the bad sense, the second and third are the good senses of the word. Righteousness is both imputed and imparted, and in both respects it is Christ Himself "who of God is made unto us...righteousness."

In verses 16 and 20 the apostle has presented both meanings; by faith we are justified, that is declared righteous, and by the imparted and indwelling Christ we are made righteous. In verse 21, Paul uses "righteousness" in this complete sense, and as against those who would either justify the sinner or rule the saint by law he declares that in either case they frustrate the grace of God and make Christ's death a useless immolation.

Part 4. iii. 1-5. The apostle's fourth objection is that the gift of the Holy Spirit is by faith and not by law-works. The Holy Spirit is presented in Galatians in two ways: (1) As "the Spirit of His Son," sent into our hearts to give us the sense of our place as full-grown sons, arrived at our majority; the proof that we are not minors under bondage to the law as were the Old Testament saints. iv. 1-7. (2) As the power of a holy life; our deliverer from the dominion of the flesh. v. 16-26.

The point is that law-works can add nothing to an individual who is justified perfectly before God; who is dead to the law; in whom Christ lives, and who, finally, has received the Spirit of sonship and victory.

Part 5. iii. 6-24. The apostle's fifth step is to clear up the relations between the Abrahamic and the Mosaic covenants. The demonstration is made:

(1) That redemption is under the Abrahamic covenant, the gospel having been preached to Abraham in the promise, "In thee shall all nations be blessed." iii. 8. Abraham believed, "and it was imputed to him for righteousness." Abraham was saved then by faith, and as many as are of faith are blessed with him and are his children. (See Part 1, Section II.)

(2) The law, on the contrary, does not save but curses; and it curses not some but all.

(3) How then may any be saved? The answer is that "Christ hath redeemed us from the curse of the law,'" etc., so that the "blessing of Abraham" which, so to speak, was on its way to us but was stopped by the righteous sentence of the law, might (the sentence of the law having been executed upon Christ) come on the Gentiles through Jesus Christ.

(4) Furthermore, the Abrahamic covenant was confirmed four hundred and thirty years before the law was given, and it cannot reach back and annul a previously confirmed covenant. One, therefore, who takes justification under the Abrahamic covenant, cannot be deprived of it upon the one hand, nor made more secure in it upon the other hand, by the law.

(5) This suggests the query, "Wherefore then the law?" The answer is twofold: It was added because of transgressions till the Seed should come; so including all under sin, and shutting them up to faith as the alone way of hope; and it was a pedagogue or tutor to rule minor children until Christ should come. "As a pedagogue has his wards in guidance and training for the aim of their future majority, so the law has taken us into a guidance and training of which Christ was the aim, that is, of which the aim was that in due time they should no longer be under the law." —H. A. W. Meyer.

Section V. The Rule of the Believer's Life is Gracious, not Legal. iii. 25 to v. 26. This section discusses the principles which govern the life and sanctification of the believer. These principles are as follows:

First, he is no longer under the schoolmaster; the law (verse 25). This rebukes modern Galatianism. Very few are now found to declare that justification is by the law. The more subtle error, that the believer, though not justified by law, is nevertheless still under law as a rule or principle of life, is still widely taught. Doubtless the law, as part of Scripture given by inspiration of God, is "profitable for instruction in righteousness" to any believer who might be so ignorant as not to know the holy requirements of the law; but Paul will by no means allow that in any possible case the "schoolmaster" has any authority over a Christian." But after that faith is come we are no longer under a schoolmaster" (verse 25), is his broad, unqualified statement.

Secondly, the apostle gives the reason why the tutelage of the law has ended for the believer: "For ye are all sons of God, through faith in Christ Jesus.'" (Verse 26, Revised Version.)

"Sons" is not synonymous with " children." The former means maturity, the latter relationship merely. The "sons" are the "children" come of age. The Old Testament saint was a child, but not (in the New Testament sense) a son. Regeneration makes children; the baptism with the Spirit puts the "children" into "sonship." This Paul illustrates by the contrast between the position of a godly Jew under the law and that of a believing Jew (or Gentile) now. (The student should use the Revised Version in all passages bearing upon sonship.) The point is that before Christ came the children of God were under law, the law being to them as guardians and stewards to minor children; but now believers, by the baptism and indwelling of the Spirit, are, in Christ Jesus the Son, made sons—full-grown, adult children, who are no longer under the authority of a guardian or steward, but under the immediate personal! authority of) then Pathen. iii. 26 tol v. 7. The Father's will is, then, the rule of the believer's life. To make it effective "the Spirit of His Son" is sent forth into believing hearts. iv. 6. If Paul had been writing to Hebrews he would perhaps have said, "This is the blessing promised in the new covenant: I will put my laws into their hearts."

Thirdly. To go back to law now is to leave the place of sons and go back to that of young children who differ in nothing from bondservants. iv. 8-11. The readiness of the Galatians to do this perplexes the apostle. iv. 12-20.

Fourthly. To make the matter perfectly clear, Paul reverts to Abraham who had two sons, Ishmael by Hagar, Isaac by Sarah. But Hagar, a bondwoman, could only bring forth a bondslave. She, with her offspring, therefore, stands for Sinai or the law system, which is one of bondage, and which has to do with the fleshly or natural man. Isaac, the son of promise, born of the freewoman, becomes, on the other hand, the true type of sonship. But a question arose: Should there be one law, one inheritance, for the servant and the son? In other words, is it possible for the natural man and the spiritual man to abide under one system? Obviously not. "The natural man receiveth not the things of the Spirit of God, for they are foolishness unto him." 1 Cor. 11.14. Liberty, to the natural man, means simply lawlessness—the pleasing of self. He can understand law. But to put the son, the spiritual man, under law is to entangle him with a yoke of bondage, like an adult man under a guardian. The two systems of law and of grace cannot, therefore, be combined. Exclusion is the only remedy; "Cast out the bondwoman and her son.'" iv. 21-31.

It is precisely the principle of 1.Tim. i. 9: "Knowing this, that the law is not made for a righteous man, but for the lawless and unruly, for the ungodly and sinners, for the unholy and profane."

The apostle follows the illustration from Hagar and Sarah with suited rebukes and exhortations down to v.15 inclusive.

Fifthly. Paul now states the second great principle of the believer's life, growth, and sanctification. The first was based on sonship in union with Christ the Son. This made him free from the law. ili. 26 toiv. 31. One baptized into Christ, made a living part of Him, a member of His body, of His flesh, and of His bones, must share His position. The second (v. 16-24) great truth concerning the Christian is the indwelling of the Holy Spirit, and the effect of that fact upon his entire life. The contrast with the legal position is absolute. A child but not a son, the man under law had not received the spirit of sonship. The governing principle of his life was, therefore, obedience to external authority; conformity to a written law. But the believer of the church age is indwelt by the Spirit. This fact governs the walk (v. 16) gives victory over the flesh (v. 17) and delivers from legality (v.18). Furthermore, the energy of the indwelling Spirit produces character. v. 22, 28. Godly character under the dispensation of law was "walking in all the commandments and ordinances of the law blameless" (Luke i. 6); character under the dispensation of the Spirit is "Love, joy, peace, long-suffering, gentleness, goodness, faith, meekness, temperance." And the apostle would have the Galatians know that the new character is not the product of their effort, but the fruit of the Holy Spirit.

Section VI. Exhortations and Conclusion. v. 25 to vi. 18. This section covers, briefly, the central principles which are to regulate Christian conduct.

EPISTLE TO THE GALATIANS

1. To whom was this Epistle written?

_____

_____

2. Describe Galatia and the Galatians.

_____

_____

_____

3. Why did Paul write Galatians?

_____

_____

4. Is anything said to indicate that the Galatians had fallen into immorality or sectarianism?

_____

5. Define the errors into which the Galatians had fallen or were in danger of falling.

_____

_____

_____

6. Why were these errors serious?

_____

_____

7. Why is the Epistle to the Galations of permanent value?

_____

_____

8. State in your own words how. Paul proves that the gospel. which he preached was of divine authority.

_____

_____

_____

_____

9. State in your own words what reasons we have for receiving Paul's. writings as the Word of God.

_____

_____

_____

_____

10. Why is the preacher who perverts the gospel accursed?

_____

_____

_____

11. Give in your own words the substance of Section I.

_____

_____

_____

_____

12. Give in your own words the substance of.Section II.

_____

_____

_____

_____

13. Give in your own words the substance of the fourfold argument of Paul in Section III.

_____

_____

_____

_____

14. Into how many parts does Section IV. fall?

_____

15. State in your own words the substance of Part 1

_____

_____

_____

_____

16. State in your own words the substance of Part 2.

_____

_____

_____

_____

17. State in your own words the substance of Part 3.

_____

_____

_____

_____

18. State in your own words the substance of Part 4.

_____

_____

_____

_____

19. State in your own words the substance of Part 5.

_____

_____

_____

_____

20. Give in your own words the substance of Section V.

_____

_____

_____

_____

21. What is the difference in position between a believer under the dispensation of law and a believer under the dispensation of grace?

_____

_____

_____

22. How does Paul illustrate this difference?

_____

_____

23. Into whom is the believer said to be baptized?

_____

_____

24. What are we said to become through faith in Christ Jesus?

_____

_____

25. How do we, as sons of God, come into the realization of our sonship?

_____

_____

26. How does Paul illustrate the impossibility of mingling law and grace in one system?

_____

_____

27. Does "Sinai" stand in the allegory for the moral law, the ceremonial law, or both?

_____

28. Why, then, cannot the natural man and the spiritual man live under one system?

_____

_____

29. What is "falling from grace?"

_____

_____

30. Why is the cross a "stumbling-block" to legalists?

_____

_____

_____

31. What danger are we liable to in this freedom from law?

_____

_____

_____

32. Is Paul's doctrine, therefore, "a dangerous doctrine," as some say?

_____

_____

_____

33. Is the danger in the doctrine or in ourselves?

_____

_____

_____

34. How may we live in victory over the flesh?

_____

_____

_____

35. What antagonism exists between the indwelling Holy Spirit and the flesh?

_____

_____

_____

36. How does the believer profit by that antagonism?

_____

_____

_____

37. Because the flesh is in us, are we compelled to do the works of the flesh?

_____

_____

38. Could one living in the practice of the sins described in v. 19, 20 be a son of God?

_____

_____

39. Write from memory the "fruits of the Spirit."

_____

_____

_____

_____

40. Is it biblical to speak of "building" character?

_____

_____

41. How, then, is Christian character produced?

_____

_____

_____

42. What illustration of the true method of producing the Christian character do you find among the last teachings of our Lord?

_____

_____

_____

43. By what means do they that are in Christ Jesus "crucify the flesh?"

_____

_____

_____

44. How does verse 25 help toward answering Question 43?

_____

_____

_____

45. What is to be done to a Christian who falls into sin?

_____

_____

_____

46. Quote a passage from First Corinthians which defines the word "spiritual" in Gal. vi. 1.

_____

_____

_____

47. How do you reconcile vi. 2 with vi.

_____

_____

_____

48. What great law of retribution is announced in vi. 7,

_____

_____

_____

49. Is this written to Christians or sinners?

_____

_____

_____

50. Does "corruption" in vi. 8 mean the loss of the soul?

_____

_____

_____

51. If a Christian has "sown to the flesh," is there no escape from the operation of this law?

_____

_____

_____

52. What great promise encourages to well-doing?

_____

_____

_____

53. What effect upon the relations of a Christian to the world has the cross of Christ?

_____

_____

54. Explain v. 24 in the light of vi.

_____

_____

_____

55. What is "the Israel of God"?

_____

_____

_____

56. Give your definition of Paul's meaning in vi.

_____

_____

_____

57. State, now, the central principles of Christian conduct, as laid down in Section VI.,

_____

_____

_____

(1) Towards Cvhristians;

_____

_____

_____

(2) Towards the world.

_____

_____

_____

LESSON: LII

ROMANS

GENERAL REMARKS

After writing Galatians, but at some time during the remainder of his three months' stay at Corinth, the Apostle Paul wrote the great Epistle to the Romans. We know almost nothing of the church of Rome during the apostolic period. It is not even known at what time, nor by what means, it was planted. The Roman Catholic tradition affirms that Peter was its founder and resident bishop. This claim rests purely upon tradition. It is incredible, if it were true, that Paul should send no salutation to his brother apostle. Neither is it known, except by inference from such passages as Rom. i. 13; x. 1-3, whether the church at Rome were predominately Jewish or Gentile. From the whole tenor of the Epistle, however, it seems beyond question to have been overwhelmingly Gentile. But all these questions, are of little importance to a right understanding of the Epistle, for it is not addressed to the church at Rome but "to all God's beloved, called saints, who dwell in Rome." It is not, then, a church epistle. Its theme is stated in i. 16, 17: "For I am not ashamed of the gospel, for it is the power of God unto salvation to every one that believeth; to the Jew first, and also to the Greek."

Accordingly, the Epistle does not concern itself with the revelation of the distinctive position of the church, as Ephesians; nor with church life and order as the Corinthian Epistles, but with the explanation of the gospel in relation to personal salvation, blessing and conduct. In fact, the church is mentioned but once. xvi. 23. The fact that great numbers of Jews dwelt at Rome, over whom the apostle yearned, led to the insertion of the great passage (ix. i. to xi. 36) which Professor Stifler rightly called "the theodicy" ("God is right'), in which God is vindicated in His present dealing with Israel, and the Gentile saints are instructed concerning their own position with reference to the Jews, and informed that God has not "cast off His people" but that He will yet save "all Israel."

The Epistle, therefore, explains, illustrates and defends the gospel; applies it to the blessing of the individual, whether Jew or Gentile; instructs the Gentile believers concerning their relation to the Jew, and lays down principles governing the Christian life.

The occasion of the writing of Romans is to be gathered from the apostle's statements in 1. 8-13 and xv. 14-33. He had long desired to visit the saints at Rome, and now that hope seems to be nearing realization. He is about to go to Jerusalem with gifts from his Gentile churches to poor Jewish saints, and purposes then to go to Spain. That journey will give him the long-coveted opportunity to see the saints in Rome, impart to them some gift, and discharge his debt to Rome by preaching the gospel there also.

Naturally, the apostle would wish to announce before his coming the doctrines of truth revealed to and preached by him. Accounts of his controversies with Judaizing teachers would have reached the ears of the Roman saints, and the apostle would desire them to have his own statement of the doctrines which were assailed by the Judaizers.

Just at this time, too, a safe messenger was available in the person of Phoebe, a deaconess of the church at Cenchrea, who was about to visit Rome. These are the natural occasions of this great Epistle. But, back of all these occasions, the Holy Spirit, the Author (as Paul was the writer) of Romans, knew that this honored servant of Christ was about to enter upon a series of experiences which would for a long time deprive His penman of the quietness of spirit and of circumstances which he was now enjoying at Corinth, and which were necessary for such a work.

ANALYSIS

The chief divisions of Romans are so obvious that even a cursory reading reveals them. The central theme is: The gospel as the revelation of the righteousness of God which is given to all men, whether Jew or Gentile, upon the alone condition of faith in Christ. This theme is developed in a seven-fold way, exclusive of the introduction. The analysis, therefore, is as follows:—

INTRODUCTION AND THEME. I. 1-17

Section I. THe Whole World Guilty Before God. i. 18 to iii. 20.

Note. In the study of this section the student should carefully observe the ground of the condemnation of the four classes into which the apostle divides humanity. The ground of condemnation is not sin as sin merely, but sin in the face of varying degrees of light.

"For the wrath of God is revealed from heaven against all ungodliness and unrighteousness of men who hold down the truth [the truth which they know] in unrighteousness."

In Section I. the apostle applies this principle of condemnation to four classes, thus dividing the section into four parts.

Part 1. Atheism condemned because the being of God is proved by the visible universe. i. 19, 20.

Part 2. Idolatry condemned because it is a willful departure from the once known true God, and because of the abominable results of it. i. 21, 31.

Part 3. Ethical moralizers (*i.e.*, the heathen philosophers), who discern the folly of idolatry and the spiritual nature of the Supreme Being, condemned because, with conscience thus enlightened, they do not obey conscience. ii. 1-16.

Part 4. The Jew, the man of privilege, who has the law, and who is the custodian of the oracles of God, condemned by the very law in the knowledge of which he boasts, but which he has transgressed. ii. 17 to iii. 20.

Section II. Justification by Faith in Christ Crucified the Gospel Remedy for Human Guilt. iii. 21 to v. 11. This section is in three parts:

Part 1. The doctrine of justification by faith, apart from law, stated. iii. 21-31. This part holds the very heart of the gospel. The student should therefore become thoroughly familiar with it.

Here four great words require definition—righteousness, justification, faith, and propitiation. Righteousness is used in three senses in Scripture.

(1) Self-righteousness or the doing of the things required in the law. This consisted not in unvarying obedience to the moral law, for, save Christ, no man ever achieved that; but in the scrupulous offering of the sacrifices, and in the observance of the forms of the ceremonial law. Luke xviii. 9-14; Phil. iii. 4-9; Heb. ix. 9,10.

(2) The "righteousness of God." By this (which is one of the key-words to Romans) is meant, not God's own rightness of character and conduct, but that rightness, as manifested in Christ,

(a) imputed and

(b) imparted to the believing sinner.

Under law, God required righteousness from man; under grace, He gives righteousness to man. The following definitions are suggestive and helpful. The righteousness of God is:

- "That righteousness which God's righteousness requires Him to require." —Cunninghame.
- "That righteousness of which God is the Author; which is of avail before God; which meets and secures His approval."— Hodge.
- "That righteousness which the Father requires, the Son became, the Holy Spirit convinces of, and faith secures."— Brookes.
- "The sum total of all that God commands, demands, approves and Himself provides."— Moorehead.
- "Christ Jesus, who, of God, is made unto us righteousness."— Paul.

(3) Righteousness is used of the transformed character of the believers. Rom. viii. 4; 1 Cor. xv. 34; Phil: i. 11, etc.

Justification is the result of that act of God which credits to every sinner who exercises faith in Christ, all that Christ is in person, character, and work. This act is called imputation. It does not impugn God's justice, because Christ has already identified Himself with the sinner by taking up his liability and answering for it to God's law.

Faith is a trustful acceptance of Christ in all that God declares concerning Him. John iii. 34; v. 24, Revised Version; 1 John v. 9, 10:

Propitiation. This word is the translation of a Greek word used both in the Septuagint (the Greek version of the Old Testament) and by the writers of the New Testament, for "mercy seat." In Exodus xxv. 17, 18, 21: Heb. iv. 5, etc. It was upon the mercy seat that the atoning blood was sprinkled on the great day of atonement. Levit. xvi. 14. The idea is not that God was made loving toward the sinner by the shedding of sacrificial blood, but that the sacrificial blood evinced the sinner's acceptance of the righteous sentence of God's holy law, so that God could still be just and yet be propitious to the sinner. The sinner's faith in Christ includes "faith in His blood" (iii. 25); that is, faith in Christ as "the Lamb of God" voluntarily offering Himself on the sinner's behalf in vindication of God's holy law. The cross enables God to "be just, and the justifier of him that believeth in Jesus."

Part 2. The doctrine of justification by faith illustrated by the instances of Abraham and of David.

The student will bear in mind that the doctrine is not merely the assertion that justification is by faith, but that it is by faith wholly apart from law. The illustrations prove both points. Abraham was justified by an act of faith centuries before the law was given, and at least fourteen years before circumcision was given. He was justified apart from any question either of law obedience or circumcision obedience. David, on the other hand, a man under law, but who had most shockingly broken the law, is equally justified, and surely without works. Note, also, that Abraham is used not only to illustrate the truth that justification is by faith apart from law merit, but also to illustrate the kind of faith which brings justification. He believed that what God had promised He was able to perform (iv. 16-21) ; we believe that what God had promised He has performed (iv. 23-25). In both cases the facts believed are supernatural. A faith which does not include a belief that Jesus died for our offenses and was raised again for our justification is fatally defective; it is not saving faith.

Part 3. The blessed results of justification by faith. v. 1-11.

These results are seven. Being justified by faith we have (1) peace with God, verse 1; (2) a standing in grace, verse 2; (3) a joyful expectation of the glory of God, verse 2; (4) the ability to glory in untoward things because of what they accomplish in us, verse 3; (5) the love of God imparted to us by the Holy Spirit, verse 5; (6) the Spirit Himself given to us, verse 5; and (7) instead of guilty fear of God, joy in Him, verses 9, 11,

Section III. Crucifixion with Christ and a New Life in the Holy Spirit the Gospel Remedy for Inherent Sin. v. 12 to viii. 13.

In this great section the apostle takes up the deepest need of humanity. The race, without one individual exception, is guilty because of sins done. For that need the gospel remedy, as we have seen, is Christ's death for sinners. But back of sins committed stands the man who committed them. The death of Christ has answered for his guilt, but the man himself remains. What manner of man is he by nature? What is his history? What shall be done for him? For example, now that he has been justified by faith, without law-works, shall he receive divine help henceforth to keep the law? If his natural heart is bad, shall it be changed into a good heart?

Note. The student will observe that from v. 1 to the end of Romans there is no more question of the safety of the believer. His justification by faith alone, without one atom of merit in him, has forever settled the question of his safety. God has been shown as not only merciful, but also as absolutely just, in thus justifying a believing sinner, because the whole question of his guilt has been so dealt with through Christ as to maintain the authority of the law. As the apostle says (iii. 31): "Do we, then, make the law of none effect through faith? God forbid; nay, we establish the law." God's holiness, God's law, and God's love, are perfectly vindicated, and He may justly justify the believer. The section upon which the student now enters, therefore, is occupied, not with making the believing sinner safe, but with making him holy.

The section is in five closely related parts.

Part 1. The race, descended from Adam, receives from him the heritage of sin; and the justified man is through Christ made righteous. v. 12-21.

The universality of sin in creation is proved by the universality of death. That this death is not the penalty of transgression under law is shown by the fact that death reigned from Adam to Moses as completely as since Moses. There was universal penalty, and therefore universal sin. The contrast is:

Adam,   sin,   death.
Christ, righteousness   life

Note. The doctrines of the believer's union to Christ and of Adamic headship, fully developed in the Corinthians, are implied in Romans. The student should have in mind 1 Cor. xii. 12-27 and xv. 22, 45.

Part 2. In the reckoning of God, the believer's union with Christ began with Christ's death, and continues in His resurrection. vi. 1-10.

Part 3. The believer must reckon to be true, what God reckons. vi. 11-23.

The believer, in effect, must say: "Since God takes account of me as a man who was dead and is risen from the dead to walk in newness of life, I, too, will think of myself as a man who was put to death by crucifixion and is now living solely unto the God who raised me from the dead. ° I will treat myself as God treats me." Verses 11, 12.

This "newness of life" is not only a new quality of life received from Christ, but, practically, a new yieldedness. Just as faith is the state which brings to the sinner justification, so yieldedness is the state which brings holiness to the justified saint. Verses 13-23. It is impossible to see this too clearly. "We were the servants of sin" (verse 17) because the yielding was to sin. The fruit then was death. The new yieldedness is of self unto God and of the members unto righteousness, and the new fruit is holiness. The justified man, therefore, takes a twofold position; he accounts himself to be a living man who was dead, and he "yields" himself to God to be made holy.

Part 4. The relation of the justified man to the law. vi. 14; vii. 1-25. (1) He is not under the law but under grace. Verse 14. In that fact lies the promise of his deliverance from sin. The law could tell him to be good, but could not make him good. Grace can. But the reason he is no longer under the law is that he is dead to it by his co-crucifixion with Christ. He was like a wife married to law; but the wife died and is no longer under the authority of that husband. Now, in resurrection, she is married to another husband, Christ. The fruit of the former marriage (through no fault of the former husband, but through sin) was death, but now we may bring forth fruit unto God. vii. 1-6. Indeed, the believer should know that he could not become holy by the law. The law is holy, just and good, but in his unjustified state it only aroused the evil that was in him, and so slew him. It did show him his exceeding sinfulness, but did not make him good. As for the effect of law on a justified man the apostle will give his own experience. He could delight in it in his new self, he could will to produce its righteousness, but he could not perform what he willed because of the old law of sin in his members,

The effort and conflict only brought him into defeat and anguish. He got no deliverance so long as he looked to law. viii. 14-24.

Part 5. The justified man finds deliverance and victory through Christ by the Holy Spirit. vii. 25 to viii. 13.

The deliverance from the dominion of sin which could not be found through the law (vii. 22, 23), nor through an awakened , and sensitive conscience (vii. 12, 16, 19), nor through a resolved will (vii. 18) is found through Jesus Christ (vii. 25). The method of deliverance is then disclosed.

(1) There is no condemnation to them who are in Christ Jesus. viii. 1, R. V. Christ has so perfectly met the question of our personal guilt, and, in the reckoning of God, our old man so perfectly died in Christ's death, that neither because of our sinful acts, nor because of such manifestations of the self-life as are set forth in chapter vil., are we subject to condemnation. It is a restatement of justification after the discussion of Adamic and inherent sin. It is as if the apostle said, "Well, in spite of this tragic failure of my efforts to be holy, my justification holds; there is no condemnation."

(2) Through Christ we have received the Holy Spirit and He is a "law" superior to the law of sin and death. Deliverance from the dominion of sin (the flesh, the old man) is wrought, not by law, nor conscience, nor will power, but by the indwelling of an omnipotent deliverer, the Holy Ghost. The law could not do this, for it imparted no new power; it only called upon the flesh to do what the flesh was too weak to do. Therefore God condemned the sinful flesh to crucifixion in the offering of His Son. Now, through the Spirit of life, the righteousness which the law required is fulfilled in (not "by") us, because we walk in yieldedness to the Spirit's will.

The gospel is thus seen to be in two great divisions. The guilt of the believer, as having committed sins, is met by imputing to him the righteousness of God; his deeper need, as inherently sinful, is met by imparting to him righteousness through the Holy Spirit. The first is justification, the second sanctification. :

Note. Sanctification is treated in Scripture in a threefold way.

(1) Positionally, the believer is at once "sanctified [set apart for God] through the offering of the body of Christ once for all." Heb. x. 10, 14; Heb. ii. 11. Of this the Spirit is the seal and earnest. Eph. I. 13. From the moment of faith the believer is accounted holy. Heb. iii. 1; 1 Thess. v. 27; 1 Cor i. 2.

(2) Experimentally, the believer is being sanctified through the work of the risen Christ as High Priest, the indwelling Holy Spirit, and the Word. Eph. v. 25, 26; John xiii. 8; 1 Cor. vi. 11; John xvii. 17; 2 Cor. vii. 1; 1 Thess. v. 22, 23; 1 John i. 9.

(3) Completely, at the appearing of the Lord. 1 John iii. 1, 2.

A sanctified man in the second, or experimental, sense is not, therefore, a sinlessly perfect man, but a justified man, who, "yelding his members instruments unto righteousness, and himself unto God as alive from the dead," "walks not after the flesh, but after the Spirit." Such an one will be cleansed from all known and realized sin; though his growth in knowledge and grace, and his constant fellowship with the Father and with His Son, Jesus Christ, will continually bring to his knowledge as sinful, things not before seen as such. "Cleansing," it should be noted, is more than forgiveness; it is deliverance from that particular form of sin. Both operations of grace are seen in 1 John i. 9.

Verses 5-13 constitute a greatly important and precious discussion of the principles of the walk of the sanctified man in the Spirit. The student should study these verses in the Revised Version for its greater accuracy in avoiding the use of the word "carnal," which does not mean "the flesh," or what we are by nature, but is properly used of an unspiritual Christian. See 1 Cor. iii. 1-3, and note the threefold classification in 1 Cor. ii. 14 to iii. 4. The "natural man" is unsaved; the "carnal" man is justified, but not spiritual; the "spiritual man" is the justified man Spirit-controlled.

In Rom. viii. 5-13 the apostle recurs to the condition of the man in the flesh, and contrasts it with the condition of the man in the blessing of the full gospel. This man is not "in the flesh" (verse 9), though the flesh is in him (verses 12, 18); and it is his privilege, through the might of the indwelling Spirit, to keep in the place of death that flesh which, in the reckoning of God, is dead (verse 13). The whole force of the passage is to emphasize the indwelling of every believer by the holy, omnipotent Spirit of life, and the life of high spirituality thus made possible.

Section IV. The Full Result in Blessing of the Gospel. viii. 14-39.

Having stated the full results of justification.(v. 1-11) and the gospel method of sanctification (v. 12 to viii. 13), the apostle may now sum up in one sweeping statement the full blessedness of the gospel which he began (i. 16, 17) by declaring to be "the power of God unto salvation." Though in strictness, as we have seen, the first thirteen verses of chapter viii. form the conclusion of the long argument which begins with the declaration (vi. 14), "sin shall not have dominion over you, for ye are not under the law, but under grace;'" still the eighth chapter in itself forms a complete statement, and should be studied as a whole. It falls into natural divisions, as follows:

Part 1. To believers in Christ there is no possible condemnation. Christ has died for their sins, and they have died to sin by the same cross, viii. 1.

Part 2. Having been accounted righteous through the work of Christ for them, believers are made righteous through the. work of the Spirit in them. viii. 2-13.

Part 3. viii. 14-16. The Spirit makes actual to believers their. new position as sons of God. (1) He leads them; (2) by Him they are able to cry, "Abba," Father; (3) He witnesses with their spirits to their sonship.

Part 4. vii. 17-30. The apostle reveals the amazing fact that because believers are children of God, they are also heirs of God, having joint heirship with Christ. But this joint heirship begins at once, and includes suffering with Him in this present time as well as glory with Him at His return. But there is so little suffering in comparison with the greatness of the glory, that, indeed, there is no real comparison.

The whole creation fell with its head, Adam (Gen. iii. 17, 18); it: is subject to vanity; under the bondage of death; and groans and travails in pain. Wealso, for a time, groan, teas we have the first fruits of the Spirit, for we have not yet our spiritual bodies. The Spirit groans also in inarticulate intercessions, because He, too, is indwelling this body in which we groan with the groaning creation (though He helps our infirmities). But the creation is to be delivered into the glory of the liberty of the sons of God. It is ours and is "waiting" for us. Thus, though we are still called to suffer we suffer in hope—hope of our "revealing" as sons of God; hope of our renewed, spiritual bodies, hope of entrance with Christ into our joint inheritance, the delivered creation—and so we "with patience wait," even though suffering. Besides, faith interprets "all things' as actively cooperating for our good, and this gives comfort and fortitude.

And then follows another revelation of truth for the stay of suffering saints; we are in a process the end of which is sure. That end is absolute conformity to Christ. "For whom He foreknew, He also foreordained to be conformed to the image of His Son, that He might be the first born among many brethren." And then the process is disclosed: "And whom He foreordained, them He also called, and whom He called, them He also justified, and whom He justified them He also glorified." There is no possible loss of the soul in which, and in behalf of which, this wonderful process has begun.

Part 5. viii. 31-39. This magnificent passage brings out the full triumph of the believer in Christ. In a word, God is for him. Spener calls that statement "the best of the glad tidings." God is "for" the sinner who believes on the Lord Jesus Christ. The apostle rises to his highest note of exultation, "Who can be against us?" And not only that, but who shall even lay anything to the charge of God's elect? How can we be brought again to the bar of justice who have already been—not acquitted but—justified, declared flawlessly righteous? Can anyone charge us before God in the face of Christ's perpetual intercession? No, for absolutely nothing in heaven, earth or hell can separate us from Christ's love.

Section V. THE GOSPEL Does Not Set Aside the Distinctive Covenant Obligations and Promises of God to Israel. ix. 1 to xi. 36.

This great passage is really a parenthesis, Chapter xii., which begins, "I beseech you, therefore, brethren, by the mercies of God that ye present your bodies," etc., is the resumption of the line of thought and revelation abruptly interrupted at the end of chapter vili. But, as Prof. Stifler has pointed out with a clearness and force unequaled by any other commentator on Romans, logic required the apostle to insert this section at this precise point. It is convenient for us to forget the Jew. It is easy, too, for usually Christians know almost nothing of distinctive Jewish covenant and promise. Furthermore, there still lingers in some minds the old and often disproved notion that Christians are now the true Israel. But to the apostolic church the question of the relation of Judaism to the new institution, the church, was the most living and burning of questions. Having, therefore, brought the entire race into one common condemnation as sinners, and opened the one and only salvation in the gospel, the question

inevitably emerges, What, then, becomes of the Davidic covenant, confirmed by the oath of God and renewed to the mother of Jesus by the angel Gabriel? What becomes of the repeated, specific, and absolutely unconditional promises of the restoration of all Israel to the land of their fathers, and the establishment again of the monarchy in the person of a Messiah, who should be son and heir of David? This section is the apostle's answer. Justas James, in the Jerusalem council, showed that the acceptance of the Gentiles by faith without circumcision not only did not contradict the prophets, but "agreed" with them, since they had predicted the restoration as occurring after the return of the Lord (Acts xv. 14-17); so Paul, only more at length, explains that this gospel age is an interregnum fully foreseen by the prophets, and that, so far from having done with national Israel, the Deliverer shall yet come out of Zion and "all Israel" (not "every Israelite") shall be saved.

The difficulty, therefore, is deeper than that respecting the Davidic covenant merely. It has to do with the older and more vital Abrahamic covenant. The promise of salvation was to Israel, and now Israel was not being saved. The parts are as follows:—

Part 1. The apostle's solicitude. ix. 1-3.

Part 2. The recognition and description of the seven-fold supremacy of Israel. ix. 4, 5.

Part 3. The distinction between the natural and spiritual seed of Abraham. ix. 6-13. This is the passage which has, to the utter confusion of all interpretation of the Old Testament, been perverted to teach that Gentiles become the true Israel by believing on Christ. It is, indeed, distinctly taught (Gal. iit. 7, 8) that believers, without distinction of race are "sons of Abraham"; but (1) Christians are never said to be sons of Jacob (or Israel); and (2) Christ recognized the precise distinction between a natural and a spiritual Jew which Paul here establishes. See John viii. 37 contra 39. There was a natural Israel and a spiritual Israel—an Israel within Israel; that is the point of the apostle's argument. He is not thinking of Gentiles at all. He is accounting scripturally for the evident fact that the gospel which was promised to Israel is not saving Israel. His point is that it is saving the spiritual Israelites. This he develops in Part 4. ix. to xi. 10.

The apostle illustrates his point that not all Israelites were the true Israel by Isaac and Ishmael, who were both sons of Abraham; and Jacob and Esau who were both sons of Isaac. Jacob, despite his carnality, had faith. Esau was a " profane person."' In ix. 27, he begins to show, from the prophets themselves, that these very things were foretold, (1) that mercy should reach the Gentiles; (2) that there should be a believing remnant in Israel. The reason the Jews were not being saved was that they were rejecting righteousness on the principle of faith, and were seeking it on the impossible principle of works. ix. 25 to x. 21. Then (xi. 1) he returns to the remnant, the true spiritual Israel of whom he was himself an illustration. So far, then, from the strange notion that the believing Gentile becomes an Israelite, Paul shows that the believing Jew becomes a Christian. Instruction then follows for Gentile believers. They have been grafted into the good olive tree (Christ) and the natural branches broken off for unbelief. But the natural branches shall yet be grafted into "their own" (see ix, 5) olive tree. When? When the fullness of the Gentiles "be come in" (see Acts xv. 14-16; Luke xxi. 24) and then (xi. 27) shall the prophecy of Jeremiah xxxi. 27-40 be fulfilled; a prophecy which includes both conversion and restoration to the land.

Section VI. Christian Life and Service. xii. 1 to xv. 33.

This great section resumes the thought interrupted at the end of chapter viii. by the Jewish parenthesis. The student should now go back and reread chapters v., vi., vii., and viii,, turning then immediately to xii. 1. The "mercies of God" are the gospel mercies which began (iii. 19) with a sinner speechless before God in utter guilt and helplessness, and left him justified, sanctified, and with naught before him but the glory of God. (viii.) Now the apostle would have the believer enter into the experience of the blessedness stated in vi. 14, and fully developed in viii. 1-39.

Part 1. xii. 1-3. He therefore recurs to the sole condition to be performed by the believer, all else being the alone work of the Spirit. That condition he had stated in vi. 13, 16 as "vieldedness." He uses (xii. 1) the same word (in the Greek) translated "yield" and "yielded" in vi. 16, 19. The' same word, "present," is also used in Luke ii. 22 and Eph. v. 27. The point of the exhortation, therefore, is that the believer "yield" or "present" his body as absolutely as the mother of Jesus "presented" her babe unto the Lord in Luke ii. 22. From that moment until He became a slain sacrifice He was "a living sacrifice." He literally lived by the will of His Father, doing nothing merely to please Himself, still less anything to be seen of man. Rom. xii. 1 is, therefore, a restatement of Rom. — vi; 16.

The student should remember that up to viii. 39 Romans is doctrinal. At xii. 1 the practical and experimental begins (though, illustratively, there is experience in Rom. - vii.). And it is of the last importance to note that, as justification begins with an act—faith, so true Christian experience begins with an act—the deliberate, definite presentation of the body to be subject absolutely to the will of another.

Part 2. xii. 4-8. Since service is to be mentioned, the doctrine of the body is briefly mentioned in connection with gifts. Each believer is to abide in his own gift.

Part 3. xii. 9-21. The general principles of Christian behavior.

Part 4. xiii. 1-14.) The behavior of the believer toward civil governments and the world.

Part 5. xiv. 1 to xv. 13. The life of brotherhood regulated.

Section VII. The Outflow of Christian Love. xv. 14 to xvi. 27.

EPISTLE TO THE ROMANS

1. What distinctive name does Paul give to the gospel?

_____

2. What as to the human ancestry of our Lord?

_____

_____

_____

3. What three proofs of His deity are referred to in i. 4?

_____

_____

_____

4. Why was not the apostle "ashamed of the gospel"?

_____

_____

5. What two things are said to be "revealed" in the gospel?

_____

_____

6. State in your own words what is meant by i. 19, 20.

_____

_____

7. State in your own words the ground of condemnation of the degraded heathen.

_____

_____

8. What seven steps marked the fall of heathendom from the knowledge of the true God? 1. 21-23.

_____

_____

_____

_____

_____

_____

_____

9. What four steps of degradation in idolatry are enumerated in i. 23?

_____

_____

_____

_____

10. What did God do?

_____

_____

11. State in your own words the ground of condemnation of the heathen moralizers. ii. 1-16.

_____

_____

_____

12. State in your own words the ground of condemnation of the Jew.

_____

_____

_____

13. What is the final effect of the law?

_____

_____

_____

14. State in your own words the meaning of the expression "the righteousness of God."

_____

_____

_____

15. How does the righteousness of God become the righteousness of a condemned sinner?

_____

_____

_____

16. Who have sinned?

_____

_____

17. What does "justified" mean?

_____

_____

18. Who are justified?

_____

19. What is justification "by"?

_____

_____

20. What is justification "through"?

_____

_____

21. What is meant by "propitiation"?

_____

_____

22. Is propitiation through faith in the perfect life of Christ?

_____

_____

23. State in your own words how God is "just" when he justifies a sinner who trusts Christ?

_____

_____

24. What has obedience to the law to do with a sinner's justification?

_____

_____

25. Who is chosen as illustrating justification by faith?

_____

_____

26. What kind of faith is "counted for righteousness"?

_____

_____

27. Will God allow some faith and some works as the ground of justification?

_____

_____

28. Who is "the man unto whom the Lord will not impute sin"?

_____

_____

29. Did Abraham's circumcision help on his justification?

_____

_____

30. State in your own words what quality of faith justifies.

_____

_____

_____

31. Does faith which accepts the example of Christ, but refuses to believe in His propitiatory death and in His resurrection, save?

_____

_____

32. State the seven results of justification.

_____

_____

_____

_____

_____

_____

33. How did sin enter the world?

_____

_____

34. What passed upon all men?

_____

_____

35. What does the fact that men died before the law was given prove?

_____

_____

36. What "came upon all men by the offense of one"?

_____

_____

_____

37. Why did the law "enter"?

_____

_____

_____

38. What does sin reign unto?

_____

_____

_____

39. What does grace reign unto?

_____

_____

_____

40. Why shall we not continue in sin?

_____

_____

_____

41. What is the judgment of God upon "our old man"?

_____

_____

42. What is to be the Christian's thought of himself in view of vi. 2-11?

_____

_____

_____

43. What is "sin" in Romans vi?

_____

_____

_____

44. What is the believer to do that he may enter into a real experience of death to sin and freedom from its dominion?

_____

_____

45. What effect has our death with Christ upon our relation to the law?

_____

_____

46. What effect had the law when we were under it?

_____

_____

47. State in your own words the conflict described. vii. 15-23.

_____

_____

48. Who were the two "I's" in that passage?

_____

_____

49. What was the result of the effort to be holy in Rom. vii.?

_____

_____

50. Why is there "no condemnation" to those who are in Christ Jesus?

_____

_____

51. What "law'" makes free?

_____

_____

52. What is the "law of sin?"

_____

_____

53. What is the "law of death?"

_____

_____

54. What is the Spirit said to do in believers who "walk after" Him?

_____

_____

55. Are Christians "in the flesh"?

_____

_____

56. Is "the flesh" in them?

_____

_____

57. Enumerate the things the Spirit is said to do in chapter viii.

_____

_____

_____

_____

58. What is the teaching of chapter viii. concerning suffering?

_____

_____

_____

59. What is the present state of the creation? (See Revised Version.)

_____

_____

60. Give the steps in completed redemption.

_____

_____

_____

_____

_____

61. Will any "whom He did foreknow" be lost?

_____

_____

62. What could separate us from the love of Christ?

_____

_____

_____

63. What was Paul's feeling toward Israelites?

_____

_____

64. What distinction does Paul make between a believing and unbelieving Jew?

_____

_____

65. What prophecies of blessing to Gentiles does Paul quote?

_____

_____

_____

66. Why were Israelites being lost?

_____

_____

67. Is it true that Israel, as such, is cast away forever?

_____

_____

68. Who is the "good olive tree"?

_____

_____

69. How long will the blindness of Israel last?

_____

_____

70. When the fullness of the Gentiles has come what prophetic event will occur?

_____

_____

71. What is the reasonable service of a sinner saved by grace?

_____

_____

72. What will be the characteristics of the yielded life (a) toward other Christians? (b) toward the world?

_____

_____

_____

73. Enumerate, in your own words, the operations of the Holy Spirit in Romans.

_____

_____

_____

74. Define the relation of the law (a) to the sinner; (b) to the. saint.

_____

_____

_____

75. What must the sinner do to secure justification?

_____

_____

_____

76. What must the saint do to secure sanctification?

_____

_____

_____

77. Define sanctification.

_____

_____

78. What new truths, not heretofore mentioned by the apostle, are discussed in Romans?

_____

_____

_____

LESSON LIV

PHILEMON

Note. The Prison Epistles. After writing Romans the apostle began that fateful journey to Jerusalem the details and results of which have come before us in the study of Acts. The student will do well at this point to again read Acts xx.—xxvii. The question has been much disputed whether all of the remaining Epistles of Paul were written during one continuous imprisonment from A.D. 62 to A.D. 68, or whether Paul was released "at his first answer" (2 Tim. iv. 16), and after about a year of liberty again imprisoned and speedily martyred. It may be said that there is no biblical reason for saying that Paul was released. Undoubtedly the tradition from Clement, who was Paul's disciple, to Eusebius, confirms the theory of two imprisonments. Those who hold to the tradition count as the Prison Epistles Philemon, Colossians, Ephesians and Philippians. First Timothy and Titus are by them supposed to have been written between the first and second imprisonments, and Second Timothy during the second imprisonment, just before the martyrdom. These questions can never be authoritatively settled. What is known certainly is that the remaining Epistles were written after Paul's arrival in Rome. The student should endeavor to fix in his mind the circumstances of Paul as a prisoner —his associates, occupations and friends. These facts are gathered from the account in Acts and from personal particulars in the Prison Epistles.

GENERAL REMARKS

This beautiful letter carries its own explanation. Onesimus, a slave of Philemon, a Christian of Colosse, had robbed his master and fled to Rome. There he came under the influence of Paul and was converted. Paul sends him back to Philemon with this letter. It is of priceless value as a teaching :

(1) in practical righteousness,

(2) in Christian brotherhood,

(3) in Christian courtesy, and

(4) as an illustration of the working of the law of love in the apostolic church.

Of this Epistle Meyer remarks: "The aim of the letter is pursued with so much Christian love and wisdom, with so great psychological tact, and, without sacrifice of the apostolic authority, in a manner so thoughtfully condescending, adroit, delicate and irresistible, that the brief letter—which is, in the finest sense, "seasoned with salt" as a most precious and characteristic relic of the great apostle—belongs, even as regards its Attic refinement and gracefulness, to the epistolary masterpieces of antiquity."

ANALYSIS

The analysis of this brief Epistle is not essential, but it may be thus divided:

Section I. Address and Greeting. Verses 1-3.

Section II. Tribute to the Character of Philemon, Verses 4-7.

Section III. Intercession for Onesimus. Verses 8-21. In this section verses 17-20 give a beautiful illustration of imputation. All Onesimus's debt is to be put on Paul; all Paul's acceptableness to be put on Onesimus.

Section IV. Salutations and Conclusion. Verses 22-25.

EPISTLE TO PHILEMON

1. Under what circumstances did Paul live at Rome?

_____

_____

_____

2. Give the names of his friends and associates there.

_____

_____

_____

3. What was the occasion of the letter to Philemon?

_____

_____

_____

4. Where did Philemon live?

_____

_____

5. Who and what was Onesimus?

_____

_____

_____

6. What effect had the gospel on the relationships of Christians?

_____

_____

_____

7. What does the Epistle disclose as to the station of Philemon?

_____

_____

8. What difference in the relation of Onesimus to Philemon did the conversion of Onesimus effect?

_____

_____

_____

9. Did it change their legal relationship?

_____

_____

_____

10. Explain in your own words how verses 17-20 illustrate justification.

_____

_____

_____

_____

Note. It is exceedingly probable that Paul, now personally present with Roman saints, would be often called upon to expound the doctrine of justification by faith, which formed so central a part of the teaching of his great letter to the Romans; and it is not improbable that, writing Philemon on behalf of one who had wronged him, the apostle consciously made of this occasion an apt illustration of the doctrine of imputed righteousness: "If he hath wronged thee, or oweth thee aught, put that on mine account...receive him as myself."

LESSON LV

COLOSSIANS

GENERAL REMARKS

Colosse was, in the apostolic period, a small town much decayed from its former importance, and has long since disappeared. The name survives in human interest because it was the home of Philemon, of the church which gathered in his house (Phil. 2), of Onesimus and Epaphras, and because to that relatively unimportant church Paul addressed this letter—of immense value in every age of the church, and never more than now.

The church was not founded by Paul. Epaphras (Col. i. 7; iv. 12) seems to have been in a particular sense the " servant" (the word is usually rendered " minister') of this church. But the whole tone of the Epistle indicates the full recognition at Colosse of Paul's apostolic authority, since he nowhere vind' cates it (as to the Galatians) ; and it would appear from hi letter to Philemon (verse 19) that he was Philemon's father in the gospel.

The occasion of the Epistle is manifest from its contents. Epaphras was Paul's fellow-prisoner at Rome; and from him Paul had learned the state of the church. This, as to fundamentals, was excellent. (i. 3-8.) But in a subtle way error was at work. The false teaching here, as we gather from Paul's refutation of it in chapter ii., was not Judaic legality emanating from Jerusalem, as in Galatia, but philosophic legality, emanating probably from Alexandria. The strictly Judaic legality consisted in letter-bondage to the law—that is, to written Scripture. The philosophic legality consisted in being "wise above what was written;" or as the apostle puts it, "intruding into those things which he hath not seen, vainly puffed up by his fleshly mind." The error seems to have been a philosophizing theosophy—the early form of that gnosticism which later wrought havoc with the faith. Of these errorists Heinrich A. W. Meyer

says: "They came most keenly into conflict with the exalted rank and the redeeming work of Christ, to whom they did not leave His full divine dignity, but assigned to Him merely a rank in the higher order of spirits, while they exalted the angels as concerned in bringing in the messianic salvation, entertaining demiurgic ideas as to the creation of the world." They looked on matter as evil, and hence practiced asceticism to mortify the deeds of the body.

Note. By demiurgic is meant that theory of these gnostics which ascribes creation to a lower spiritual being whom they called the demiurge. The effect of gnosticism was to put God at an infinite distance from man; to fill that distance with orders of angelic beings grading downward, and to give Christ only a place among the higher of these beings. Gnosticism has passed away; but the efforts to degrade Christ from His full deity, to make a merit of asceticism ("touch not, taste not," etc.), to conceive of the body and the natural physical desires as inherently wrong or ignoble, and to make of religion a form, in which days and times are invested with especial religious meaning—these survive; and against them Colossians is a perpetual and unanswerable declaration. In other words, pure Christianity lives between two dangers ever present: the danger that it will evaporate into a philosophy— philosophies of the atonement, philosophies of the incarnation, etc.—and the danger that it will freeze into a form. Paul's answer to both is— Christ. Knowing, then, of these dangers besetting the Colossian church, the apostle would desire to strengthen their faith at the assailed points. Looking beyond the immediate occasion, the all-seeing mind of the Spirit would desire to leave an authoritative instruction concerning the ever-present danger in which faith would stand from philosophy and formalism. The immediate occasion was the departure of Onesimus and Tychicus (iv. 7, 8) for Colosse.

ANALYSIS.

The Epistle falls into seven sections, and these into many parts.

Section I. Introduction. i. 1-8.

Section II. The Aposroric Prayer. i. 9-14. The student will note very particularly what the apostle asks for on behalf of the Colossians, and for what he gives thanks. It is a model prayer.

Section III. The Exaltation of Christ as Divine Creator and Redeemer, and as Indwelling the Saints. 1. 15-29.

Part 1. The seven distinctions of Christ. i. 15-19.

(1) As incarnate He makes visible ("images") the invisible God.

(2) He is the "firstborn" (i.e., the Goel or elder brother of the Old Testament).

(3) By Him and for Him all things, visible and invisible, were created. (As against the gnostic notion that He was one among created things).

(4) He antedates all things.

(5) By Him all things "consist"—literally 'hold together."

(6) He is the Head of the body, the church.

(7) And finally, all fullness dwells in Him.

Beyond that it is impossible to go. This, then, is the inspired answer to all and every attempt to make Christ less than God or to conceive of matter in a dualistic sense, as not made by Him; or, on the other hand, to identify Him with matter in a pantheistic way. Gnosticism, pantheism, polytheism, eternity of matter, Arianism, Unitarianism, Kenoticism,—in short, every error concerning the adorable Person of Christ is met by this passage.

Part 2. The outward and objective work of Christ for sinners. i. 20-23.

(1) Christ alone is the channel of reconciliation. i. 20; John xiv. 6; 1 Tim. ii. 5.

(2) The blood of "His cross makes peace. The sinner sees in that blood the love of the God whom he has offended, and the offenses borne away; God sees in the cross that which enables Him to be just and yet justify the sinner—in that sacrifice the sinner and God meet.

(3) The mysterious reach of that atonement—"things upon the earth or things in the heavens"—is, perhaps, not altogether within our present comprehension.

(4) For the believer that reconciliation is fully accomplished.

(5) He will present us holy, etc., if we "continue in the faith grounded and settled, and be not moved away from the hope of the gospel."

Note. There should be a semicolon after "death" in verse 22. The thought is that reconciliation through His death is now accomplished; but our state, as "holy without blemish and unreprovable" depends upon our continuance in the faith, etc. "The faith" never means our personal trust in Christ, but the body of revealed truth. (See Jude, verse 3; Rev. v.) The hope of the gospel" is not the hope to be saved; that, for the believer is always regarded as accomplished.

Part 3. The inward and subjective work of Christ for saints. i. 24-29.

(1) The church as the living body of Christ, sharing His position in glory (John xvii. 22; Rom. viii. 30), is exalted to the high privilege of sharing also His afflictions.

Note the word used, thlipseon, does not mean atoning sufferings. Christ's sufferings were threefold. He suffered from God for sin; from man for righteousness' sake; and, as human, from personal weakness, weariness, temptations, sorrows, etc. In the first sense, He suffered alone; in the second sense, we are privileged to share His sufferings; in the third sense, He shares our sufferings.

"The apostle's conception is that all the sufferings and afflictions which are involved in the carrying on of Christ's work in the world, whether experienced by Himself or His followers, are His sufferings." Some of the totality was borne by Him

in His earth life; some are left behind for his body."
—Dwight.

(2) And this is according to that mystery now revealed, "which is Christ in you." This tremendous revelation makes clear what the believer's "glory" is to be; the manifestation of the indwelling Christ!

Note. The indwelling of Christ is not to be confounded with the indwelling of the Spirit. The apostle presently (iii. 3, 4) reveals the mode of Christ's indwelling. It is by Himself as our life. (See 1 John v. 11, 12.)

Section IV. Christ Exalted as the Embodiment (or Incarnation) of the Godhead, with Whose Life and Death the Believer is Identified, and in Whom the Believer is Made Perfect. ii. 1-23.

Part 1. The "mystery of God" is Christ. ii. 1-6.

Note. A "mystery" in Scripture is not something hidden, but the revelation of something which had been hidden. Matt. xiii. 11, 16, 17; Col. i. 26, 27. The "mystery of God" is that He is revealed in Christ, and that all hidden things are revealed or will be revealed in Him.

Part 2. The twofold danger which menaces "the faith." ii. 8-23.

Note. The student is now in the very heart of the Epistle. To say these things was the real occasion of the writing. And because these perils are present in every age and to every individual the Epistle has an abiding value.

(1) "The faith"—the body of revealed truth—is in danger from "philosophy and vain deceit." — (Literally "empty deception." Empty, because mere speculation; "having no real contents. "—Meyer.) Doubtless the apostle has in view especially the particular phase of philosophy becoming current at Colosse. But he does not limit his warning to that. It is a general warning against the intrusion of philosophy into the domain, solid and real, of revealed. religion. As he has. said.in 1 Cor. it. 7-9, it is a sphere into which the human mind cannot intrude. All is matter, not of discovery, but of revelation. And even when the revelation has been made, the natural mind cannot understand it. 1 Cor. ii.14. In this sphere, therefore, philosophy, as Luther said, "spoils whatever it touches." In verse 18 Paul describes the method and effect of this philosophy, "dwelling in the things which he hath not seen, vainly puffed up in his fleshly mind, and not holding the Head."

(2) The second danger is (as was said in "General Remarks") the danger of making a merit, as recommending one more perfectly to God, of ordinances, even circumcision and baptism; or of holy-day observances, even sabbaths; and of severities to the body, fastings, dietary rules, "handle not," etc. All of these, the apostle says, are of "no value against the indulgence of the flesh" (verse 23). Indeed, they minister directly to the pious flesh. These are the "traditions of men, the rudiments of the world." In Galatians the apostle has used this expression of the system of law-work. It covers all the externalities of religion, considered as adding merit to the believer. Certainly spiritual religion expresses itself in many outward ways, but these add nothing to the believer's position or security. The especial danger of these things lies in their "show of wisdom" and in their appeal to the natural desire of the flesh to "have something wherein to glory." The gospel, however, is the end of man's glorying. A condemned sinner, speechless before a holy law, who has been saved wholly by another, has no ground for glorying in the flesh.

Note. The student should note with special care the application in ii. 11-13, of the doctrine of Romans vi. of the Christian's identification with Christ. Here, the identity is pushed back of His death, where, in Romans, it began. The believer is considered as circumcised in Christ's circumcision, and baptized in Christ's baptism.

Section V. The Union of the Believer with Christ in Resurrection Life, and in His Glory. iii. 1-4. The believer's present life is to be keyed to his position as risen with Christ. It is the teaching of Rom. vi. 11, 13: "Dead indeed unto sin, but alive unto God." "Yield yourselves unto God as those that are alive from the dead." In other words, it is a great doctrine made the basis of a new type of living.

Another little: known truth is revealed here. Christ is the believer's life. Verse 4. It is commonly believed, indeed, that Christ gave us life; but that life is thought of as detached, as a germ or principle of life imparted, so that the believer has eternal life as a flower pot might hold a living seed. But the deeper, more precious truth is that the life which is in Christ is also in the believer—as the life of a spring of water is in the streamlet which flows from it; or, to use our Lord's own illustration, "I am the vine, ye are the branches."

Section VI. Right Christian Living, Based on the Death and Resurrection of Christ. iii. 5 to iv. 6. The student will note the bearing of "therefore" in verse 5. "Mortify therefore"—because ye are dead and your life is hid with Christ, so that now Christ is your life.

Section VII. Tidings and Greetings. iv. 7-18.

EPISTLE TO THE COLOSSIANS

1. Where was Paul when this Epistle was written?

_____

_____

2. What was the occasion of it?

_____

_____

3. By whom was it sent?

_____

_____

4. Who was joined with Paul in the Epistle?

_____

_____

5. What proof of faith did the saints at Colosse give?

_____

_____

6. Who and what was Epaphras?

_____

_____

7. Give the clauses of Paul's prayer, i. 9-11?

_____

_____

8. What comes before work in the apostle's desire for them?

_____

_____

9. State in order what the apostle thanked God for, on behalf of the Colossians.

_____

_____

_____

10. Give, from memory, the seven distinctions of Christ in Section III.

_____

_____

_____

_____

_____

_____

11. Explain, in your own words, the difference between being reconciled to God, and being unblamable and unreproveable in His sight.

_____

_____

_____

12. State. in your own words the meaning of "mystery" in Scripture.

_____

_____

_____

13. What is the "mystery which hath been hid from ages and from generations"?

_____

_____

_____

14. What is the proof that Paul was not known by face to the Colossians?

_____

_____

15. State in your own words the two dangers against which saints are warned in chapter ii.

_____

_____

_____

_____

16. State why philosophy works harm in matters of revelation.

_____

_____

_____

17. What was the meaning in the ages before Christ of dietary regulations, holy days and the Sabbath?

_____

_____

_____

18. Is the Christian to have a conscience toward men in respect of religious forms and observances?

_____

_____

_____

19. What practical application is made of the believer's oneness with Christ in death and resurrection?

_____

_____

20. Make a list of the Christian virtues and graces mentioned in ii. 5 to iv. 6.

_____

_____

_____

_____

21. What persons are mentioned in this Epistle as being with Paul in Rome?

_____

_____

_____

LESSON LVI

Ephesians

General Remarks

The circumstances under which Ephesians was written are identical with those of Philemon and Colossians. Indeed, the present Epistle was sent by the same messenger, Tychicus.

Unlike the other Epistles, Ephesians cannot 'be said to have had its occasion in any local conditions. None are mentioned. Indeed, it is more than doubtful whether the Epistle is properly called "to the Ephesians." The earliest and best manuscripts have no address. Basil, Jerome, and Tertullian, all state that such was the state of the manuscripts in their day. The Vatican manuscript has the words "in Ephesus," added in the margin by another hand.

Colossians (iv. 16) mentions an Epistle to the Laodiceans. It has been conjectured that the letter known to us as Ephesians, is really the Laodicean letter. Laodicea was very near Colosse, so that Tychicus would naturally be charged with the care of a letter to that church. It seems incredible that there should be no greetings, if the letter were really to the church where Paul had labored so long. "The letter itself implies that he knew of them only by hearsay (i. 15; iii. 2). The question is no vital one, however, for Ephesians is the most universal of the Epistles. Probably it was sent to the Laodicean church without being addressed to any church. It was divinely intended to be impersonally personal: "To the saints and to the faithful in Christ Jesus"—at Laodicea, or Ephesus, or anywhere, at any time. The doctrine of the Epistle accords with this view. It contains the highest church truth, but has nothing about church order. The church here is "His body"; not, as in Philippians, the local church. So the revelation of truth is for the individual Christian, as a member of the body of Christ. There are no groups, no sects, as in Corinth; no false teachers, as in Galatia. But Ephesians is the summit of revelation for the members of the body of Christ. Essentially, three lines of truth make up this Epistle: the truth of the believer's exalted position in Christ; the truth concerning the body of Christ; and the truth concerning a walk according to that position. According to the New Testament method the position is first stated, then the principles of the walk. This is one of the contrasts between law and grace. Under law, the position was the reward of the life; under grace, the position is a free gift, and the life flows from it, as the result of a new nature, and of the indwelling Spirit.

There is a strong spiritual affinity between Ephesians and the book of Joshua. The "heavenly places" of Ephesians are to the Christian what "the land" was to the Israelite. In "the land" the Israelite had conflict (comp. Eph. vi. 12), but also possession, rest, victory, the fulfillment of promises. Josh. xxi. 43-45; Eph. i. 3, iii. 14-19, vi. 23, vi. 16.

Certain expressions in Ephesians require definition. These are:

1. "Heavenly places." It is the word usually translated "heavenly," as in Matt. xviii. 35; John iii. 12, and Heb. iii. 1. The translation "places" is, perhaps, the most misleading which could have been used. "In the heavenlies" has been suggested as better. But this also—besides being meaningless—conveys the misleading notion of some place other than earth. Literally, it is "in the heavenly." The word is so rendered in 1 Cor. xy. 48, "they also that are heavenly." .The Christian is "heavenly" by calling (Heb. iii. 1), by citizenship (Phil. iii. 20), by inheritance (1 Peter i. 4) and by resurrection life (Eph. ii. 6), as a member of that body of which the Head i actually in heaven. The heavenly (or "in heavenly places"), therefore, is the sphere of the believer's present association with Christ. This is shown by the constant context, "in Christ Jesus." The believer is now associated with Christ in life (Col. iii. 4; 1 John v. 11, 12), position (Eph. ii. 6), suffering (Rom. viii. 18; 2.Tim, ii. 11,

12; .Col. i. 24; Phil. i. 29), service (John xvii. 18; Matt. xxviii. 18-20) and betrothal (2 Cor. xi. 1-3),

Note. The believer is to be associated with Christ in glory (John xvii. 22; Rom. viii. 18; Col. iii. 4), inheritance (Rom. viii. 17), authority (Matt. xix. 28; Rev. iii. 21) and marriage (Eph. v. 22-33; Rev. xix. 1-9).

The believer's "spiritual blessings" (Eph. i. 3), therefore, are to be possessed or experienced only as he lives in the sphere of his joint life, joint position, joint suffering, joint service and joint marriage-pledge with Christ. In so far as he lives as a natural man whose interests are earthly, and avoids the path of co-service and (if need be) co-suffering, he will know nothing experimentally of the exalted blessings of Ephesians. "It is sufficient that the servant be as his Master." Christ took account of Himself as a heavenly Being come down to earth to do His Father's will.

ANALYSIS

The Epistle falls into four sections, and these into orderly parts.

Section I. Apostolic Greeting. i. 1-2. The words "at Ephesus" are not in the best manuscripts.

Section II. Positional. The Doctrine of the Believer's Standing as Redeemed by Christ, and as "In Christ," a Member of His Body. i. 3 to iii. 21.

Part 1. The seven great elements of the believer's present position. i, 3-14. These are the believer's election, securing his ultimate holiness, blamelessness, and love character; his predestination, securing his sonship; his acceptance, in the full measure of Christ's own acceptance; his redemption through Christ's blood, securing the absolute forgiveness of his sins; his exaltation to fellowship with God in His future purposes; his inheritance, and, finally, the gift of the Spirit.

Part 2. The apostolic prayer, that saints might enter into an actual apprehension and experimental knowledge of their exalted position in the church, the body of Christ. i.15-23. Incidentally, as always in inspired prayers, there is an unfolding of truth.

The truth revealed is that Christ, raised from the dead and set at God's own right hand, is made "head over all to the church, which is His body." This marks the distinction between the group of saved ones gathered about Christ during His ministry on earth, and the church. That group formed, indeed, the first "members," but only after the "Father of glory,' (verse 17) had set Christ at His own right hand (verse 20), and the Holy Spirit had been sent upon them (1 Cor. xii. 12, 18).

Part 3. The explanation of the method of Gentile salvation out of death in trespasses and sins, into the position of fellow heirs, and of the same body with Christ. ii. 1—ii. 12. The student should compare this part carefully with Romans i.—iii. There, as here, all are sinner; but in Romans sin is treated as guilt; in Ephesians, as a state of death. In Romans the guilty sinner is justified by faith; in Ephesians the dead sinner is given life through faith. In Romans the sinner is before the bar of justice; in Ephesians he is "far off." In Romans the blood is the ground of his justification; in Ephesians the blood makes him "nigh." [In Ephesians the cross makes nigh (ii. 13); makes peace (ii. 14); abolishes the ordinances which made a middle wall between Jew and Gentile (ii. 15), and reconciles (ii. 16).]

Our title to draw nigh is the blood; our actual access is by the Spirit (ii. 18). Then follows the revelation of another aspect of the church. It is the body, but it is also a temple, and a habitation of God.

The student will note that all this was given to Paul by revelation (iii. 8), and that the other ages (or dispensations) had no such revelation (iii. 5). It would be idle, therefore, to look in the Old Testament for the doctrine of the church. The Old Testament prophet foresaw the salvation of the Gentiles, but not the gathering of the Gentiles into the body of Christ. Israel was a true "church in the wilderness" (Acts vii. 38)—that is, a "called-out assembly"—but was not, like the called-out assembly of the New Testament, "baptized into one body."

Section III. The Walk and Service of the Believer. iii. 13—vi. 24.

Part 1. The fivefold prayer for the members of Christ's body. iii. 13-21. In the study of this marvelous prayer the student will be profited more by meditation than by mere exercise of mind. It unfolds both the believer's need and his privilege. It is inconceivable that the Spirit should form in the heart of Christ's apostle a prayer which could not be answered. The first petition, "That He would grant you, according to — the riches of His glory, to be strengthened with might by His Spirit in the inner man," does not refer to power for service. It is rather spiritual vigor, freshness and fullness of life—a state of spiritual vitality, which is meant. The second petition, "That Christ may dwell in your hearts by faith," is for the active occupation of the heart with Christ as its object. It is what Christ meant by "abiding." The heart, exercised and judging all things with reference to Him, like the heart of a devoted husband or wife in absence from the beloved one, "abides." Probably all Christians desire this state of heart and make many efforts to attain it. All such efforts are vain.

It is only as "strengthened with might by His Spirit in the inner man" that faith is so quickened as to fill the heart with the presence of Christ. In the same way the third petition, "That ye, being rooted and grounded in love," etc., is for a love life only possible to those who, vitalized by the suffusion of the whole inner being with the Spirit, have their hearts occupied with Christ. In other words, there is an inevitable order in the possession of these marvelous fruits of redemption. The fourth petition gives the next stage in this life of privilege, comprehension of the love of Christ in its four symmetrical dimensions. How many Christians, alas, make vain efforts to realize the love of Christ by recounting His mercies. How useless are such efforts! The comprehension of that love is the spontaneous blessing of those who, "

strengthened with might by His Spirit in the inner man," have hearts filled with Christ, and whose spiritual life, therefore, is "rooted and grounded in love." But one possibility of blessing now remains—to be "filled with all the fullness of God." The divine order in the obtainment of this supreme blessing may be seen by reference to Col. ii. 9 with John i. 16. The "fullness" is all in Christ, and from Him passes to us on the principle of "grace for grace." Every grace of the divine character which we receive makes capacity and hospitality for larger graces. In other words, the filling with all the fullness of God is not by one act of divine power, but "grace for grace."

The worship passage (verses 20, 21) ascribes the marvelous succession of blessings to the power of God, not the effort of man.

Part 2. The walk and service of the believer as a member of the body of Christ. iv. 1-16. The student will note that the apostle does not refer to the law as fixing the character of the believer's walk, but to his exalted calling as one perfectly redeemed, sealed with the Spirit, and made a member of the body of Christ. The very first characteristic of such a walk is lowliness. Observe that lowliness is not humility. Humility is a state of soul toward God; lowliness an attitude toward man. Matt. xi. 29; Rom. xii. 16; Phil. iii. 3. The apostle adds the seven existing unities. In these all believers are one. Verses 4-6. In grace and gift they differ. Verse 7; Rom. xii. 5, 6.

This introduces the subject of gifts for service. The ascended Lord gave gifts. Not the indwelling Spirit, as in John xx. 22, but the baptizing Spirit, as in Acts ii., 1 Cor. xii., etc., imparts gift. Five gifts are enumerated. (Compare 1 Cor. 12.) These are the greater, or ministry gifts. Verses 8-11. Note the divine purpose in the bestowment of gift. Verses 8-16.

Part 3. The walk of the believer as a "new man" and dear child of God, indwelt by the Spirit. iv. 17—v. 17. The key verses are iv. 17, 22-24, 30; v. 1. The believer is no longer a mere Gentile (compare ii. 11 and 1 Cor. xii. 2, R. V.), and should, therefore, be inaccessible to the silly argument of the worldling, "they" do such and such things. As to the outward life the believer is to "put on" Christ. As to the inner life the Holy Spirit is there, and that marvelous fact gives the key to what should be allowed and disallowed. For the rest the believer is God's "dear child."

Section IV. The Walk and Warfare of the Believer when Filled with the Spirit. v. 18—vi. 24.

Part 1. The Spirit-filled walk. v. 18—vi. 9. A new key, a new enabling, is given with verse 18. Up to this verse the believer has been regarded as perfectly redeemed, brought out of death, put into the highest conceivable position and relationships, and indwelt by the Holy Spirit. But verse 18 makes an immense advance. To have the Spirit is one thing, to be filled with the Spirit quite another thing. All believers have the Spirit, not all are filled with the Spirit. But it is the privilege of all to be so filled. Nay, it is an imperative: "Be ye filled with the Spirit."

The immediate results are stated. The walk is at once lifted to its highest possibilities. Now it is not precept, but power. A melodious heart (verse 19); an inveterately thankful heart (verse 20); an humble heart (verse 21), are the direct effects of the filling. All this is at once made practical by application to the most sacred of human relationships—marriage. This application is unflinching, but reciprocal. The wife in obedience is to be as the church to Christ; the husband in love, as Christ to the church. Needless to say that only Spirit-filled believers can realize this reciprocity of absolute love, and absolute obedience. This opens the great subject of the church as the wife of Christ—the summit of divine revelation. With vi. 1 the apostle passes to the relationships of parent and child, and master and servant.

Part 2. The Spirit-filled believer in conflict. vi. 10-18. Three gradations of conflict are revealed in Paul's Epistles, as possible to the believer.

(1) The conflict of the old man and the new man in the believer. This is the subject of Romans vii. 14-25. Between the old Saul and the new Paul there is inevitable strife. But it is a conflict in which there is no victory.

(2) The conflict of the indwelling Spirit with the old man. Gal. v. 16, 17; Rom, vii. 4, 13) This. is an advance in experience. The believer no longer seeks to overcome the old self with the new self, but trusts the Holy Spirit for victory.

(3) The conflict of the Spirit-filled believer with "wicked spirits in heavenly places." Satan chooses a new battle ground when the believer, filled with the Holy Spirit, enters into victory in the sphere of the natural life.

Temptation now is in the sphere of the spiritual. The dangers of spiritual pride, of subtle unbelief, of resting in experience instead of in the Word, must now be encountered. For this conflict, a panoply or armor is provided, and a weapon also.

Part 3. Closing words. vi. 19-25. Such is this great Epistle. The student is affectionately exhorted not merely to become acquainted with its teachings, but to enter into a personal apprehension of them.

EPHESIANS

1. State the circumstances under which Ephesians was written.

_____

_____

_____

2. What was the occasion of this Epistle?

_____

_____

_____

3. State from memory why it is questioned whether the Epistle should be called " Ephesians."'

_____

_____

_____

4. Why is the question relatively unimportant?

_____

_____

5. State from memory what three great lines of truth are taught in Ephesians.

_____

_____

_____

6. Why is the believer's position stated before instructions for right living?

_____

_____

_____

7. What book of the Old Testament groups with Ephesians?

_____

8. Give from memory, in your own words, a definition of the expression, "heavenly places."

_____

_____

_____

_____

9. In what four respects is the believer said to be "heavenly"?

_____

_____

_____

10. State from memory in what ways the believer is now associated with Christ.

_____

_____

_____

11. State from memory in what ways the believer is to be associated with Christ hereafter.

_____

_____

_____

12. Into how many and what sections does the Epistle fall?

_____

13. State from memory the seven chief elements of the believer's present position in Christ.

_____

_____

_____

_____

_____

_____

14. State in your own words why the group of disciples who believed on and followed Christ during His earthly ministry were not a church?

_____

_____

_____

_____

_____

15. Prove from Scripture that Christ had not at that time assumed His place as " Head over all things' to the church.

_____

_____

16. What is said to be the state of the unbelieving sinner in Ephesians?

_____

_____

17. In what respect does this aspect differ from that in which the sinner is regarded in Romans?

_____

_____

18. What proof does Ephesians give that church truth was revealed to Old Testament writers?

_____

_____

_____

19. Was not Israel a "church in the wilderness"?

_____

_____

20. What distinction exists between the wilderness church and the New Testament church?

_____

_____

_____

21. Who is the "spirit that now worketh in the children of disobedience"?

_____

_____

_____

22. What is said to characterize the walk of the unbeliever?

_____

_____

23. What is the first character of the walk of the believer?

_____

_____

24. What are the offices of the Holy Spirit in chapter i.?

_____

_____

_____

25. Who are "sealed"?

_____

_____

_____

26. How far back is the believer's salvation traced in chapter i.?

_____

_____

27. What is stated in chapter ii. to have moved God to save us?

_____

_____

28. How far back is the believer's salvation traced in chapter ii.?

_____

_____

29. Of what are we to be an object lesson in the ages to come?

_____

_____

_____

30. What have works to do with salvation?

_____

_____

_____

31. What is the position of the Gentile unbeliever?

_____

_____

32. What makes the believer "nigh"' to God?

_____

_____

33. What is the measure of the believer's nearness to God? i. 6.

_____

_____

34. Who are the "twain" of ii. 15?

_____

35. Does the cross abolish the distinction between unsaved Jews and unsaved Gentiles? ii. 16.

_____

_____

36. What is meant by "you that were afar off"?

_____

_____

37. What is meant by " them that were nigh"?

_____

_____

38. What is the difference between being "made nigh" and "having access"?

_____

_____

_____

39. Who gives us our title to a place in God's presence?

_____

40. By whom are we brought into the experience of that presence?

_____

41. In what aspect is the church presented in chapter i.?

_____

_____

42. In what aspect is the church presented in chapter ii.?

_____

_____

_____

43. How does God inhabit the church?

_____

_____

_____

44. What particular revelation and ministry was committed to the Apostle Paul?

_____

_____

_____

45. Of what is the church an object lesson in chapter 11.?

_____

_____

_____

46. To whom is the church an object lesson?

_____

_____

47. Give, entirely in your own words, the substance of Paul's prayer in chapter iii.

_____

_____

_____

_____

48. What is the second general principle governing the believer's walk?

_____

_____

49. What is the believer's calling?

_____

_____

_____

50. State in your own words the difference between lowliness and meekness.

_____

_____

_____

51. What is meant by "the unity of the Spirit"?

_____

_____

52. Give from memory the seven respects in which all true believers are one. |

_____

_____

_____

_____

_____

_____

53. In respect of what do individual believers differ? iv. 7.

_____

_____

54. Enumerate from memory the five ministry gifts.

_____

_____

_____

_____

_____

Note. The student will observe that in 1 Cor. xii. "gifts" mean qualifications for special service bestowed by the Spirit upon individuals; while in Eph. iv. "gifts" mean persons endowed by the Spirit to do the work of apostles, prophets, etc. In 1 Cor. xii. endowments are given to persons by the Spirit; in Eph. iv. the endowed persons are given to the church by Christ. Every true minister is Christ's gift to the church. The list in Ephesians by no means supplants the list in Corinthians.

55. State the four purposes for which apostles, prophets, evangelists, pastors, and teachers are given to the church.

_____

_____

_____

_____

Note. The expression "the faith" (iv. 13; I Tim. iv. 1; Jude 3. etc.) does not mean personal faith or trust, but the body of revealed truth.

56. What is the third principle of the believer's walk in Ephesians?

_____

_____

57. What is to be "put off" by the believer?

_____

_____

58. Who is to be "put on"?

_____

_____

59. What sin against the Holy Spirit is forbidden?

_____

_____

60. Is it biblical for a believer in this dispensation to i Eins of grieving "away" the Spirit?

_____

_____

61. What is the fourth principle of the believer's walk in Ephesians?

_____

_____

62. What is the fifth principle of the beliesets s walk in Ephesians?

_____

_____

63. State the distinction between what is said of the ae Spirit in i, 18 and in v. 18.

_____

_____

_____

64. What is the sixth principle of the believer's walk in Ephesians?

_____

_____

65. What relation of the church to Christ is developed in chapter v.?

_____

_____

66. In what does that differ from the relation expressed in 2 Cor. xi. 2?

_____

_____

67. What are the immediate results of being filled with the Spirit?

_____

_____

_____

Note. The student will note carefully the contrast between the negative exhortations to forsake the grosser sins in chapter iv., and the exhortations to manifest the sweetest graces in chapter v.

68. With what class does the apostle use the law as an "instruction in righteousness"?

_____

_____

69. Into what conflict does the Spirit-filled believer enter?

_____

_____

70. In what lies his safety and victory in that conflict?

_____

_____

71. Give the various offices of the Spirit in Ephesians.

_____

_____

_____

_____

72. Give the names of God in Ephesians.

_____

_____

_____

_____

73. Are any of these names used in Ephesians for the first time?

_____

_____

LESSON LVII

PHILIPPIANS

I. GENERAL REMARKS

The circumstances under which this Epistle was written are not affected by the controversy as to whether the apostle endured two imprisonments or only one. All agree that it is one of the prison epistles. It was doubtless in the providence of God that an inspired writing, the key word of which is "rejoice," should be written out of circumstances the least joy inspiring. So written, the letter is a demonstration that the peace and joy of the Christian are supernatural in their origin.

The immediate occasion of the Epistle is disclosed in iv. 10-18. The church at Philippi, always forward to remember the material needs of the apostle, as he sought to preach where Christ was not named, have not forgotten that as a prisoner in Rome those needs continue. They have sent relief to him by Epaphroditus. In its simplest aspect, therefore, Philippians is the letter of a missionary to a church which has contributed to his support.

But, though the relief sent by the Philippians to Paul, and the return of Epaphroditus, the messenger, gave thus the natural occasion of the Epistle, the apostle will by no means exalt the gift out of its due place. He will not permit the Philippians to think they have done a "great thing" in sending of their "carnal things" to one who has "sown unto them spiritual things." (1 Cor. ix. 11.) Three things should be observed of this aspect of the Epistle.

(1) The apostle makes full and gracious — acknowledgment of this aid and of past help of the same kind.

(2) He gives to such ministry an exalted place. It is "an odor of a sweet smell, a sacrifice acceptable, well pleasing to God"; and also "fruit" which will abound to the account of the Philippians. But

(3) it does not put the apostle himself under a slavish, unmanly obligation. He does not "desire a gift'; he does not " speak in respect of want"; he can "suffer need" or "abound," according as God may will. It is Christian manliness. See, also, 1. Cor. ix. 7-11; 2 Cor. 8-10. In other words, Paul will not permit the occasion to determine the contents of the Epistle.

The theme of Philippians is Christian experience. Redemption, justification, perfect safety—these are assumed. It is assumed, too, that the local church is in due order—"saints in Christ Jesus which are at Philippi, with the bishops and deacons"—and that heresies are not- at work among them. Untroubled, in the case of this church, by irregularities of doctrine or of practice, the Spirit sets forth the inner state and outward behavior which should characterize those who look back to the cross as establishing their perfect security, and forward to the second coming of Christ as the consummation of their perfect felicity. It is significant that the key word of right and normal Christian experience is "joy." Suffering is freely mentioned; conflict is reckoned with; imperfection is confessed; but, despite these incidents of the saved life, joy dominates.

In view of all this the key verse is i. 21, " For to me to live is Christ, and to die is gain." The startling contrast between right Christian experience and usual Christian experience is shown by the fact that the latter could be best described by precisely inverting the apostle's testimony—" For to me to live is gain, and to die is [I hope] Christ."

Normal (or right) Christian experience is, therefore, the reproduction of Christ. And this not by imitation, nor by striving to imagine what Christ would do if in our circumstances. It is the outworking, in our circumstances, of the life, nature, mind, of Christ Himself dwelling in us. ["He which hath begun a good work in you." i. 6, "Filled with the fruits of righteousness, which are by Jesus Christ." i. 11. "Let this mind be in you which was also in Christ Jesus." ii. 5. "For it is God which worketh in you, both to will and to do." ii. 13.]

II. Analysis

The natural divisions of the Epistle are sufficiently indicated by the chapter divisions. It falls, therefore, into four chief sections.

Section I. Christ the Believer's Life, Rejoicing in Victory over Suffering. Chapter i.

The apostle's circumstances are wholly adverse. He is Nero's prisoner. His energetic nature is forbidden its accustomed activity. His life itself is subject to the whim of a bloody despot. Until help came from Philippi he was in actual need. But in and over all these things he rejoices. He is not occupied with these things. His heart is filled with others. Upon every mention of the Philippians he thanks God. i. 3. He never prays without mentioning them, and his prayers are filled with joy because of what Christ has done and will do in and through them. i. 4-11. Besides (i. 12, 13) he will tell them that the imprisonment itself is working the furtherance of the gospel. Through his bonds the gospel has penetrated Caesar's court— that place alike inaccessible and vile. 2 Tim. iv. 16; Phil. iv. 22. And not only so, the steadfastness and preservation of the bound apostle have restored confidence to fearful and disheartened brethren, so that now they are much more bold to speak than they had been. i. 14.

Even though the Judaizers, and those who strive about words, are also stirred up to activity, the apostle will rejoice, for they preach Christ. Some may be saved despite a leaven of malice in the preacher. i. 14-18. He rejoices, too, in confidence that whether through life or through death Christ will be magnified in his body, for he has the prayers of the saints and "the supply of the Spirit of Jesus Christ." i. 19, 20. And, since the worst Nero can do is to put him to death, he will tell them what he thinks of death. To live is Christ, to die is gain, so he cannot choose. His desire is to go, but for others

it is more needful that he should continue to manifest Christ through suffering, so he will abide.

Section II. Christ, the Pattern of the Believer's Life Reproducing Himself in Lowly Service.

In chapter ii, the apostle now turns more directly to the Philippian saints. Great as are his present causes of rejoicing, it rests with them to fill his cup full. As a working and worshiping brotherhood they must be of one mind. They must avoid doing things by faction, or for ostentation. ii. 3, R. V. This should be pondered deeply. We must. do nothing in the church by working up a "faction" or party in favor of it. We must do nothing out of vainglory (literally, "ostentation"). But if these evils are to be excluded brethren must not be opinionated, nor occupied with their own ideas, or service. They must be open minded. ii. 1-4.

In all this Christ must be the believer's pattern. Let it be repeated that Paul never conceives of Christ-likeness, as producible by imitation. "Let this mind be in you, which was also in Christ." 11.5. It is not the intellect of Christ which is meant, but Christ's attitude toward the Father's will, and toward service. That posture of soul was one of entire self-effacement, at whatever cost of humiliation or suffering. The proof and illustration of that attitude is His incarnation, lowly service and death. God will work in the Philippians the same mind. Their responsibility is to "let" Him do it. This involves willingness and yieldedness.

The seven steps in Christ's humbling are set forth. ii. 6-8. He was in the form (en morthe: "the form by which a person or thing strikes the vision; the external appearance." Thayer.) of God, He thought that glorious appearance of deity not a prize to be held eagerly, but emptied Himself (of that " form") and took upon Him the form of a servant, and was madé in likeness asa man. Then, as a man he did not stand upon his rights nor seek human: greatness and distinction, but became a humble man; and, in the cross (a slave's death) touched the bottom of possible obloquy and humiliation. There His (human) exaltation began. By divine decree the human name of Jesus is exalted above every other name. ii. 9-11.

The application follows; "Wherefore," etc. The believer is not exhorted to work for his salvation, but, since God inworks in willing and doing, the believer is to outwork in righteous living and testimony. The outward life is to be the manifestation of an inner life, which is divine in nature and energy. ii. 12, 18. What such a life will be is defined in verse 14-16.

Two touching (because they are unconscious) illustrations follow. Timothy and Epaphroditus. ii. 19-30.

Section III. Christ, the Object of the Believer's Life; Rejoicing in Victory over Imperfections. Chapter iii.

In this great section Christ is the believer's object, as in Section II. He was the believer's pattern.

The key to this chapter is found in two phrases. "I count not myself to have apprehended"—" I press toward the mark." The believer is deeply conscious of imperfect spirituality, knowledge, growth; but he is conscious too, that he is on the way to perfection and full stature. The goal is the second coming of Christ and the first resurrection. It is the thought of 1 John iii. 1-3. We are now the sons of God, but imperfectly developed. When Christ appears we shall be like Him. Meantime, having this hope set on Him, we purify ourselves.

The difficulty many find in interpreting this chapter is due to the failure to perceive that the apostle goes back to the beginning and traces his experience. He was a Hebrew of the Hebrews, having every kind of Hebraic excellency. Then Christ came to be his object. Verse 7 may interpret his state of soul in Acts ix. 5, 6,11. He counted the highest conceivable self-righteousness, "loss for Christ." And that was not the passing thought of the moment of his conversion, but a continuing passion. iii. 8-10. It is not that he doubts that he is

in Christ, nor that he will be in "the resurrection from among the dead.'"" See Greek and Revised Version. Past and present are fused in his vehemence. At iti.12 he leaves the past and takes up the present. He does not count himself to have attained. He is not of those who say that "the (first) resurrection is passed already" (2 Tim. ii. 18), nor that he is already perfected. He does not even count himself perfectly to have grasped Christ's whole meaning in laying hold of him, Paul, for salvation and service. He longs to grasp the fullness of Christ's thought and purpose for him. To that end he presses forward; and, since occupation with the past, whether good or bad, is a hinderance, he "forgets" it. The calling of Godis an upward (not "high") calling. At the end is a prize—Christliness perfected. iii.12-14.

This brings in a truth which demands the exercise of charity. On this upward path, which begins with regeneration and ends in glory, are believers in all stages of progress. Some are stumbling in spiritual infancy, others are full grown (verse 15, not " perfect").

What, then, is the rule of fellowship? "Whereunto we have attained let us walk." It is the principle of James iv. 17. "To him that knoweth to do good and doeth it not, to him it is sin." It is impossible, without sin, for one who has come to spiritual manhood and perception, to revert, for the sake of uniformity of practice, or of any other seeming advantage, to a less developed state. But, neither may such become unduly impatient with those of lower spirituality, for—"if in anything ye be otherwise minded, God shall reveal even this unto you." iii. 15, 16. But this law of charity must not degenerate into a mere good-natured tolerance of evil practice or doctrine. Many walk (professing Christians are meant), who are enemies of the cross of Christ. They may say beautiful things about the character of Christ, and the words of Christ, but they are marked by their rejection of the atonement, and by mere earthliness of life. iii. 17-19.

The sum of the matter is that the believer's citizenship is in heaven; and the proper expectation of thu instructed Christian is neither death nor judgment, but the coming of "the Saviour, the Lord Jesus Christ; who shall change the body of our humiliation, that it may be fashioned like unto His glorious body." I. Cor.) xv. 51, 52; I Thess. iv. v.16-18.

This section therefore presents the Lord Jesus as the believer's object in three ways—for righteousness (iii. 7-9), for present fellowship in resurrection power and in suffering (iii. 10), and for the redemption of the body and the perfecting of holiness, either through the first resurrection (if the believer dies) or through transforming power at His coming.

Part 1. gives the perfect attitude looking toward service. ii. 14-16.

Part II. the perfect attitude looking toward character. iii. 9-21.

Section IV. Christ, the Strength of the Believer's Life, Rejoicing in Victory over Anxiety. Chapter iv.

Verse 1 belongs logically to the preceding chapter. The emphatic word is "so." "So stand fast in the Lord:" that is, according to the attitude of the apostle in chapter iii.

After a most tender rebuke and exhortation the apostle strikes again the vibrating chord of joy. iv. 4. In verse 5 for "moderation" read, "yieldingness." Verses 6 and 7 give the sovereign cure for anxiety. Verse 6 states the human side, verse 7 the divine side. The emphatic words are "for nothing," "in everything," and "by prayer." Very few enter this blessedness because very few are willing to give up all anxiety and overt concerns. They think they ought to be anxious about their sins, or their necessities, or their relations.

Verse 9 gives the rule for the abiding presence of the God of peace. Here "do" is the emphatic word.

For the rest, the apostle was glad the Philippians had thought of his necessities, but he would not have them suppose he had been cast down, or put into anxiety, by those necessities.

Through Christ, his strength, he could be content in any state. "Therewith" in verse 11 should be omitted. It completely spoils the sense. Paul had not learned to be content with his state, but in his state. But he was no stoic, and so was glad when abundance came. As inspired of God, he sends back the mighty promise of verse 19.

It remains to notice that in an epistle especially devoted to Christian experience there should be such scant mention of the Holy Spirit, since all right Christian experience is the realization, through the Spirit, of blessings which we have in Christ. Along with this may be mentioned the absence in a marked degree of doctrinal teaching. The explanation is simple. Normal Christian experience is not occupation with doctrine, however important or precious, nor with the Holy Spirit. It is an occupation with Christ. The Spirit-filled saint is not Spirit-conscious, but Christ-conscious. " He shall take of mine and shew it unto you." This is not to discredit the importance of doctrine, for all experience is the realization in blessing of the truths of doctrine. It is only to say that the most exquisite accuracy of doctrine, and the complete filling with the Spirit, have their issue in complete fellowship and preoccupation with Christ.

PHILIPPIANS

1. Where and in what circumstances was Paul when he wrote Philippians?

_____

_____

_____

2. What was the occasion of the Epistle?

_____

_____

3. State all that is known of Epaphroditus.

_____

_____

_____

4. How does Paul in this Epistle shew his habitual courtesy?

_____

_____

_____

5. How does he preserve his manly independence?

_____

_____

_____

6. What is the theme of Philippians?

_____

_____

_____

7. What doctrines are assumed?

_____

_____

_____

8. What three classes compose a fully organized New Testament church?

_____

_____

_____

9. Which class is named first?

_____

_____

10. What is the key word of Philippians?

_____

11. What is the key verse of Philippians?

_____

_____

12. Define, in your own words, the source of right Christian experience.

_____

_____

_____

13. Does the apostle tell us to imitate Christ?

_____

_____

14. Give the analysis of Philippians.

_____

_____

_____

_____

_____

15. Summarize from chapter i. the causes of Paul's rejoicing.

_____

_____

_____

16. Was his imprisonment a hindrance to the gospel?

_____

_____

17. Was it a hindrance to his own growth or blessing?

_____

_____

18. Explain, in your own words, the meaning of i. 14,

_____

_____

_____

19. Why did Paul rejoice in preaching, which was mingled with envy and controversy?

_____

_____

_____

20. Where is a Christian when he has departed this life?

_____

_____

21. Is Christ in the grave?

_____

_____

22. What common faults are rebuked in ii. 3?

_____

_____

23. Give from memory the seven steps of Christ's humiliation.

_____

_____

_____

_____

_____

_____

24. What is the revised rendering of ii. 7?

_____

_____

_____

25. Does this mean that Christ emptied Himself of deity, or of the manifestation of deity?

_____

_____

26. How may we be like Christ in self-effacement?

_____

_____

_____

27. Is the believer to work for his salvation?

_____

_____

28. State, in your own words, the principles of life and service laid down in ii. 12-16.

_____

_____

_____

_____

_____

29. State the seven natural superiorities of Saul the Pharisee.

_____

_____

_____

30. In comparison with the righteousness which Christ gives to all who believe, what does Paul call the highest possible human goodness?

_____

_____

_____

31. Does Paul rest content with his perfect standing in Christ?

_____

_____

32. When Paul, as a convicted sinner, came to Christ, what were the two supreme objects of his desire? (verse 9; verse 11.)

_____

_____

33. Now that he is in Christ, and sure of the first resurrection, what are his desires?

_____

_____

34. What distinction, in sympathy and fellowship, does the apostle make between weak and uninstructed Christians, and those professing to be Christians, who are enemies of the cross of Christ, and who live for earthly things?

_____

_____

35. Where is the believer's citizenship?

_____

_____

36. For whom is he to be looking?

_____

_____

37. State, in your own words, the three aspects in which Christ is the believer's object.

_____

_____

_____

_____

38. What must the Christian do to be freed from all anxiety?

_____

_____

_____

39. What does God do to free the Christian from all anxiety?

_____

_____

_____

40. How may we have the God of peace with us?

_____

_____

_____

41. What is God's estimation of material help given to His servants?

_____

_____

_____

42. Does God promise to give anything we may desire?

_____

_____

43. What limiting word is contained in His promise of supply?

_____

_____

44. How many times is the Holy Spirit mentioned?

_____

_____

45. How many times is prayer mentioned?

_____

_____

46. How many times joy and rejoicing?

_____

_____

47. State the petitions in Paul's prayers in Philippians.

_____

_____

_____

_____

48. What names of deity are used in Philippians?

_____

_____

LESSON LVIII

F<small>IRST</small> T<small>IMOTHY</small>

G<small>ENERAL</small> R<small>EMARKS</small>

In the examination upon this Epistle the student is required to give from his own research the known facts concerning Timothy. Nothing, therefore, is said upon that head here.

For Timothy Paul felt the tenderest personal affection, and he constantly employed him, despite his youth, ill-health, and timidity, in the weightiest matters. The date, place of writing, and occasion of the First Epistle, are much in dispute. If Paul suffered two imprisonments it seems clear that the Epistle was written after the first, and before the second. If there was but one imprisonment, it seems equally clear that the Epistle was written before the apostle's last journey to Jerusalem.

The question has, however, no bearing whatever upon interpretation. From 1 Thessalonians to Philippians (inclusive) there is a recognizable progress of doctrine, which is best discerned and followed by studying the Epistles in their chronological order. But in the two Timothys and Titus the subjects are church order and discipline, and the path of the servant of Christ in a time of declension and disorder. Doctrine, considered as the revelation of new truth, is not specifically affected. In a very real sense, therefore, the three pastoral Epistles are disconnected from the great body of Paul's writings.

First Timothy supposes the existence of local churches (as at Ephesus, i. 3), and lays stress upon the vital importance of sound doctrine and of order in church life. The key phrase is: "That thou mayest know how thou oughtest to behave thyself in the house of God." iii. 15. Timothy, however, was not addressed as either an elder or pastor, but as Paul's spokesman at Ephesus. He spoke in Paul's place, and by his authority. He was not an apostle, but was an apostolic legate. i. 3; Phil, 11. 19-23; 1 Thess. iii. 2, etc. The Epistle therefore, has the abiding importance of setting forth the mind of Christ concerning sound doctrine, church order, and discipline; and in our study fitly follows Philippians, which is addressed to saints "with the bishops and deacons." It is easy to forget, in occupation with heavenly truths, that in the will of God the earthly life and service of saints is to be in the fellowship of local assemblies.

Doubtless, we are not under law. Doubtless, harm may be wrought by turning First Timothy into a new Leviticus. But doubtless, also, this precious Epistle gives the mind of Christ for the ordering of His churches. In so far as their work and worship are dominated by the counsels and spirit of this letter will church life abide in peace and power. It is noteworthy that every characteristic error of Romanism concerning ministry and office in the church is expressly rebuked in this Epistle.

Analysis.

Many analyses of First and Second Timothy have been suggested. It remains true that they defy structural analysis The student should, however, group the more important teach ings under definite heads as follows:

I. Bishops (or elders).
  (1) Qualifications.
  (2) Duties.
  (3) Privileges.

II. Deacons.
  (1) Qualifications.
  (2) Duties.
  (3) Privileges.

III. Doctrines.
  (1) Doctrines taught or commended.
  (2) Doctrines condemned.

IV. Practices.

    (1) Commended.

    (2) Condemned.

V. Discipline.

    (1) For what causes.

VI. Ministry of the Word.

    (1) By whom.

    (2) To whom forbidden.

    (3) Instructions.

VII. Warnings.

FIRST TIMOTHY

1. Gather from the Acts and Epistles the following particulars as to Timothy:

    (1) Parentage.

_____

_____

    (2) Early training.

_____

_____

    (3) Place of residence at conversion.

_____

_____

    (4) Through whom converted.

_____

_____

    (5) Health.

_____

_____

    (6) Personal characteristics.

_____

_____

_____

    (7) Chief events in his life.

_____

_____

_____

_____

2. For what purpose was Timothy left at Ephesus?

_____

_____

3. Of whom is it said that they had "turned aside unto vain jangling"?

_____

_____

4. What is the lawful use of the law?

_____

_____

_____

5. What is the unlawful use of the law?

_____

_____

_____

6. What saying is worthy of all acceptation?

_____

_____

7. What two things must be "held" by one who would war a good warfare? See i. 18, 19, Revised Version.

_____

_____

_____

8. Is the faith likely to be held incorrupt after the conscience becomes defiled?

_____

_____

9. In church worship what does Paul put 'first of all'?

_____

_____

_____

10. Of what truths was Paul "ordained a preacher"?

_____

_____

11. What must men who pray in the assembly have?

_____

_____

12. What must men who pray in the assembly be "without"?

_____

_____

13. How should women dress for the gatherings of the church?

_____

_____

14. What functions in the gatherings of the church are forbidden to women?

_____

_____

Note. The student will distinguish "teaching"—i.e., the authoritative declaration of doctrine—from "prophesying," which is defined as speaking "unto edification, and exhortation, and comfort." 1 Cor. xiv. 3. "All may prophesy." 1 Cor. xiv. 24, 31; xi. 5.

15. The student will here insert the groupings of passages under the heads suggested in the lesson outline.

_____

_____

_____

16. What "mysteries" of the faith are enumerated in chapter iii?

_____

_____

_____

17. What corruptions of the faith are predicted for "the latter times"?

_____

_____

_____

18. From what sources will those corruptions proceed?

_____

_____

_____

19. What mark of "a good minister of Jesus Christ" is given in chapter iv.?

_____

_____

20. What saying " worthy of all acceptation"' is given in chapter iv.?

_____

_____

21. Upon what is a minister to meditate, and to what give himself wholly?

_____

_____

_____

Note. "Elder" in v. 1 means elderly person—not necessarily an official person.

22. What persons are to be supported by the churches?

_____

_____

_____

23. What is said of those who do not support their own households?

_____

_____

_____

24. What doctrinal errors are condemned in this Epistle?

_____

_____

_____

25. Cite the passages which show the divine solicitude that doctrine be preserved incorrupt.

_____

_____

_____

_____

LESSON LX

Titus

General Remarks

Internal evidence assigns the same date to First Timothy and Titus. In the main the same circumstances gave the occasion to both. Timothy was left in Ephesus, and Titus in Crete, to instruct and guide those churches in their organized, corporate life. To each, therefore, was given a letter of instructions and authentication. Neither had the smallest personal authority over the churches of Jesus Christ; both were delegated by the apostle who was the "sent one" of the ascended and glorified Christ. These letters of instruction have naturally much in common. Their characteristic differences grow out of somewhat different conditions in the churches to which, respectively, they were sent. To Timothy Paul writes, "I besought thee to abide still at Ephesus, when I went into Macedonia, that thou mightest charge some that they teach no other doctrine." To Titus, "For this cause I left thee in Crete, that thou shouldst set in order the things that are wanting, and ordain elders in every city." Both Epistles concern doctrine and order; but First Timothy lays special stress upon incorrupt doctrine, Titus upon ecclesiastical order. Both are filled with wise and tender instructions such as bear rule in the assemblies, or labor in word and doctrine.

Analysis

Like First Timothy, the Epistle to Titus does not fall into structural divisions. Groupings may be made, as in the study of First Timothy. The student should especially note the passages which fix the order of experience and blessing—ii. 11-13, 14; iii. 4-8.

TITUS

1. State, in your own words, all that is known of Titus.

_____

_____

_____

_____

2. State, in your own words, what you understand Paul to mean by i. 1-3.

_____

_____

_____

3. Why was Titus left in Crete?

_____

_____

4. State the Scriptural qualifications of elders (bishops).

_____

_____

5. From what source was the truth in danger in Crete?

_____

_____

6. What test of profession is given in chapter i.?

_____

_____

7. What behavior should characterize aged men?

_____

_____

8. What behavior should characterize aged women?

_____

_____

9. What behavior should characterize young women?

_____

_____

10. What behavior should characterize young men?

_____

_____

11. What behavior should characterize servants?

_____

_____

12. What is it which "adorns" doctrine?

_____

_____

13. What does grace bring?

_____

_____

14. What does grace teach?

_____

_____

_____

15. For what should Christians be looking?

_____

_____

16. State the distinction between "that blessed hope" and "the glorious appearing."

_____

_____

17. What proof of the deity of Christ does ii. 13 give?

_____

_____

_____

18. State the three purposes for which Christ "gave Himself for us."

_____

_____

Note. Four precious truths meet in ii. 14. Atonement, redemption, sanctification, good works.

19. What is the relation of the believer to the civil authority?

_____

_____

_____

20: What graces should characterize the bearing of Christians toward others?

_____

_____

_____

_____

21. Couple ii. 11 with iii. 4, and give the inspired definition of grace.

_____

_____

_____

22. What part in our salvation had our works? Why did God save us?

_____

_____

_____

23. How are we justified?

_____

_____

_____

24. Upon whom are good works enjoined?

_____

_____

_____

25. What things are "unprofitable and vain?" Is heresy sin?

_____

_____

_____

26. What duty toward heretics is enjoined?

_____

_____

_____

LESSON LX

SECOND TIMOTHY

GENERAL REMARKS

This touching and solemn letter was written by Paul to his "*dearly beloved son," shortly before the martyrdom by which the great apostle to the Gentiles sealed his testimony. iv. 6-8. Its contents are in striking contrast with those of First Timothy. That Epistle had in view the church as "the pillar and ground of the truth" (1 Tim. iii. 15), and Timothy is charged with the duty of establishing the church in incorruptness of doctrine and orderly organization. Now the apostasy of the church is assumed, and Timothy is charged to commit the truth "to faithful men, who shall be able to teach others also." 2 Tim. ii. 2. Then the corporate walk of the church was the object of solicitude; mow the individual path of the servant of Christ is pointed out. First Timothy looked forward to the "latter time," corruptions of papistry; Second Timothy looks forward to the "last days" of general apostasy. Compare 1 Tim. iv. 13 with 2 Tim. iii. 1-138. In the former passage it is said that "some" shall depart, etc. In the latter the things specified are general.

The key phrase of First Timothy is: "'That thou mayest know how thou oughtest to behave thyself in the house of God, which is the church of the living God." iii. 15. The key phrase of Second Timothy is: "Study to show thyself approved unto Gods?) 1115:

In Second Timothy it is already necessary to exhort against being "ashamed" of "the testimony of the Lord," and of persecuted witnesses to that testimony. i. 8. Paul declares himself unashamed, and commends Onesiphorus because he was not ashamed of Paul's chain. Already the churches in Asia (e.g., Ephesus, Smyrna, Pergamos, Thyatira, Sardis, Philadelphia, Laodicea), had forsaken the Pauline teaching. i. 15. The church is no longer spoken of as "the pillar and ground of the truth," but is called a "great house" in which there are not only vessels unto honor but unto dishonor... 11.20. This brings in a new principle of separation. In Corinthians the believer was called to separation from the unbelieving world; but in Second Timothy he must purge himself from complicity with " vessels unto dishonor" within the professing church.

In First Timothy and Titus disorders and heresies were dealt with by authority. 1 Tim. v. 20; vi. 17; Titus i. 10-13; ii. 15; iii. 10, 11; in Second. Timothy the servant of the Lord is restricted to meekly teaching "those that oppose themselves" (ii. 24-26), and reproof and rebuke is to be "with all long suffering and teaching." iv. 2.

Moreover, the servant of the Lord is warned that the time will come when sound doctrine will not only be disbelieved, but no longer endured. Instead of receiving (however ungraciously) such ministry as Christ may raise up by conferring spiritual gifts, "they" (not "some") will choose such teachers as please them. iv. 3, 4.

The resource of the servant of the Lord in such times is pointed out—the Scriptures. This is most noteworthy. While it is true that in all his writings the apostle makes evident his absolute subjection to the authority of the Scriptures (by which he meant the Old Testament), it is in Second Timothy that he especially exalts their authority as final to a servant of the Lord. ii. 15; iii. 15-17; iv. 2. To the Old Testament authority he adds that of his own inspired teaching. i. 13; 11. 2, 8; ili. 14. The "form of sound words" is insisted upon, since Paul testifies that the Spirit taught him the very words in which he gave forth revelations which had been commuitted.to him. 1 Cor, ii. 13.

In a word, the apostolic presence is about to be withdrawn. That presence had carried with it authority, because the apostles were inspired and sent forth as the spokesmen of Christ. Looking forward now to his approaching removal by death, the apostle points the servants of the Lord to the Scriptures as inspired, authoritative, able to make wise unto salvation, and competent to teach, reprove, correct, instruct, and to thoroughly furnish the man of God unto every good work. Not one word does he say of a successor to his apostleship, nor of the authority of a church, body of churches, council, or creed. The Scriptures, and they alone, are authoritative. When the time comes that the churches will not hear the preaching of the Word, nor endure sound doctrine, the servant of the Lord must turn.to the unsaved, and "do the work of an evangelist." iv. 2-5.

ANALYSIS

As with First Timothy, this Epistle does not fall naturally into divisions.

THE JEWISH-CHRISTIAN EPISTLES

INTRODUCTORY NOTE

It is obvious that in Hebrews, James, and First and Second Peter, we have a group of writings in many striking respects different from the Pauline Epistles on the one hand, or those of John and Jude on the other. It is important to notice that this difference is in no sense one of conflict. There is no disagreement between Paul and the other writers named. All present the same Christ, the same way of salvation, the same morality. All,

too, appeal to the Scriptures as of final authority. There is not a doctrine in Hebrews, in James, in Peter, which is not also implied or expressed in the Pauline writings. The difference is one of extension, of development. The foundational truths, the doctrines of salvation through the sacrifice of Christ, by faith; of the person of Christ as truly God and truly man; of the divine origin and absolute authority of Scripture; of a new life through Christ; and of godliness as the evidence and result of true faith—these are truths common alike to Paul and to the Jewish-Christian writers.

But Paul, as the student has seen, received revelations of truth which open the mystery of the church as the body and bride of Christ; which govern the local churches; which unfold the doctrine and work of the Holy Spirit; and the distinctive position, walk, warfare, and hope of the believer.

The Jewish-Christian Epistles, therefore, as presenting the great fundamentals of the Christian faith, belong to Gentile as well as to Jewish believers, and could be hindered of blessing only if taken as the summit and final word of revelation for this dispensation. That word was given to the great apostle to the Gentiles. Doctrinally, the Jewish-Christian, writings group with the Gospels and with Acts i.—ix.

SECOND TIMOTHY

1. Cite the passages which prove that Paul was now a prisoner.

_____

_____

2. Of what is Timothy exhorted not to be ashamed?

_____

_____

3. Was the apostle in doubt of his own salvation?

_____

_____

4. Was he saved according to his works?

_____

_____

5. In what connection does he place his works in iv. 7, 8?

_____

_____

6. What three characteristics of the Spirit are given in chapter i.?

_____

_____

_____

_____

7. Before what event was God's purpose to save us formed?

_____

_____

8. How and when was that purpose made manifest?

_____

_____

_____

9. Of what was Paul appointed a preacher and an apostle and a teacher?

_____

_____

10. Define those three functions.

_____

_____

_____

11. To whom was Paul appointed to minister?

_____

_____

12. What grounds of assurance does Paul give in chapter i.?

_____

_____

13. What definition of saving faith do you find in i. 12?

_____

_____

14. Why does Paul exhort Timothy to remember the "words" of his teachings?

_____

_____

15. What "good thing" had been "committed" to Timothy?

_____

_____

16. Through whom do believers keep their knowledge of the truth?

_____

_____

Note. "Keep," in Scripture, means not only retain, but observe, obey. See, e.g., Deut. xxx. 16; John xv. 10-12.

17. What relationship with the Holy Spirit is asserted in Second Timothy?

_____

_____

18. What seven names are given to the Christian in chapter ii.?

_____

_____

_____

_____

_____

_____

19. What is said of the Christian in his character of a son?

_____

_____

_____

20. What is said of the Christian in his character of a soldier?

_____

_____

21. What is said of the Christian in his character of a wrestler? ("Strive for masteries." ii. 5)

_____

_____

22. What is said of the Christian in his character of a husbandman?

_____

_____

23. What is said of the Christian in his character of a workman?

_____

_____

24. What is said of the Christian in his character of a vessel?

_____

_____

25. What is said of the Christian in his character of a servant?

_____

_____

26. To what is false doctrine compared in ii. 17?

_____

27. Give, in your own words, an example of such separation as is commanded in ii. 21.

_____

_____

_____

28. What benefit accrues to one who thus separates himself?

_____

_____

_____

29. Does the separation of ii. 21 mean withdrawing from the church of God, or only from complicity in practices dishonoring to God?

_____

_____

30. What general evils will characterize the professed church in the last days?

_____

_____

_____

31. What do you understand by the "power" of true godliness?

_____

_____

_____

32. What four characteristics of false teachers are mentioned i i 1, 28?

_____

_____

_____

_____

33. What promise is given in chapter ii. of divine interposition when apostasy has reached the stage described?

_____

_____

_____

34. What is said as to the origin of the Scriptures?

_____

_____

_____

35. What seven things are affirmed of the Scriptures?

_____

_____

_____

_____

_____

_____

36. What are ministers commanded to preach?

_____

_____

_____

37. What applications of the word are they commanded to make?

_____

_____

_____

38. What prediction is made as to hearers?

_____

_____

_____

39. What is said of their ears?

_____

_____

40. What " work" is the servant of the Lord to do when Christians will no longer endure sound doctrine?

_____

_____

_____

41. What three things could the apostle say of himself at the end?

_____

_____

_____

42. What, therefore, was "laid up" for him?

_____

_____

43. To whom is the same reward promised?

_____

_____

44. What led to the desertion of Demas?

_____

_____

LESSON LXI

HEBREWS

GENERAL REMARKS

Hebrews is without superscription or signature. From the earliest times its authorship has been ascribed to Paul, but also from the earliest times the Pauline authorship has been questioned. Since the book itself makes no mention of the writer the question of his identity is better left in abeyance. The occasion of the Epistle is not stated, nor is there any other indication of the date than that it was written before the destruction of the temple, while it could still be said, "And every priest standeth daily ministering, and offering the same sacrifices, which can never take away sins." x.11. The hortatory passages reveal the purpose of the Epistle. It was written for the instruction of Jewish Christians, who were in danger of going : back to Judaism. The continued existence of the temple and priesthood made this danger a very real one. Indeed, it is clear from many passages in the Acts that even the strongest and most assured among the Jewish believers in Palestine were holding to a strange mingling of Christian doctrine and Jewish practice. See, *e.g.*, Acts xxi. 18-24. The doctrine of Hebrews is that the sacrifice of Christ "took away" the Levitical sacrifices by fulfillment and substitution, and that the entire Mosaic economy came to an end by fulfillment. The book may be called an inspired commentary on the types. The method of the writer is to take up one after another of the good and precious things of the Old Testament religion, and to leave Christ in their place and stead. Those were good, but Christ is better. "Better," therefore, is the key word of Hebrews. It is a series of contrasts between good and better, between the shadow and substance, between type and anti-type. Christ is "better" than angels, chapters i., ii.; than Moses, chapter ili.; than Joshua, chapter iv.; than Aaron, chapters v.—

vii.; than the Mosaic covenant, chapter viii.; than the Levitical sacrifices, chapters ix., x. The primary object of the writer was to establish in the hearts of Jewish believers faith in Christ as Fulfiller and Finisher of Judaism as a system. As a presentation of Christianity the doctrine of Hebrews is strictly elementary. The writer has in view the sphere of Christian profession. Jews were in danger of taking on Christianity without a full Christ. There were many sects in Judaism. Men were Pharisees, Sadducees, Essenes, Herodians, etc. But none of these involved the forsaking of Judaism. Therefore, impressed by the power, sanctity, joyfulness, and unselfishness of the earliest believers, earnest-hearted men might join their company without accepting Christ as deity (chapters i., ii.), or as having perfected by one offering all who believed on Him (x. 1-14).

In this respect Hebrews groups with the Gospel of Matthew. In that Gospel, from the thirteenth chapter onward, the disciples are viewed as a professing body. Accordingly, in both Hebrews and Matthew, warnings of apostasy, unreality, and peril are frequent. Hebrews vi. 4-8 and x. 26-30 are examples. Safety is shown to depend upon faith in Jesus Christ as a complete Savior. Apostasy is possible up to the very act of salvation. And those who, having come to the very threshold of that act, turn back are hopelessly lost. That gives the important contrast between sin and apostasy. Sin may be forgiven, but apostasy turns from the Forgiver. Such a case is supposed in vi. 4-6. That that passage does not describe salvation is evident from verse 9. Good as are the things of verses 4 and 5 the "things which accompany salvation" are "better." The test of reality is that if we have true faith we "hold the beginning of our confidence firm unto the end." iii.14. These hortatory and warning passages are parenthetical. They interrupt, but do not advance the course of the argument. They give to Hebrews an extraordinary freshness and liveliness, as if the Epistle were a verbatim report of a spoken discourse.

We shall not, therefore, find in Hebrews the doctrine of the church. It would have been apart from the purpose of the writer to arouse the anti-Gentile prejudices of these men of prejudice until they had first become established in the faith of Jesus Christ. It is like Peter's preaching on the day of Pentecost. Indeed, church truth was to the very end of temple and city unwelcome and undeveloped in Jerusalem. To the very end it continued to be one of those truths of which our Lord speaks in John xvi. 12, "Ye cannot bear them now."' Heb. v. 11-14. Hebrews, therefore, does not go beyond the "heavenly calling," in which the fathers also shared according to the teachings of Christ (Luke xiii. 28; Heb. xi. 10, 16; iii. 1), and the way into the holiest made manifest. The essence of Judaism as a preparatory religion was the veil which hid God. Heb. ix. 3-8. Once each year, on the great day of atonement, one Israelite, the high priest, was in grace permitted to enter the holiest with sacrificial blood, which he offered for himself and for the sins of the people. When Christ died the veil was rent from the top to the bottom; the way into the holiest was open to any sinner who came through the blood of Christ. It was a "new and living way through the veil." Heb. x. 20. From that moment all Jewish ceremonies, sacrifices, and priesthood became, not a means of access, purification and communion, but mere obstacles and hindrances,

It follows that the key phrase of Hebrews is, "Having therefore, brethren, boldness to enter into the holiest by the blood of Jesus." But the student will find neither the perfected doctrines of Christianity, as in Galatians and Romans, nor the perfected position of the Christian, as in Ephesians and Colossians. The church, as in Matthew, is barely mentioned. The believer is not shown as "accepted in the beloved" and "made nigh," but is exhorted to "draw near." The student will, however, observe that while Hebrews presents only foundational truth it presents that truth with extraordinary force and

clearness. The great outstanding truth of Hebrews is that "without shedding of blood is no remission," that Christianity gathers its saving power from atoning blood. The Old Testament sacrifices are shown to have been typical and anticipatory, and the offering of the body of Christ "once for all" to have so completely met the whole question of the believer's sin as that he is thereby "perfected forever."

Christ is presented in His glory as Deity taking part with flesh and blood. His offices in Hebrews are Apostle, High Priest, Sacrificer, and Sacrifice. In resurrection He is the Great Shepherd of the sheep, who appears in the presence of God for us, ever living to make intercession—our Forerunner who makes good our future position there; and as our coming-Deliverer. He is not seen as the Head of the body, the church, nor as espoused Bridegroom. Neither is He seen as indwelling the believer by His imparted life.

The Scriptures are greatly exalted. Throughout they are ascribed to the Holy Spirit. Human authorship disappears. See, e.g. iii. 7; ix. 8; x. 15. They are, therefore, treated as divinely perfect and authoritative.

The Spirit is seen in inspiration, impartation of gifts, as enlightening and convicting, and as standing in a momentary priestly relation to the sacrifice of Christ (ix. 14); but not as indwelling, sealing, baptizing, or sanctifying the believer.

Sanctification is positional, not experimental.

God is seen in relationship with the Son, and, through Him, with the "many sons."

ANALYSIS

Hebrews falls into ten sections and five parentheses. The student will do well to mark the parenthetic passages in his Bible by a brace on the margin. Having done so, let him read the book at one sitting, disregarding the parentheses. Afterward let him study the book by sections with the parentheses.

Section I. Christ, the Son of God, is Better than the Prophets. i. 1-3.

Section II. Christ, the Son of God, is Better than the Angels. i. 4-14; ii. 5-9.

(First Parenthesis. ii. 1-4. The sinner exhorted not to neglect the great salvation.)

Section III. Christ, the Son of God, Incarnated for the Redemption of the Sons of God and for Priesthood, ii. 10-18.

Section IV. Christ, the Son, Better than Moses, the Servant. iii, 1-6.

(Second Parenthesis. iii. 7—iv. 13. The saint exhorted to enter the life of rest.)

Section V. Christ, our High Priest, Better than the Aaronic High Priests. iv. 14—v. 10 and vi. 20—viii. 5.

(Third Parenthesis. v. 11—vi. 19. The saint exhorted to go on to full growth. v. 11—vi. 3. The professor warned of the awful possibility of apostasy. vi. 4-8. The saint comforted and assured. vi. 9-20.)

Section VI. The New Covenant, Better than the Old, Supersedes It. viii. 6-13.

Section VII. The Sacrifice of Christ, Better than the Levitical Sacrifices, Supersedes Them. ix. 1—x. 22.

(Fourth Parenthesis. x. 23-39. The Jewish professor warned that since the Levitical sacrifices are "taken away," there is "no more sacrifice for sin," and it is either Christ or judgment. x. 26-31. The saint comforted and encouraged. xx. 32-39.)

Section VIII. The Supremacy of Faith. xi. 1-40.

(Fifth Parenthesis. xii. 1-17. The saint assured in respect of the Father's chastenings. The final warning by the case of Esau.)

Section IX. The Christian Position and Hope Superior to the Mosaic. xii. 18-29.

Section X. Horatory. xiii. 1-25.

HEBREWS

1. Who was the writer of Hebrews?

_____

_____

2. What was the date?

_____

_____

3. Before what historical event was Hebrews written?

_____

_____

4. What passage proves the truth of your last answer?

_____

_____

5. To whom, primarily, was Hebrews written?

_____

_____

6. In what special danger were zealous Jews after the coming of Christianity?

_____

_____

7. Why were the warning parenthetical passages inserted?

_____

_____

_____

8. State the general distinction between Hebrews and the Pauline Epistles.

_____

_____

_____

9. State from memory the offices of Christ in Hebrews.

_____

_____

_____

_____

_____

10. What is the central doctrine of Hebrews?

_____

_____

_____

11. What is the key word?

_____

_____

12. What is the key phrase?

_____

_____

13. State in your own words why x. 19 is the key phrase.

_____

_____

_____

14. State from memory in what respects Christ is " better" than Old Testament things.

_____

_____

_____

15. State the difference in the Authorized Version and Revised Version renderings of i. 1-3.

_____

_____

_____

16. What are the seven unique superiorities of Christ enumerated in i. 2, 3?

_____

_____

_____

_____

_____

_____

17. What passages in Hebrews declare that Christ " sat down on the right hand of the majesty on high"?

_____

_____

_____

18. What has Christ which is " more excellent" than anything the angels have?

_____

_____

_____

19. What passages of the Old Testament are quoted in chapter i. as teaching the deity of Christ?

_____

_____

_____

20. Is He distinctly called God?

_____

_____

21. What are the angels said to be?

_____

_____

22. What "man" is meant in Psalm viii. 4-6?

_____

_____

23. What, in the fulfillment of that prediction, do we see "not yet'?

_____

_____

_____

24. What, meantime, do we see?

_____

_____

25. What was the purpose of Christ's sacrifice as stated in chapter 1.?

_____

_____

_____

26. What moved Him to "taste death "?

_____

_____

27. What other object than atonement had the sufferings of Christ?

_____

_____

28. What effect upon Christ had His sufferings?

_____

_____

_____

29. For how many men did Christ taste death?

_____

_____

_____

30. Are all, then, brought to the glory of sons?

_____

_____

31. What danger is the subject of the first parenthesis?

_____

_____

32. For what two purposes did the Son of God become incarnate?

_____

_____

_____

33. What human experiences of Christ assure us of His sympathy in our weaknesses and temptations?

_____

_____

34. In what two great offices are we exhorted to "consider" Christ?

_____

_____

_____

35. What is the central thought of apostleship? Mark iii. 14, 15; Acts ix. 15.

_____

_____

36. What is the central thought of priesthood? Heb. v. 1, 2.

_____

_____

37. Why is Christ counted worthy of more honor than Moses?

_____

_____

38. From what Old Testament Scripture is Hebrews iii. 7-11 quoted?

_____

_____

39. Who is said to be the author of those words?

_____

_____

40, What danger is the subject of the second parenthesis?

_____

_____

41. Why could not the children of Ferae enter their Canaan rest?

_____

_____

42. When they refused to enter what penalty fell?

_____

_____

43. Did they cease to receive the care and protection of God?

_____

_____

44. With what feelings did He regard them forty chases det

_____

_____

45. Of what was the Canaan rest a type?

_____

_____

46. Give the revised rendering of iv. 8.

_____

_____

_____

47. Did Joshua give Israel spiritual rest?

_____

_____

48. In what passage, long after Joshua, did God continue to promise rest?

_____

_____

49. What is stated in parenthesis two as the positive condition of entering into the rest of God?

_____

_____

50. What is stated as the negative condition?

_____

_____

Note. 'The student should observe that in parenthesis one the salvation of a sinner is the object of solicitude; in parenthesis two, the rest of a saint.

51. What qualities and offices are ascribed to the Word of God in chapter iv.? 3

_____

_____

_____

52. Where is our High Priest?

_____

_____

53. Who is our High Priest?

_____

_____

54. What effect upon our High Priest have our infirmities?

_____

_____

55. What common experience with us had He?

_____

_____

56. In what respect did His temptations differ from ours?

_____

_____

_____

Note. The correct rendering of Hebrews iv. 15, last clause, is: "but was as we like tempted in all points, sin apart." Christ, like the first Adam, was an unfallen man, and like the unfallen Adam, subject to external temptations. But He had not "sin" in the sense of Romans vii. 17-23.

57. Give, from iv. 14, 15; v. 1-9; ix. 11-14, a summary of Christ's priesthood under the following particulars:

(1) His person.

_____

_____

(2) His character.

_____

_____

(3) His place.

_____

_____

(4) His priestly work.

_____

_____

(5) His appointment.

_____

_____

(6) His intercession.

_____

_____

(7) His sacrifice.

_____

_____

58. What is the essential distinction between high priesthood after the order of Melchisedek and after the Aaronic order? vii. 2, 23, 24.

_____

_____

59. Why is Melchizedek a suitable type of an unchanging priesthood? vii. 3.

_____

_____

60. Why is he a suited type of a greater than the Aaronic priesthood? vii. 4-10.

_____

_____

61. What Old Testament passage warned Israel that there would arise a Priest after the order of Melchizedek?

_____

_____

62. Did the law secure perfection?

_____

_____

63. Why was the law called "weak and unprofitable'? Rom. viii. 3.

_____

_____

64. Was the law in itself "weak," etc.? Rom. vii. 12, 14.

_____

_____

65. What did the law " make perfect'?

Note. The supplied word "did" in vii. 19 spoils the sense and should be omitted. Hebrews vii. 19 and Gal. iii. 21-24 are parallel in thought.

Note. "Testament" in Hebrews should be "covenant," except in ix. 16, 17.

Note in vii. 22 the suretyship of Christ. The theological concept of Jesus as surety for us before God— "Before the throne my Surety stands"— is a complete inversion of the Biblical idea. Christ is God's surety to us. The "new covenant" is a covenant of certainties, of assurance. viii. 10-12. It contains seven great unconditional "I wills;" and it is made sure to us by Christ, its Mediator. ix. 15.

66. Go over chapter vii., and draw up a list of contrasts between the priests under the law and the priesthood of Christ.

_____

_____

_____

_____

67. What did the priests under the law "serve unto?"

_____

_____

_____

68. What did God enjoin upon Moses when he was about to make the tabernacle?

_____

_____

_____

69. How many times does Hebrews mention the temple?

_____

70. How many times does Hebrews mention the tabernacle?

_____

71. Give your thought as to the significance of your last two answers.

_____

_____

_____

72. Of what, in the New Testament, is the temple typical?

_____

_____

73. In what respect is the new covenant "better" than the old?

_____

_____

_____

74. In the promise of the new covenant did God find fault with the old covenant, or with Judah and Israel?

_____

_____

75. For what did God blame them?

_____

_____

76. Where did God put His laws under the old covenant?

_____

_____

_____

77. Where did God put His laws under the new?

_____

_____

_____

78. Where did He write them under the old?

_____

_____

_____

79. Where did He write them under the new?

_____

_____

80. Give the seven clauses of the new covenant.

_____

_____

_____

_____

_____

_____

81. Are the two covenants to coexist? vii. 12; viii. 13.

_____

_____

82. Describe in your own way the tabernacle.

_____

_____

_____

_____

83. Where was the first veil?

_____

_____

84. Where the second veil?

_____

_____

85. Into how many rooms was the tabernacle divided?

_____

_____

86. What were these called?

_____

_____

87. What, according to chapter ix., was the spiritual significance of the second veil?

_____

_____

88. What, according to chapter x., was the spiritual significance of the second veil?

_____

_____

_____

89. Of what was the "holiest of all" a type?

_____

_____

_____

90. Into the holiest of all who might enter, and how often?

_____

_____

_____

91. What was the effect upon the second veil of the death of Christ?

_____

_____

_____

92. Where is the Christian's place of worship and communion?

_____

_____

_____

93. What is his title to enter the presence of God?

_____

_____

_____

94. What could not the many sacrifices of Judaism effect?

_____

_____

_____

95. What nine things are mentioned in chapters ix.—x. as having been accomplished by the sacrifice of Christ?

_____

_____

_____

_____

_____

_____

_____

_____

96. What do you understand by "dead works"?

_____

_____

97. In what sense is the word " sanctified" used in chapter x.?

_____

_____

98. What should we draw near "with"?

_____

_____

99. What should we draw near "in"?

_____

_____

100. Might a Jew, after the sacrifice of Christ, continue to offer the Jewish sacrifices, claiming Old Testament promises? x. 26}

_____

_____

101. Is there any sacrifice for one who rejects the Son of God and His blood?

_____

_____

_____

102. What " remains" for one who has received the knowledge of the truth, and yet rejects the Son, the blood, the covenant and the Spirit?

_____

_____

_____

103. What could God do that He has not done for such an one?

_____

_____

104. Is "confidence" a dangerous thing?

_____

_____

105. By what do the justified live?

_____

_____

_____

106. What is lacking, then, to those who "draw back"?

_____

_____

107. Are those who "believe" in the same class with those who "draw back?" x. 39.

_____

_____

108. Quote xi. 1, according to Revised Version.

_____

_____

_____

109. What, according to xi. 1, are the effects of faith?

_____

_____

110. What did Abel do by faith?

_____

_____

111. Why was his sacrifice "more excellent" than Cain's?

_____

_____

112. What did Abel "obtain"?

_____

_____

113. Did God testify of Abel's character or sacrifice?

_____

_____

114. Is it possible for an unbeliever to "please God"?

_____

_____

115. What five things did Abraham do "by faith"?

_____

_____

_____

_____

116. Did not some of the men and women of Heb. xi. lose their faith before they died?

_____

_____

_____

117. What three steps mark faith's dealing with promises? xi. 13.

_____

_____

_____

118. Why do not men of faith return to "that country from whence they came out"? xi. 16.

_____

_____

119. What illustration is given in chapter xi. of supernatural power working in answer to faith?

_____

_____

120. Of faith in resurrection?

_____

_____

121. Of faith "concerning things to come"?

_____

_____

122. Of faith breaking the charm of sinful pleasure?

_____

_____

123. Of faith giving courage and serenity?

_____

_____

124. Of faith in redemption by blood?

_____

_____

125. Of faith to accomplish great things?

_____

_____

126. Of faith to endure hard things?

_____

_____

127. What relation to our faith has Jesus?

_____

_____

128. Of what relationship to God is chastening the proof?

_____

_____

129. What purpose has God in chastening His children?

_____

_____

130. What terrible warning is given concerning " the grace of God"?

131. Give the marginal rendering of xti. 17.

132. What "mount" is meant in xii. 18?

133. Of what is that mount typical?

134. Give a reference in Galatians to prove the typical significance of that mount.

135. Does the believer come to that mount at all?

136. What is meant by the Mount Zion?

137. What three classes of beings (other than deity) are said to inhabit "the heavenly Jerusalem"?

138. To which class does Gabriel belong?

139. To which class do the persons in Heb. xi. belong?

140. To which class do the saved of this dispensation belong?

_____

_____

141. Enumerate the seven things commended in xiii. 1-9.

_____

_____

_____

_____

_____

_____

_____

142. When Israel was following the tabernacle in the wilderness what was done with the bodies offered on the day of atonement?

_____

_____

143. What, then, to a Jewish Christian would be the significance of xiii. 12, 13?

_____

_____

144. What other sacrifices than that of Christ belong to Christianity?

_____

_____

145. Have the sacrifices of xili. 15, 16 any relation to the believer's sin, or acceptance?

_____

_____

146. What effect, then, have they upon God?

_____

_____

147. Cite the passages which refer to the second coming of Christ.

_____

_____

LESSON LXII

James

General Remarks

The student will not fail to observe in this precious Epistle a very marked instance of what has been said concerning the limitations of the Judeo-Christian writings. Hebrews, even, in comparison with the scope of James, seems cosmical.

James, called "the Just," is mentioned by Paul with Cephas and John as "pillars" in the church at Jerusalem. It is gathered from the several passages which mention him that in his practice he was austere, legal and ceremonial. Distinction is always to be drawn between the writers of Scripture and the Scriptures. The writers were men of like passions with ourselves and compassed with human limitations. Doubtless they are distinguished, especially the apostles of our Lord, by great spirituality, devotedness and holiness. But it is the Scriptures which are "given by inspiration of God;" it is Christ alone who is flawless. But James, saturated with the Hebrew idea of righteousness of life, was obviously the suited exponent of the ethical emphasis of Christianity. Doubtless his solicitude was great lest such of "the twelve tribes scattered abroad" as had professed the name of Christ should become corrupted in measure by the lax morality of the Gentile world, or even by the imperfect ethical ideal of new converts out of corrupt Gentilism. This solicitude gave both the occasion and purpose of the Epistle. He is aware that they are under stress of temptations which would never assail them in Jerusalem. Against the general tendency to relaxation of life he sternly insists that only by a godly life can true faith be manifested; and. against the special tendency to accept the crude ideas of practical righteousness current among those newly come out of Gentilism he reminds them that they know better. The key verses, therefore, are: "Even

so faith, if it hath not works, is dead, being alone" (ii. 17); and "Therefore, to him that knoweth to do good and doeth it not, to him it is sin" (iv. 17). James is not treating upon justification before God, but of "justification of life'—that is, manifestation before men. He tests profession by practice. The key phrases, therefore, are: "Yea, a man may Say," and "Ye see'" or "Seest thou?"

Paul tells how a sinner is justified before God wholly without works; James, how a saint is justified before men by faith-inspired works. Each apostle illustrates his doctrine from Abraham, Paul points to the moment when Abraham believed (Gen. xv. 6); James to the testing of Abraham's faith a full twenty years later (Gen. xxii. 1-18). Paul, pointing to his faith, exclaims: "For what saith the Scripture? Abraham believed God, and it was counted unto him for righteousness." Rom. iv. 3. James, pointing to his offering of Isaac, exclaims, "Seest thou how faith wrought with his works, and by works was faith perfected?"

The great theme of James, then, is faith tested and perfected by works. "Temptation," in James, means not solicitation to evil, but testing. The believer prays to be kept from temptation; he counts it all joy when the varied circumstances of life test the reality of his faith. It remains to observe that by "works" James means far more than a negative morality. He means the active exercise in practical ways of the lovely graces of the Christian character. Patience, faith, prayer, humility, love, benevolence, self-control—all these graces are made the subjects of exhortation in the brief first chapter. Every one of the beatitudes is expressed or implied in James.

James presents the legal view of sin (ii. 10, 11), but is careful to guard the gospel liberty of the believer. ii. 12. His style is obviously formed upon our Lord's, and is pointed, sententious and abounding in exquisite natural illustration. (e.g., i. 6, 10, 11; iii. 3-5, 11, 12; iv. 18, 14.) While works, as the test and proof of faith, and solicitude for the highest Christian ethic give the primary purpose of James, his secondary purpose is to maintain the perfect equality of the Christian brotherhood. Against the vulgar and essentially unchristian deference to wealth and success, James lifts a calm, pure voice of protest, rising to terrible warnings. Perhaps there never was a time when the testimony of James, rightly understood, had a more necessary application than now.

ANALYSIS

Section I. The Testing of Faith. i. 1—ii. 26.

Section II. the Inner Life Tested by the Utterances of the Tongue. iii. 1-18.

Section III. The Rebuke of Worldliness. iv. 1-17.

Section IV. The Rich Warned. v. 1-6.

Section V. Hortatory. v. 7-20.

JAMES

1. To whom is the Epistle addressed?

_____

_____

2. Give briefly, in your own words, all that Scripture tells us of James.

_____

_____

_____

3. Give in your own words a description of his character.

_____

_____

4. Is James i. 2 in conflict with Matt. vi. 13?

_____

_____

5. What is the first grace which James exalts?

_____

_____

_____

6. What the second grace which James exalts?

_____

_____

_____

7. Who may have wisdom?

_____

_____

8. How may they have wisdom?

_____

_____

_____

9. What is meant by "nothing wavering"? i. 6.

_____

_____

10. What is the third grace exalted?

_____

_____

11. What is the fourth grace exalted?

_____

_____

12. What is the right effect of conversion upon one of low degree?

_____

_____

_____

13. What is the right effect of conversion upon one of high degree?

_____

_____

_____

14. Why is one who endures temptation "blessed"?

_____

Note. "Endurance" in Scripture means to resist the bad influence of temptation or suffering; to remain unfallen.

15. Does God tempt man to evil?

_____

_____

16. What is James's account of the origin of our fleshly sins?

_____

_____

_____

17. What is Christ's? Mark vii. 21-23. ,

_____

_____

_____

18. Does any passage of Scripture ascribe that class of sins to Satan's temptations?

_____

_____

19. Who is the Author of every good?

_____

_____

20. Does God sell good?

_____

_____

21. How does James state the doctrine of regeneration?

_____

_____

22. How are we likely to deceive ourselves?

_____

_____

23. Does James say that the "doer of the work" is saved by his doing?

_____

_____

_____

24. What, then, is the reward of the doer?

_____

_____

_____

25. What are the two parts of pure religion?
(1) Positive?

_____

_____

(2) Negative?

_____

_____

Note. The student will distinguish between "religion" and "salvation." Salvation is a gift of God; religion is a work of man. Religion is the proper occupation of the saved.

26. By what name of our Lord does James rebuke distinctions between rich and poor in Christian gatherings?

_____

_____

27. Is such discrimination in favor of the rich a lack of grace, merely, or a sin? ii. 9.

_____

_____

28. State, in your own words, the aspect of justification presented by Paul in Romans?

_____

_____

_____

29. State, in your own words, the aspect of justification presented by James?

_____

_____

_____

30. Give from memory the key verses?

_____

_____

_____

31. Give from memory the key phrases?

_____

_____

_____

32. What test of a right heart life does James give?

_____

_____

33. Is it possible always to control the tongue? iii. 7, 8.

_____

_____

34. What two kinds of " wisdom" are contrasted? ;

_____

_____

_____

35. What is the first quality of the wisdom which is from above?

_____

_____

36. What is the second quality of the wisdom which is from above?

_____

_____

37. What is the third quality of the wisdom which is from above?

_____

_____

38. Of what is wisdom "full"?

_____

_____

39. What is wisdom "without"?

_____

_____

40. What will be the effect upon the tongue of a heart filled with the "wisdom that is from above"?

_____

_____

41. What, then, is the Christian way to control speech?

_____

_____

42, What are the sources of divisions among Christians?

_____

_____

_____

43. What, chiefly, defeats prayer?

_____

_____

_____

44, What is world friendship?

_____

_____

Note. Chapter iv. 5 should read: Think ye the Scripture saith in vain, The Spirit that he hath caused to dwell in you jealously desireth you?

45. In what connection does James present the second coming of Christ?

_____

_____

46. What, according to James, should be the attitude of believers toward the promise of His second coming?

_____

_____

47. Make a list of the Christian graces of character which are commended in James.

_____

_____

_____

48. Make a list of Christian practices which are commended.

_____

_____

_____

49. Make a list of the practices which are condemned.

_____

_____

LESSON LXIII

First Peter

General Remarks

The student will bear in mind what has been said of the general character of the Jewish-Christian writings. The same limitations will be observed in the two Epistles by Peter. Largely, also, his characteristic excellences are the same.

First Peter was written from Babylon on the Euphrates. That the mystical Babylon is not meant is shown by the order of provinces in i. 1. To one in the city of Babylon the order stated would be the actual order of proximity. It will be noted, however, that while James writes to the dispersed of Israel only, and that from the ancient home of the race, Peter takes his place as one of those who are "scattered abroad." He addresses these scattered Jewish believers as "strangers." They really are so in the midst of Gentilism, and he would remind them that their spiritual separation is to be as actual. i. 1; ii. 11.

In all else, there is, however, a striking contrast between Peter's point of view and James's. James distrusts all profession and sternly tests it. He looks upon the professed believer through the eyes of men. Peter assumes the reality of profession. Or, rather, he addresses sincere believers as such, and—like Paul and John—assumes that personal faith is a matter of personal consciousness. 1. 2-5, 18-25; ii. 9, 10, etc.

Like James, he is filled with sympathy for the peculiar trials through which a Christian Jew must pass. Like James, also, he interprets it as a necessary and precious testing of the reality of their faith. i. 6, 7; 11. 19-25; iv. 12-19.

But, as Peter was greatly less legal in his personal and racial view than James (Gal. ii. 12)——a fact due perhaps to his contact with Paul outside Jerusalem, where the apostle of liberty was at his best—the Spirit could without violence make him the penman of a freer, more joyous, and ample message. The Epistle of James is divinely perfect so far as it goes, but it does not go so far as First Peter. James (to give another point of contrast) writes to "the twelve tribes;" Peter, too, thinks primarily of Jewish Christians, but in ii. 10 he steps fairly upon Gentile ground; and his whole doctrine is inclusive of all believers, whether Jew or Gentile. It is a striking illustration of the way in which the Spirit respects the personality of His amanuenses. There is no flaw in the prophecy of Obadiah; but for sweep of vision, majestic fullness of revelation, and incomparable fire and glory, it does not equal the prophecy of Isaiah.

The great theme, then, of First Peter is the sufferings of believers interpreted by the greatness of their salvation, their future glory, and the example and appearing of Christ. Along with this the apostle insists upon a walk in accordance with that salvation, glory, and example. His method is warm, hopeful, encouraging.

Peter's characteristic words are "precious" and "glory" ("glorify"); and he lays triumphant emphasis upon the atonement, and the work of the Holy Spirit. James does not once mention the blood of Christ, and the Holy Spirit but once, and that in an obscure and difficult passage. Ina word, First Peter may be considered as doctrinally intermediate between Paul and James, but nearer to Paul than to James.

Analysis

First Peter does not yield to rigid and exact analysis; but, speaking broadly, the following divisions are discernible.

Section I. Christian Suffering and Conduct in the Light of the Believer's Complete Salvation and Heavenly Inheritance. i. 1—ii.3.

Section II. Christian Suffering and Conduct in the Light of the Believer's Holy and Royal Priesthood, and of the Example of Christ. ii. 4—iv. 19.

Section III. Christian Service and Conduct in the Light of the Coming of the Chief Shepherd. v. 1-14.

FIRST PETER

1. What is Peter's doctrine of election?

_____

_____

2. State in your own words how the offices of the Trinity are defined in i. 2.

_____

_____

_____

3. "According" to what is election?

_____

_____

4. "According'" to what is the believer's "living hope"?

_____

_____

5. "According'" to what is the believer's inheritance?

_____

_____

6. Where is the Christian's inheritance?

_____

_____

7. Upon what does the believer's continued security rest?

_____

_____

_____

8. How does the power of God keep the believer?

_____

_____

_____

9. Since, then, it is God who keeps, and since faith is the method, of whom is faith?

_____

_____

10. State from memory the three aspects of "salvation"' in the New Testament.

_____

_____

_____

11. Which of these aspects is in view in i. 5?

_____

_____

12. In Heb. ix. 28?

_____

_____

13. In 2 Tim. i: 92

_____

_____

14. In I Pet.i. 8, 9

_____

_____

15. In Titus iii. 4, 5?

_____

_____

16. May one rejoice in salvation, though in heaviness through circumstances?

_____

_____

17. Of what is " manifold temptation "' a trial or test?

_____

_____

18. Why is this testing "precious"?

_____

_____

19. In what state must the Christian be if he is to "rejoice with joy unspeakable and full of glory"?

_____

_____

20. Who are represented as having "searched" concerning our salvation?

_____

_____

21. What did the prophets "search"?

_____

_____

22. What bearing, then, has Peter's statement (i. 10-12) upon that theory of inspiration which affirms that "inspiration was in the prophet's concept, not in his writings'?

_____

_____

_____

23. What is the measure of holiness?

_____

_____

_____

24. State Peter's doctrine of redemption.

_____

_____

_____

25. State in your own words the process of purification in 1.

_____

_____

_____

26. State Peter's doctrine of regeneration.

_____

_____

_____

27. What is his sentence upon "flesh"?

_____

_____

28. Does he consider " flesh" at its best or worst?

_____

29. What does Peter say of the Word in chapter i.?

_____

_____

_____

30. What does Peter say of the Word in chapter ii.?

_____

_____

31. Who is the "living Stone" of ii. 4?

_____

_____

32. Who is the "living Stone" of ii. 5?

_____

_____

33. Give the references to Christ as the "Stone" (or Rock) in the Old Testament.

_____

_____

_____

34. Give the references to Christ as the "Stone" (or Rock) in the Gospels.

_____

_____

_____

35. Give the references to Christ as the "Stone" (or Rock) in the Epistles.

_____

_____

_____

36. According to Peter what is Christ the Stone to the believer?

_____

_____

37. According to Peter what is Christ the Stone to the unbeliever?

_____

_____

38. What is said of the position of the believer in chapter ii.?

_____

_____

39. What is the responsibility of the believer?

_____

_____

40. What, according to chapter i., was the relation of Christ's death to us?

_____

_____

41. What, according to chapter ii., was the relation of Christ's death to us?

_____

_____

42. What, according to chapter iii., was the relation of Christ's death to us?

_____

_____

43. What distinction between two kinds of suffering is made in ii. 20?

_____

_____

44. What distinction between two kinds of suffering is made in iii. 17?

_____

_____

45. What distinction between two kinds of suffering is made in iv. 12-16?

_____

Note. The following paraphrase of the difficult passage, iii. 18-21, may help the student: Christ...put to death in the flesh, was quickened again into life by the same Spirit by whom, through Noah, He preached in the days while the ark was preparing unto the spirits now in prison; in which ark few, that is, eight souls were saved, as we may say, by water. And the same figure may be applied to our Christian ordinance of baptism, which symbolizes the purification of our consciences, and is not (like circumcision) a mere putting away of the filth of the flesh.

46. Give the names of deity in First Peter.

_____

_____

47. What work is attributed to the Father?

_____

_____

48. What work is attributed to the Son?

_____

_____

49. What work is attributed to the Holy Spirit?

_____

_____

50. Give all the names by which the believer is called.

_____

_____

_____

51. By what name is Christ related to our service?

_____

_____

52. What gift does Peter claim?

_____

_____

53. What office in the church?

_____

_____

54. What is enjoined upon elders?

_____

_____

55. What is forbidden them?

_____

_____

56. What is said of Satan?

_____

_____

LESSON LXIV

SECOND PETER

GENERAL REMARKS

In respect of circumstances and point of view a strong likeness exists between Second Timothy and Second Peter. In both the writers are aware that martyrdom is near; both are singularly sustained and joyful in view of their approaching suffering; and to both it is given to see the abounding sinfulness and apostasy in the professing church in the last days.

In many ways, however, Second Peter will be found complementary of Second Timothy. For example, Paul warns Timothy of the apostasy of the laity; Peter traces that apostasy to false teachers. Both together complete the picture. The taught became intolerant of sound doctrine and chose teachers to please themselves, "having itching ears." On the other hand, such teachers "bring in damnable heresies?" (2 Tim. iv. 2, 8; 2 Pet. ii. 1); and the people who began by turning "away their ears from the truth....shall be turned unto fables." 2 Tim. iv. 4. Or, in Peter's phrase, "Many shall follow their pernicious ways; by reason of whom the way of truth shall be evil spoken of." It will be observed that Peter states the chiefest of the "damnable heresies," the bringing in of which by false teachers he predicts. "Even denying the Lord that bought them." The denial is not of "the Lord," nor of "Christianity," but of the Lord as Redeemer. It is the denial. of the apostolic doctrine of redemption " with the precious blood of Christ, as of a lamb"—that is, of atonement interpreted by Old Testament types. We shall see in John's Epistles the final apostasy traced to even a more fundamental denial than this— the denial of the truth as to Christ's person. Peter also points to the denial of the return of Christ (involving a denial of any necessity for His return) as characteristic of the apostasy of the last days. Meantime his solicitude

for the true believers is that they shall go on to full growth in character, and keep the hope of the Lord's coming operative as a living motive to holy living.

Note. 'The student will observe that the aspect of the second coming of Christ in this Epistle is the "day of the Lord," or judgment phase, rather than that which concerns the saints only, as in 1 Thess. iv.

ANALYSIS

Section I. Exhortations to Strenuousness in the Development of the Great Christian Virtues. i. 1-15.

Section II. The Scriptures Exalted as Inspired and Authoritative. i. 16-21. :

Section III. Warnings Concerning Apostate Teachers. ii, 1-22.

Among the striking illustrations in this section the apostle introduces Balaam. It is significant that three apostles refer to Balaam in connection with the apostate teachers of the last days 2 Peter (ii. 15, 16), Jude (11), and John (Rev. ii. 14). The student will note that Peter speaks of the way of Balaam, Jude of the error of Balaam, and John of the doctrine of Balaam. In a word, the reference to Balaam marks the false teachers as loving money, and as breaking down the separation between the church and the world. From Numbers xxxi. 15, 16 we gather that Balaam, unable to curse Israel, taught Balak to tempt the Israelites with Moabitish women, and that this ruse succeeded. He could not curse, but he could corrupt. Worldliness is spiritual unchastity. Rev. ii. 14; James iv. 4. The Balaam phase of the apostasy is the realization of Paul's fear for Corinth: "For I have espoused you to one husband, that I may present you as a chaste virgin to Christ. But I fear," etc. 2 Cor. xi. 2, 3. The Balaam teachers will, therefore, be greedy of money, and will corrupt the espoused bride of Christ by leading her to worldliness.

Section IV. The Second Coming of Christ, And the "Day of the Lord." iii. 1.18.

SECOND PETER

1. By what means are grace and peace multiplied to us?

_____

_____

2. Of what are we said to be "partakers"?

_____

_____

3. Through what do we become partakers of the divine nature?

_____

_____

4, State from memory the seven elements of Christian character which are to follow faith.

_____

_____

_____

_____

_____

_____

_____

Note. Render i. 5, "And beside this, giving all diligence, provide in your faith virtue," etc.

5. What efficacy is attributed to this development of character?

_____

_____

6. Is this development said to result in salvation?

_____

_____

7. What does the apostle mean by i. 14?

_____

_____

8. What does he consider his body to be?

_____

_____

9. To what event does Peter refer in i. 15-18?

_____

_____

10. To what does he compare the "word of prophecy"?

_____

_____

11. What rule of interpretation does he give?

_____

_____

12. State in your own words the warning of ii. 1.

_____

_____

_____

13. By what word does Peter characterize heresy?

_____

_____

14. What especial error will mark its teaching?

_____

_____

15. What effect of their teaching does he predict?

_____

_____

16. What fate does he predict for them?

_____

_____

17. Will this condemnation overtake a justified man?

_____

_____

18. What past dealings of God are cited to illustrate and prove future judgments?

_____

_____

19. What is meant by " the way of Balaam"?

_____

_____

20. Does the Scripture distinguish between ignorance and heresy? 2 Tim. ii. 24-26 with Titus iii. 10.

_____

_____

_____

21. What characteristics of false teachers are enumerated in ii, 1—iii. 4 in respect of—

(1) Conduct?

_____

_____

_____

(2) Speech?

_____

_____

_____

(3) Promise?

_____

_____

_____

(4) Doctrine?

_____

_____

_____

22. Are the persons described in ii. 20-22 said to have salvation or knowledge?

_____

_____

23. What would the apostle have us mindful of??

_____

_____

_____

24. What argument will "scoffers" use against the promise of Christ's coming?

_____

_____

25. Is it true that all things continue as they were from the creation?

_____

_____

26. What great event are the scoffing teachers said to be "ignorant" (unbelieving) of?

_____

_____

27. How will "the day of the Lord" come?

_____

_____

_____

28. What. is the difference between the "day of the Lord" and the "day of Christ"?

_____

_____

29. What great change is to pass upon "the earth that now is"?

_____

_____

30. What do we look for?

_____

_____

31. What effect ought the expectation of the Lord's return to have on conduct?

_____

_____

32. Why does Christ tarry?

_____

_____

33. With what writings does Peter class Paul's Epistles?

_____

_____

LESSON LXV

FIRST JOHN

GENERAL REMARKS

The three Epistles of John have a distinctive character which is best seen by comparison with his Gospel. The Gospel was written "that ye might believe that Jesus is the Christ, the Son of God; and that, believing, ye might have life through His name." John xx. 31. The first Epistle was "written unto you that believe on the name of the Son of God; that ye may know that ye have eternal life." 1 John v.13. The Gospel, in other words, was written to the world to give a foundation for faith; the Epistle to Christians to give a foundation for assurance. In both cases the passages quoted define no more than the apostle's chief or central purpose, for the contents of both books overflow and go beyond their core thought. The Gospel shows us the Father's thoughts and ways with the Son; the Epistle the Father's thoughts and ways with the sons. The Gospel leads us across the Father's threshold; the Epistle makes us at home in the Father's house. The key words of the Gospel are "faith" and "life"; of the Epistle "love" and "fellowship." In the Gospel the second coming of Christ is presented in connection with translation (xiv. 1-3); in the Epistle in connection with transformation (iii. 2). In so far as the Johannean Epistles look forward the view coincides with the second Epistles of Paul and of Peter. As with Paul so with John—the end time is preceded by antichrist. He does not go much into detail. With Paul and Peter he exalts revealed truth as the Christian's refuge and stay in those days. The especial key phrase of First John is "my little children." This gives the clue to its interpretation—it is a Father's letter to His family, unspeakably intimate and sacred.

Note. The Epistle as a whole is best studied in the Revised Version. The student will observe especially the omitted words in v. 6, 7, 8, 13. Also an important change in v. 18.

It is exceedingly important to note that John habitually deals with the Christian as a son of God in an abstract and absolute way rather than as compassed with infirmity and still bearing about the old nature. He does not, indeed, ignore the old man, but is not occupied with him. In this is the reconciliation of the apparent contradiction of i. 8 and iii. 9. The old nature is sin, and we deceive ourselves if we suppose sin to be entirely eradicated; the new nature is the seed of God, and as born again the believer cannot sin.

ANALYSIS

The first Epistle of John, unlike his Gospel, does not yield to a rigid analysis. It is not a treatise. The style is sententious. Nevertheless, a closer examination reveals the fact that the precious counsels of the Father cluster about seven messages to His "little children." It should be noticed that the word for children is the one which indicates relationship, rather than position. The passages might be translated "my little born ones." The Scottish word "bairns" expresses it. Paul, in the sonship passages, sets forth rather the idea of position.

Taking, then, these passages as giving the moral divisions of the Epistle, the analysis will stand as follows:

Section I. Introductory: John's Testimony to the Incarnation. i. 1-2.

Section II. Fellowship and its Maintenance. i. 3—ii. 12. "My little children, these things write I unto you that ye sin not. And if any man sin, we have an advocate with the Father, Jesus Christ the righteous: and he is the propitiation for our sins."

Fellowship, not salvation, is the subject of this section. Believers only are in view. Sins, in this section, are therefore the sins of the children of God. The highest privilege in the family of the Father is full, unhindered fellowship; and the one thing essential to this is that we walk in the light.

Walking in the light is living in perfect openness toward God. It is the New Testament equivalent of the Old Testament phrase, "dwelling in the secret place of the Most High." To the Israelite in the wilderness that meant the holy of holies in the tabernacle. The godly Israelite did not actually go in there; but his waking and sleeping, his toil and rest, his family life and public life, his thought and actions were dominated by the consciousness that God dwelt among His people, and that their whole life must be keyed to that great fact. Everything must be tested by the Presence. Walking in the light is having nothing apart from God the Father. 'If we walk in the light, as He is in the light, we have fellowship." It is where we walk rather than how we walk. That brings in another principle. "But all things that are reproved are made manifest by the light: for whatsoever doth make manifest is light." (Eph. v. 13.) 'The light of the presence of God shows every sin. How, then, may one increasingly conscious of sin, one making constantly new discoveries of sin, live in that light?

The answer is threefold. *First*, atonement. "The blood of Jesus Christ cleanseth from all sin." By virtue of the sacrifice of Christ and our justification by faith our sins are put away from before the just God. We therefore stand in the light, notwithstanding our consciousness of sinfulness, as knowing that atonement has answered for our guilt. 1. 7.

Secondly, we may deal with sins by confession. i.9. Here the blood of Christ is still, as always, the foundation. He is 'faithful and just" to forgive ; not (as we should say) kind and merciful. Our Father does not forgive His children's sins out of tolerant good nature; but because He is just to the Cross of Christ and faithful to His new covenant. Nothing even is said of our repentance. But there is more than forgiveness: "and to cleanse us from all unrighteousness." Both aspects— forgiveness and cleansing—meet in Psalm li. 1, 2. And observe, the cleansing is not from the defilement of the sin, but from the sin itself. A little child of the Father,

walking in the light, may so deal with specific sins through confession as to be delivered from them. It is not sinless perfection, for the light constantly reveals new sins; but known sins may be put away. This righteous self-judgment restores the believer's moral integrity, which, with the sense of forgiveness and deliverance, renews interrupted fellowship.

Thirdly. If the little children of the Father sin, they "have an advocate with the Father, Jesus Christ the righteous: and he is the propitiation." ii. 1, 2. "Advocate" may easily be a misleading word, as tending to bring up the thought of a court of justice and legal advocacy. It is the same word translated "comforter" in John xiv. 16. The thought is not that Christ makes excuses for us when we sin; Jesus Christ the righteous could not do that. Nor that He appears for us as a lawyer for one accused of crime. It is important to be very clear here.

1. It is not a forensic question, involving the public justice of God, the moral Ruler of the universe. The believer is "justified from all things from which he could not be justified by the law of Moses." Nothing can again put him in jeopardy. As to all that phase of the question "He is the propitiation"— literally propitiatory, or "mercy seat." The fault of a believer is purely a family affair, a question of the peace and purity of the household.

2. "If any [believing] man sin we have an Advocate with the Father.' It is not when we repent and seek restoration, but when we sin. This advocacy is part of the Shepherd work of Christ.

   (1) It includes intercession. A perfect illustration of this is the case of Peter: "Simon, Simon, behold, Satan hath desired to have you, that he may sift you as wheat: but I have prayed for thee, that thy faith fail not."? Luke xxii. 31, 32. And Peter's faith did not fail. He failed most shamefully.

(2) It includes restoration. "He restoreth my soul: He leadeth me in the paths of righteousness for His name's sake." Psa. xxiii. 3. "What man of you, having an hundred sheep, if he lose one of them, doth not leave the ninety and nine in the wilderness, and go after that which is lost until he find it?" Again the case of Peter furnishes an illustration." He was seen of Cephas, then of the twelve. 1 Cor. xv. 5. "The Lord is risen indeed, and hath appeared unto Simon." Luke xxiv. 34. "Feed my sheep." John xxi. 16.

(3) But Peter went out of the light for a time, and walked in darkness. This he need not have done. "If we confess our sins," etc. 1 John i. 9. "For if we would judge ourselves, we should not be judged." 1 Cor. xi. 31. Persistence in sin by one of God's children must bring chastisement, but chastisement is unto restoration 1 Cor. xi. 32; Hebrews xii. 5, 10, 11.

(4) But, because sin interrupts fellowship, the most precious and important of the believer's privileges, the Father writes unto us "that we sin not'"—literally, "be not sinning." While abiding in Him we are not sinning. 1 John iii. 6.

The apostle then takes up the tests by which we may avoid self-deception. ii. 3-11. That test (as always with John) is obedience to the commandments of Christ. It is not the Decalogue (though disobedience to the morality of the law would, of course, be sin), but Christ's law of love. See these discriminated in John xv. 10. The test is brotherly love.

Finally, lest any little child should still be in darkness as to the ground of forgiveness, or in doubt as to the fact of forgiveness, the passage ends with the second of the seven messages to little children: "I write unto you, little children, because your sins are forgiven you for His name's sake." ii. 12.

Note "Little children" in ii. 13, 18, is a different word. It means "youths"—actual young persons. "Little children" in the other passages includes all Christians of whatever age.

Section III. The Right Attitude of the Little Children of the Father Toward (1) The World Which is Openly Such, and (2) The World Which is Professedly Religious, but Actually Anti-Christian. ii. 13-28. "And now, little children, abide in him; that, when He shall appear, we may have confidence, and not be ashamed before Him at His coming."

1. The whole body of believers is addressed in three convenient classes—fathers, young men, youths.

2. All are warned of the world.

Note. Remember always that John speaks in an absolute way, presenting the perfected standard. A heart full of the love of the world is an unconverted heart. A heart full of the love of the Father would bea sinlessly perfected heart. These are the two ultimate extremes. Doubtless the love of the world fills many human hearts. Well, the Father is not there at all. The believer may have to mourn and confess some inclination still toward the world, but knows, if the test came, he would give a million worlds rather than leave the Father.

3. But there is another and more subtle danger to the little children. There is an apostate and spurious " religious" world. It is really anti-Christian. "The man of sin shall come" (2 Thess, ii. 3-10), but before that "there are many antichrists." The student will remember that "antichrist" is not to be atheistical and unreligious. He will be most religious, and a miracle worker, "having horns as a lamb." That is the greatness of the peril. Only those who have received "the love of the truth" will be safe from His deceptions. Rev. xiii. 10-15. This is the antichrist who is not yet come. But the "many antichrists" who had already come in John's time are, like the great final antichrist, far more subtly dangerous than open blasphemers.

223

The Father warns His little children of them, giving the tests.

1. "They went out from us." They are, therefore, apostate from a sound faith. Nominally Christian.
2. They teach error concerning the divine personality. They deny the Son. The believer's safety lies

   (1) in abiding in the doctrine of Christ and His apostles, "that which ye have heard from the beginning."

   (2) In abiding in Him as One who May appear at any time.

Section IV. How We May Discern the Other Little Children. ii. 29—iii.10. "Little children, let no man deceive you; he that doeth righteousness is righteous."

"Doeth" in ii. 29 and iii. 7 should be "practiseth." The trend of the life is in view. The new man, God's seed, cannot sin. Therefore, notwithstanding that we still "have sin" (i. 8), the life should be righteous. If it is not we must not expect others to believe our profession. It is James's point of view. Neither should we believe the profession of one whose habitual. life is unrighteous. It is not sinless perfection, because not until " He shall appear" will we be wholly "like Him." iii. 2. But if we have this hope we purify ourselves (by the walk in the light and confession) with His purity as the absolute standard.

Section V. The Law or the Family, or How the Little Children Must Live Together. iii. 11-24; iv. 7-21. "My little children, let us not love in word, neither in tongue; but in deed [doing] and in truth [reality]."

The message from the beginning is that we should love one another. But this love is not a sentiment or emotion, merely. We perceive God's love "because He laid down His life for us; and we ought to lay down our lives for the brethren." Brotherly love, if real, is operative, is a motor. Verse 17 applies the principle: "Whosoever hath...and seeth.'" We are to so love that a brother cannot have

a need which we do not see. We are not to compel our brother to beggary—to come and ask. This is our subjective basis of assurance. Verse 14. The law of the family is summed up in verse 23.

Section VI. The Little Children protected From False Teachers. iv. 1-6. "Ye are of God, little children, and have overcome them: because greater is He that is in you than he that is in the world."

The clue passage (iv. 1) is, "Because many false prophets are gone out into the world.'" The question is not of refusing fellowship to these, as in Section III., nor of discerning mere professors, as in Section IV.; but of protection against error. "Hereby know we the spirit of truth, and the spirit of error." iv. 6. Four marks of "false prophets" are given:—

1. Error as to the doctrine of the person of Christ, with special reference to denials of His preëxistence or deity, "is come ;'" and of His incarnation or humanity in the flesh. iv. 3.
2. "They are of the world" (worldly-mindedness).
3. "Therefore speak they of the world" (avoidance of supernaturalism).
4, "And the world heareth them" (popularity with the worldly-minded).

Section VII. The Little Children Assured and Warned. v. 1-21. "Little children, keep yourselves from idols."

The section opens with a reminder that not love, but faith, brings us into the family. v. 1. We were begotten when we believed, and love follows. In this birth, and in our faith (not love) lies, too, the potency of victory over the world. v. 4, 5. Furthermore, the Spirit is the witness to our regeneration (as also to our sonship, Rom. viii. 15, 16), and the believer has the Spirit. |

Eternal life is Christ (i. 1, 2); and we have eternal life, not as something apart from Christ, but in Christ. This is the Vine and branches and Head and members truth. v. 6-12. Upon our known childship is based our confidence in prayer (v. 14-16) and intercessory work (v. 16-20).

FIRST JOHN

1. To whom does John refer in i. 1, 2?

_____

_____

2. State, in your own words and from memory, the differences between John's Gospel and First Epistle.

_____

_____

_____

3. What is the prophetic outlook of the Epistles of John?

_____

_____

4. What is the special key phrase of First John?

_____

5. State, in your own words, the reconciliation of i. 8 with iii. 9.

_____

_____

_____

6. State the threefold fellowship of i. 3.

_____

_____

7. What is it which makes Christian joy "full"?

_____

_____

8. What is John's first statement concerning what God is?

_____

_____

9. State, in your own words, what it is to walk in the light.

_____

_____

_____

10. What, then, is it to "walk in darkness"?

_____

_____

11. Must a believer who has sinned walk in darkness?

_____

_____

12. What may we do in that case?

_____

_____

13. What did David do when Nathan rebuked his sin?

_____

_____

14. What is the effect of light on blemishes and stains?

_____

_____

15. What, then, is the threefold provision of God which enables a believer to walk in the very light which reveals his unworthiness to be there?

_____

_____

_____

_____

_____

Note. The student will give this answer fully, in his own words, without recourse to the outline. It is the very heart of the Epistle.

16. What is the distinction between "sin" in i. 8 and "sins" in i. 9?

_____

_____

_____

17. What does John say of those who say they have no "sin"?

_____

_____

_____

18. What does John say of those who say they have not sinned?

   _____

   _____

19. If the atonement has fully answered the guilt and penalty of our sins, why is the confession of sins into which we fall after conversion necessary to our fellowship with the Father?

   _____

   _____

20. What is the difference either the advocacy and the intercession of Christ?

   _____

   _____

   _____

21. What act of the believer calls into exercise the advocacy of Christ?

   _____

   _____

22. State, in your own words:
   (1) What advocacy is not.

   _____

   _____

   (2) What it includes.

   _____

   _____

23. How may we "know that we know Him"?

   _____

   _____

24. State what John means by "His commandments."

   _____

   _____

   _____

25. In whom is the love of God perfected?

   _____

   _____

   _____

26. Is "the love of God" (ii. 5) our love for God?

_____

_____

27. How is the profession tested of one who says he is abiding in Christ?

_____

_____

28. Is sinlessness the proof that we are living in the light?

_____

_____

29. Why are our sins forgiven?

_____

_____

30. Into what three classes, in respect to age, are believers divided?

_____

_____

_____

31. What is "the world" made up of?

_____

_____

32. Why should we not love the world?

_____

_____

33. Give the definition of "many antichrists."

_____

_____

(1) Origin.

_____

(2) Doctrine.

_____

_____

34. What is the second message to "little children"?

_____

_____

35. What is the third message to "little children"?

_____

_____

36. What proof does John give of the greatness of the Father's love?

_____

_____

_____

37. What proof does John give of God's love?

_____

_____

_____

38. When shall we be perfected?

_____

_____

39. What is the present effect upon Christians of belief in the second coming of Christ?

_____

_____

40. Give the Revised Version rendering of iii. 4.

_____

_____

41. What general test of profession is given us in the fourth message to little children?

_____

_____

_____

42. How do we know that we have passed from death unto life?

_____

_____

_____

43. What is the practical test of brotherly love?

_____

_____

_____

44, How may we discern false teachers?

_____

_____

_____

45. In whom does God dwell?

_____

_____

46. Does salvation begin with love, or with faith?

_____

_____

_____

47. Who are "born of God"?

_____

_____

_____

48. Do we know that we have eternal life by things which we feel?

_____

_____

_____

49. Give John's definition of faith, in regard to prayer?

_____

_____

_____

50. What definitions of sin are given in this Epistle?

_____

_____

_____

51. What names of deity occur in this Epistle?

_____

_____

_____

52. What offices of the Holy Spirit are mentioned?

_____

_____

_____

53. What is John's second great statement concerning what God is?

_____

_____

_____

LESSON LXVI

Second John

General Remarks

This brief letter is addressed to a Christian lady and her children. There is not the slightest basis for the notion that by "lady" a church is meant.

The scope of the Epistle is simple and limited, but exceedingly precious. It gives the essentials of the personal walk in the day when "many deceivers are entered into the world."

The emphatic key word is "the truth." It is John's word for Scripture. The Second Epistles of Paul to Timothy, of Peter and of John have in common the two ideas that the last days are times of apostasy and false teaching, and that the Christian's safeguard is obedience to Scripture.

Analysis

Section I. The Pathway or "Truth" and Love. Verses 1262

Section II. The Peril of Untruth. Verses 7-11.

Section III. The Superscription. Verses 12-13.

SECOND JOHN

1. In what official character does John write?

_____

_____

2. To whom does John write?

_____

_____

3. How often is "the truth" mentioned in this brief Epistle?

_____

_____

4. What vital untruth does this Epistle warn us against?

_____

_____

_____

5. How does he show that the doctrine concerning Christ's person is absolutely vital to true Christianity?

_____

_____

_____

6. Are we to fellowship, religiously, teachers who promulgate error as to Christ?

_____

_____

LESSON LXVII

THIRD JOHN

GENERAL REMARKS

What has been said of the Second Epistle will, in general, apply to this. What is peculiar to the present letter is that it contemplates a condition worse, greatly worse, than that revealed in Second John. There, the worst said is that false teachers are abroad; here, Diotrephes, a preéminent member, absolutely refuses apostolic authority. Verse 9. Taking the two Epistles together the apostasy may be traced as follows:

1. False teachers appear who corrupt the churches after the manner of Balaam. See Lesson LXIX. That is, they teach world-conformity.

2. The corrupted laity will not endure sound doctrine, but choose teachers to please themselves.

3. False teaching assails the doctrine of the incarnation either by denying the full deity, or proper humanity of Christ.

4. The apostolic doctrine is rejected.

THIRD JOHN.

1. In what character does John write?

_____

_____

2. According to what measure does John desire prosperity and health for Gaius?

_____

_____

3. What practical Christian grace is exalted?

_____

_____

4. What bearing has this Epistle upon the practice of receiving money from unbelievers for Christ's work?

_____

_____

5. What was the character of Diotrephes?

_____

_____

6. What did Diotrephes do?

_____

_____

7. How might we commit the sin of Diotrephes?

_____

_____

LESSON LXVIII

Jude

General Remarks

This brief Epistle, addressed to all true believers, is, in the arrangement of the canon, put last of these epistolary writings. This is its right moral and prophetical order. It contemplates, prophetically, the last of the last days and fitly introduces the Apocalypse, which unveils the final condition of apostate Christendom under the beast after all true believers have been caught up to meet the descending Lord.

Recurring to the indications of apostasy in preceding Epistles the student will see that every form of incipient evil therein indicated is here shown in fullness of development. This is most important to whoever would walk according to the mind of God. And for this reason: We are not competent, in our own wisdom, to judge the seriousness of incipient evil. We think of doctrinal error as insignificant and unimportant. We may even think such biblical language as Gal. i. 6-9, or 2 John 10, harsh and ungracious. But the Spirit of God sees the end of false teaching, and so warns us against its beginnings.

The student should observe that the solemn warnings and stern denunciations of the Spirit, through these great-hearted and loving apostles, is not against ignorance of truth, nor against such errors as arise from undue emphasis upon some phase of truth. The warnings and judgments have to do invariably with that truth which is so vital that without it there is no gospel, no Christianity. Speaking generally, the errors condemned are in respect of the atonement, and of the nature and person of Christ. Abundant charity covers even serious error, but there is no charity in the teaching of Christ and His apostles for that which under whatever guise of profession destroys the only hope of sinful man. We might bear with one who should roil the stream from which millions must drink or die; it would be false and abominable to bear with one who should poison it.

The student will note the apostle's account of the origin of this Epistle. He sat down to write a gospel letter; he was constrained to write what follows. It is not, therefore, Jude who speaks, but the constraining Spirit. It is most solemn.

Note. The Epistle should be studied in Revised Version.

Analysis.

Section I. Introduction. Verses 1-3. The Epistle is addressed to individual saints anywhere, in any age or country. "Sanctified" here is used in its primary sense of set apart for God. "Preserved in Jesus Christ" should be "kept for Jesus Christ." It carries out the thought of John xvii. 11, according to which our safety depends not upon our faithfulness to God, but upon the Father's faithfulness to His son's trust. Verse 3 is exceedingly important. A body of truth has been "committed'" to the saints. Paul exhorts us to "hold fast" that truth; Jude goes beyond and exhorts us to "contend earnestly" (not angrily) for it. Whenever, then, the body of revealed truth is assailed it is not open to any obedient Christian to stand neuter.

Section II. Apostasy is Possible. Verses 5-7.

Section III. TheApostate Teachers Described. Verses 8-19.

The student will understand Jude's impassioned analysis of these false teachers best by considering first his final statement, "Sensual, not having the Spirit." By "sensual" he does not mean sexual uncleanness, but "natural." It is Paul's word in 1 Cor, ii. 14. "But the natural [sensual, psychical] man receiveth not the things of the Spirit of God: for they are foolishness unto him : neither can he know them, because they are spiritually discerned." The apostate teachers in Jude are mere professors—unregenerate and destitute of the Spirit. His solemn warnings are confirmed by ecclesiastical history. The great evil to pure Christianity has been wrought neither by persecutors nor by atheists, but by professed teachers of Christianity who have been destitute of the new nature and of the Spirit. The first mark of such teachers is that they despise authority. It is not that they refuse the authority of creeds or of ecclesiastics, it is that they reject the principle of authority.

The second mark is that, even in those things of religion which the natural man may comprehend—as ethics—they are perverters. A natural man can understand high morals, but he cannot do them. His tendency, therefore, is to lower the standard to his inclination or capacity.

The third mark is that they have "gone in the way of Cain." Cain was religious, but made his own religion. He brought an offering, but it was an unbloody offering. He rejected atonement. The natural man cannot understand the beauty and the perfectness of the sacrificial death of Christ, as interpreted on the one hand by the types and on the other hand by the apostolic writings. Compelled as a religious teacher to explain it, he explains it away. Character is substituted for blood, as that which saves. Repentance is more dwelt upon than faith. Cain's lovely altar, heaped with fruit and flowers and golden grain, is more attractive than Abel's, with its dead lamb. Gen. iv. 3-11; Heb. xi. 4.

The fourth mark is that they "run greedily after. the error of Balaam for reward." See, as to this, Lesson LXIV. The "reward" may not be money. It may be influence or applause or popularity.

The fifth mark is "the gainsaying of Korah." The reference . is to the sin of Korah. Num. xvi. It is significant that the sin of Korah was threefold: insubordination to rightful authority, special denial of the authority of Moses, and assuming priestly functions.

Verses 12-13 accumulate descriptive particulars showing the character and influence of the men in view. They "feed themselves"—the true shepherd feeds the sheep. They are " clouds without water.' Water is the constant symbol of the Holy Spirit. The true minister not only serves in the power of the Spirit, but ministers the Spirit. Gal. iii. 5. These men have not the Spirit. They are "carried about of winds"—ready to change, unsteadfast (Eph. iv. 14); 'trees whose fruit withereth." They may gather great audiences and seem to do much, but nothing abides. John xv. 16. The student may extend this study through the particulars which follow. Verse 16 is especially significant.

In applying these minute details it is necessary to remember that Jude is showing the apostate teachers as they are in the sight of God. "Clouds" are often beautiful, "waves of the sea" sublime and impressive. "Great swelling words" may well be the inspired description of what we call marvelous eloquence.

The prophecy of Enoch is net recorded in the Old Testament. Enoch lived before the flood, when already the iniquity of the world was great, and when that striking judgment was impending. He warned the world of it, doubtless; but it is remarkable that he should have predicted the second coming of Christ. Verse 14.

Section IV. The Saints Assured and Comforted. Verses 20-25.

JUDE

1. Who was Jude?

_____

_____

2. How does verse 1, Revised Version, differ from verse 1, Authorized Version?

_____

_____

_____

3. What was Jude's plan for this Epistle?

_____

_____

_____

4. How did it occur that he wrote something quite different?

_____

_____

5. What light does this throw upon the method of inspiration?

_____

_____

_____

6. State differences in Authorized Version and Revised Version renderings of verse.

_____

_____

_____

7. What is meant by "the faith once for all delivered to the saints"?

_____

_____

_____

8. Why is it necessary "earnestly to contend for it?

_____

_____

_____

9. Is earnestness compatible with tenderest love and charity?

_____

_____

10. How does Jude prove that apostasy is possible?

_____

_____

11. Explain in your own words what is meant by "sensual, having not the Spirit," in verse 19.

_____

_____

12. Why are natural men incapable of understanding the spiritual meaning of Scripture?

_____

_____

13. May not great learning take the place of the Spirit in interpreting Scripture?

_____

_____

14. Explain in your own words what is meant by—
    (1) Despising dominion.

_____

_____

_____

    (2) Men corrupting what they pao naturally.

_____

_____

_____

    (3) The way of Cain.

_____

_____

_____

    (4) The error of Balaam.

_____

_____

_____

(5) The gainsaying of Korah.

_____

_____

_____

15. Who was Enoch?

_____

_____

_____

16. What did the apostles of Jesus Christ predict for the last time?

_____

_____

_____

17. What seven things are enjoined upon Christians in verses 20-23?

_____

_____

_____

18. What is Christ able to do?

_____

_____

_____

LESSON LXIX

THE REVELATION

GENERAL REMARKS

Note. The Revised Version only should be used in the study of the Revelation.

The Revelation is confessedly a difficult book, but no reverent child of God should concede that is an obscure book. God Himself has named it "The Revelation," or Apocalypse; that is, the "unveiling." So far, then, from being an incomprehensible book, a writing in which truth is hidden away too deeply for discovery, it is a bringing forth and revealing of truth. Five reasons may be given why the student should enter upon the study of the Revelation expecting to understand its messages.

1. It is (as has been said) a revelation.

2. It is not sealed. xxii. 10. Compare Dan. xii. 9.

3. A blessing is promised to him "that readeth, and they that hear." It is sometimes said that the blessing is promised, not to such as understand this prophecy, but to such as read and hear it— which is pious nonsense.

4. The analysis of the book is simple, thus facilitating comprehension. It is easier to understand what we may take apart.

5. The symbolism of the book is Biblical. When new symbols, not previously used in Scripture, are introduced they are immediately explained. E.g., i. 20; vii. 13, 14.

We here touch the chief reason why the book has often been found obscure and mysterious. Into it the Spirit has gathered the wealth of symbolism which the Bible has been accumulating through the ages. But the more part of us have read our Bibles so carelessly, and have been so especially intolerant of the teaching by type and symbol, that we come to the closing book of Scripture in practical ignorance of those things. There are, then, two courses open to the student of the Apocalypse. He may patiently take up these symbols and trace them back through the pages of Holy Writ until their meaning is clear; or he may set his fancy at work, aided by suggestions from profane history. Having read about fifty books upon the Revelation I am constrained to believe the latter has been the more usual method. In this connection, it is important to remember that this wonderful series of prophetic visions and symbols was not given to John, primarily, but to Jesus Christ. Nor was it given to Jesus Christ for the church, nor for saints, nor for Israel, but for "his servants." i.1. This is exceedingly important as bearing upon interpretation. Not all believers (alas!) are servants. It is safe to say that the Revelation will not yield its fullness of truth and blessing to the idle or the curious. Of this book may with emphasis be said what Augustine says of the whole Bible: "It reserves its deeper mysteries for such as are not light of mind."

The occasion of the book is definitely stated. The aged apostle was an exile in Patmos "for the word of God, and for the testimony of Jesus Christ." He was in the Spirit on the Lord's day and was given a vision of the risen and glorified Christ, and was commanded to write the occurrences of that day, besides seven letters to specific churches, and then a series of revelations, partly heavenly, partly earthly, of events to be accomplished after the church period should have closed,

ANALYSIS

There can be no room for legitimate question as to the general analysis of the Revelation, since it is definitely stated in Jolin's commission, 1.19. "Write—

(1) the things which thou hast seen,

(2) and the things which are,

(3) and the things which shall be hereafter."

Three classes of "things," therefore, make up the contents of the book. The only question is as to where the dividing lines shall run. As to the first there can be no question. The things John had seen were the visions of that memorable day. These he wrote in chapter i. What is meant by "the things which are"? Clearly "things" then in existence—things of Christ. Judaism was not meant, for more than twenty years before the appearance of Christ to John in Patmos the temple and city had been destroyed, and the religious organization of Israel broken up. The answer is evident. The "things" then in being in the earth, in which Christ was interested, were the churches. The Patmos vision was of Christ in the midst of the golden candlesticks (properly "lamp stands") which are explained to mean churches. His immediate command was, "What thou seest write in a book, and send it unto the seven churches which are in Asia." Accordingly, John first writes the things which he has seen—the Patmos vision, chapter i. And next he writes seven messages, or epistles, to the seven specified churches in the pro-consular province called Asia, chapters ii., iii. These chapters are about churches, and about nothing else. Furthermore, from the end of chapter iii. churches are never again mentioned. It is evident, then, that chapters 11., 111. form the second category of "things," viz., "things which are." Of necessity, then, the third category, "things which shall be hereafter,' consists of the remainder of the book, chapters iv.—xxii, That John's instructions in i. 19 formed, also, a prophetic order of events is evident. "Things which shall be hereafter," is literally, "which shall be after these things" (see Revised Version); i.e, after "the things which are," namely, the churches. We have, therefore, the general analysis of the Revelation.

Section I. "Things Which Thou Hast Seen." The Patmos Vision. Chapter i.

This section falls into parts.

Part 1. General introduction. i. 1-3.

Part 2. Special introduction to the churches. i. 4-8. Salutation from Christ in His past, present, and future offices. He was "the faithful witness;" He is the "first begotten from among the dead ones;" He is to be "the prince of the kings of the earth." i. 5-8. We are thus at once introduced to a full Christ, incarnate, glorified, coming. It is noteworthy that His coming is considered, not in relation to the church, as in First Thessalonians, but in relation to the earth (verse 7), or the "day of the Lord" aspect. The rapture of the church is seen but for one moment in iv. 1.

An important symbol occurs in this part: "the seven spirits which are before His throne." Seven is a dominant number in Revelation. It signifies fullness, completeness. It is incorrect to say that seven is the number of perfection, since that implies a moral element, whereas seven is often associated with complete immorality. Mark xvi. 9; Rev. xiii. 1, etc. The symbol means, therefore, the fullness or completeness of the Spirit. It is the sevenfold Spirit of Isaiah xi. 2.

Part 3. The vision. 1. 9-20. Here are many symbols.

Golden lamp stands—churches. i. 20.

Girdle—service. Luke xii. 87; John xiii. 4.

Fire—discriminating judgment. 1 Cor. iii.13; Mal. iii. 2, 3.

Stars—messengers of the churches. i. 20.

Note. Three interpretations are widely held as to these "messengers."

1. That they were elders.

2. That each church is given a guardian angel, and that these are meant.

3. That the seven churches named, solicitous for the aged apostle, had sent messengers to learn his state, and that these are meant. The latter is the more reasonable explanation, and does not exclude the first, since the churches might naturally send elders or pastors. It is of the less importance since

    (1) the churches, not the messengers, are in view; and

    (2) the epistles go quite beyond the seven local churches addressed. In iii. 1, however, the symbol becomes of great importance, and can only apply to those who rule and minister in the churches.

Section II. "The Things Which Are" Chapters ii., iii.

The student is at once confronted with a question of interpretation. Why should so large a portion, of so brief a book, be given to an elaborate analysis of the spiritual state of seven churches? Why, out of hundreds of churches then existing, were these special churches chosen? Why do the exhortations and promises go beyond these churches to "him that hath an ear'? Why is it evidently assumed that all these messages will be read by all Christians, and not merely each by the particular church to which it was addressed? "Hear what the Spirit saith unto the churches' (plural). The answers are, that these churches were chosen, and the messages to them arranged in this order, because, thus arranged, their then actual condition prefigured seven great phases of church history, from the close of the apostolic period to the rapture of true believers, and the apostasy of the professing church. In other words, this section is church history told in symbol, by the Spirit of prophecy. This is clear because :—

1. It is incredible that in a prophetic book (i. 3) concerning the whole period of the existence of the church of God on earth there should be no prophecy concerning it.

2. These epistles to seven churches contain that prophetic foreview if it is in the book at all. No church is mentioned after iii. 22.

3. The symbolic number seven indicates a complete statement about something. ;

4. It is incredible that so much space should have been given these churches if nothing symbolic was meant.

5. This occurs in the most symbolical book in all Scripture, a book of "signs." "He sent and signified it by His servant John." i. 1.

6. The messages to the seven churches by their terms go beyond the churches, All are exhorted "hear what the Spirit saith unto the churches."

7. And, finally, and perhaps most conclusively of all, these messages do present an exact picture of the history of the church, in precisely this order. If Ephesus (ii. 1-7) represents the average spiritual state of the churches at the close of the apostolic period (and all other information confirms it) then Smyrna fitly represents the era of the great persecutions; Pergamos of the lapse into worldliness after the conversion of Constantine; Thyatira, of fully developed Romanism, etc. The parallels are too exact and too numerous to be accidental.

These messages have, then, a fourfold application.

1. Local, to the churches actually addressed.

2. Admonitory, as touchstones by which any churches in any age may test their spiritual state in the sight of God.

3. Personal, as enabling individual saints to discern evil in themselves.

4, Prophetical, as disclosing seven progressive phases of the spiritual history of the church from (say) A. D. 96 to the end.

The student will observe carefully the following structural peculiarities of these messages.

1. Christ is always presented in a character suited to the moral state of the church which is addressed. This is of most solemn import, for it reveals the attitude of Christ toward the specific faults indicated.

2. That which is commendable in the churches, if there be anything worthy of commendation, is first mentioned. The Lord does not walk in the midst of the candlesticks merely to note that which is evil.

3. That which is blameworthy is exposed and rebuked.

4, Exhortations and promises, especially to "him that overcometh," follow. The promises to the overcomer mark the path of personal obedience in circumstances where the prevailing conditions are evil.

The divisions of this section are, of course, apparent.

Part 1. Message to Ephesus. ii. 1-7. The general state of the churches at the close of the first century. Distinguished for works, patience, the effort to maintain a clean membership, the rejection of a false ecclesiasticism. Verses 2, 3, 6.

Note. A word as to 'the deeds of the Nicolaitanes." Many Bible dictionaries make of these Nicolaitans a sect, "followers of one Nicolas." But there is not a fragment of evidence for this. It is purely a deduction from this passage and ii. 15. But if we seek in the Word itself, in harmony with the symbolical method and structure of the book, a meaning, we get light at once. It is a compound Greek word, niko-laos, signifying "conquerors, or overcomers of the people," or laity. It indicates, therefore, that already there were the beginnings of priestly assumption; the setting up of pastors or elders to be a "clergy," as distinguished from the equal brotherhood and equal priesthood of all believers. i. 6; Matt. xxiii. 8; 1 Peter ii. 9.. This interpretation is confirmed by the remarkable emphasis of Christ's condemnation, "which I also hate" (ii. 6, 15); for, historically, it is certain that the corruption of Christianity came through priestly assumption. Nothing else made papacy possible.

The general state of the churches then was admirable. But the Spirit discerned a fatal lack: "thou hast left thy first love." First love is absorbing and personal, and above all else desires the presence of the beloved object. The churches had lost that. They had substituted his "name's sake" for Himself. ii. 3. It was "the cause," now; Christianity, rather than Christ. This was not a small thing. "Somewhat" is supplied, and spoils the sense. "I have against thee because thou hast left thy first love." How great a thing this was is immediately disclosed. "I will remove thy candlestick out of his place except thou repent."

Part 2. Message to Smyrna. ii. 8-11. This church was in the midst of severe persecution. Accordingly sympathy restrains the mention of whatever might have been blameworthy. The character in which the Lord reveals Himself is itself reassuring. If they are to be slain it is no more than He has suffered. As He is alive so they shall be.

Historically, we have here the period of the ten great organized persecutions ending with the conversion of Constantine, 60 to 316 A.D. "Thou shalt have trouble ten days." The character in which Christ is revealed to these suffering ones, as also the special promises made to them, are beautifully suited to their condition.

Part 3. The message to Pergamos. ii. 12-17. Historically, we have here the period dating from the conversion of Constantine, A. D. 316, to the full development of the papacy. The rise of the papacy, and the growth of priestly and ecclesiastical tyranny was, as is well known to students, gradual.

Morally, the state is perfectly disclosed. "I know where thou dwellest, where Satan's throne [not "seat"] is." There is no difficulty in the interpretation of this symbol... Satan is "the prince of this world." John xiv. 30. Two things, then, were wrong: the church had settled down, given up her pilgrim character ("I know where thou dwellest"); and the place of her dwelling was the world. Precisely this happened. Satan had tried in vain to destroy the church, he now seeks to seduce and corrupt her. Christianity became the court religion, and baptism the way to preferment. Zeal for truth still survived. "Thou holdest fast my name, and hast not denied my faith."

Indeed, it was the period of the great creeds, Nicene and other. Two great evils were tolerated. The "way" of Balaam (2 Peter ii. 15) had become a "doctrine," a teaching. Separation was openly reprobated; bishops openly enriched themselves; the churches received lands and endowments. "Balaam" means, "devourer of the people." Nicolaitanism also had made progress. In Ephesus there were "deeds;" in Pergamos the thing has become, like Balaamism, a "doctrine." It is not only that a few ambitious men are setting up to bea "clergy," but that the thing is defended—as, indeed, it is to this day. Between Balaam, the devourer of the people, or "laity," and Niko-laos, the conqueror of the people, the simple apostolic brotherhood is crushed and rent.

Note. Nicolaitanism, needless to say, raises no question of the rightness of office, as elders and deacons, nor of gift, as prophets, evangelists, pastors, and teachers. It is making of these a class apart, having the alone right to preach, or to baptize, or to administer the bread and wine, which constitutes Nicolaitanism. That hateful heresy puts a priesthood (protestant or papal) between the simple saint and his Father. Logically, as well as historically, the next step exalts the simple Christian ordinances into sacraments, having mysterious efficacy, the benefit of which depends upon administration by priestly hands. From thence it is but a step to full grown papacy.

Nor does Nicolaitanism consist in the free appointment of pastors or elders to baptize or administer the bread and wine. Someone must do it; order requires that there be no confusion in such matters. Nicolaitanism begins only when such appointed service becomes an exclusive right.

Note. Beautiful symbols abound. It would be impossible, short of an elaborate treatise, to interpret all of these. The lesson outline will suggest the interpretation of many. The industry of the student, seeking diligently through Scripture for the sources of the symbols, will solve the mystery of many more. Some (as, e.g., 'the number of a man," xiii. 18) are not yet satisfactorily explained to the writer. Where he has light he gives it in the outline. Doubtless much which is mysterious to the church will be full of meaning to the Jewish remnant as the end time approaches.

Part 4. The message to Thyatira. ii. 18-29. Historically, Thyatira is fully developed Romanism. Balaamism had utterly devoured the people; Nicolaitanism had utterly subjugated them. Jezebel was the suited symbol. It will be remembered that she was the heathen wife of a Jewish king. Romanism is Christianity as a doctrinal system, wedded to heathen rites and ceremonies. Jezebel brought idolatry into Israel; incited the civil power to acts of cruelty, and persecuted the true prophets of God. All this the papacy did for the church.

Morally there was much that was good, but " works" take the primacy of faith. We find, also, a remnant: "the rest in Thyatira." In the worst days of Romanism great saints arose, as Elijah in the days of Jezebel. ii. 24. Now, for the first time in these messages to the churches, our Lord brings in the expectation of His coming. ii. 25. It is the Thessalonian aspect, "the morning star"—light to the watchful before the full rising of the Sun of righteousness; the rapture before the glorious appearing. Let the student remember that Ephesus, Smyrna, Pergamos, and Thyatira constitute a progressive history from the apostolic period to, say, A. D. 1500. The church is still one; sunken in priestcraft and heathen practice, but holding a true creed, and containing a remnant of most saintly souls. So precious was the unity of the church that for long Christ bore with her errors: "I gave her space to repent." ii. 21. It was useless. Worldliness (" fornication") in Pergamos had become simply the world ("adultery") in Thyatira. Union of state and church all over Christendom was universal. Morally, therefore, the Greek church, though rejecting the papacy, is a phase of Thyatira.

Part 5. The message to Sardis. ii. 1-6. Historically we have here the Protestant reformation. Of Thyatira it was said: "She repented not" (ii. 21), and a break was inevitable.

Morally, we have in Sardis the reformation, not in its lovely morning, but arrested, unprogressive, congealed. This was historically true. After the glorious beginning the Protestant movement paused. Doctrinal quarrels ensued. She had a name that she lived and was dead. She ceased to expand geographically and doctrinally. The elementary truths recovered by the fathers of the reformation were crystallized into hard creeds, and admitted no accretions of newly recovered truth. The warning is suited: "I have not found thy works fulfilled [not "perfect"] before my God." Also, "Remember how thou hast received." Protestantism had received liberty, and an open Bible. Macaulay, a secular historian, notes this singular arrest of development. " How it was that Protestantism did so much, yet did no more; how it was that the church of Rome, having lost a large part of Europe, not only ceased to lose, but actually regained nearly half of what she had lost, is certainly a most important question." Review of Ranke's History of the Popes. As in Thyatira, so in Sardis there is a remnant: "Thou hast a few names even in Sardis which have not defiled their garments."

Part 6. The message to Philadelphia. iii. 7-13. Historically we do not advance beyond Thyatira (Romanism) and Sardis (Protestantism), which go on to the end. Philadelphia is not, symbolically, an epoch, but a phase. Not a period of time, nor a distinct organization, but a presentation of all that is real in Protestantism. In other words, " Philadelphia" is in all the Protestant churches. The word means "brotherly love;" and is, therefore, the appropriate symbol of reality in Christianity. "We know that we have passed from death unto life, because we love the brethren." 1 John iii. 14. " By this shall all men know that ye are my disciples, if ye have love one to another." John xiii. 35.

Part 7. The message to Laodicea. iii. 14-22. Historically Laodicea, like Philadelphia, represents not a period of church history, but a phase of Protestantism. Morally it is characterized by that blatant and shallow optimism which will take no serious account either of the tremendous biblical warnings of apostasy, nor of the menacing signs of its presence. It is Protestantism spiritually puffed up and self-satisfied—"rich and increased with goods" and having no sense of need. Another significant sign is given in verse 20. Christ is outside the door! His authority is disowned. Doubtless not in word. They may still be saying

pretty things about Him. The point is, they have no subjection to His word, nor any sense of need of what He alone can "sell"—the gold of divine righteousness, the white garment of personal righteousness, the anointing with the Spirit. But He knocks still, if perchance any may open the door. Such will be fed. As matter of fact, Philadelphians do open the door, and to them He opens doors. iii. 8. The mass know not that they are "wretched, and miserable, and poor, and blind, and naked." That is the pathos of it—they "know not."

But Christ does not bid those who hear His voice, as He stands knocking, to "come out'? to Him. They are to let Him in—not come out. Presently He will take them out, which is a vastly different thing.

The sum of the matter, then, is that outwardly Christianity exists to the end in two forms, Thyatira and Sardis. In Sardis two phases coexist, Philadelphianism or real belief, marked by a measure of power and by loyalty to Christ's Word; and blatant, self-satisfied, ostentatious profession, or Laodicea. In every church it is notorious that the praying, working, and giving members are a well-defined few. It is these who go as missionaries, and, singularly enough, it is to the lives and work of these that the Laodiceans point in justification of their boastings of progress.

And this is the end time, for with the message to Laodicea ceases in the Revelation all reference to the church, or to the churches, as such. Saints are seen in heaven and on earth; "Babylon" is seen in awful destruction, but nothing which Christ owns as a church. There is, indeed, and most preciously, the indication of the rapture. "After this I looked, and, behold, a Door was opened in heaven; and the first voice which I heard was as it were of a trumpet talking with me, which said, Come up hither." iv. 1. From that moment the view-point of the seer changes. John still sees things on earth, but looks down upon them from the heights of glory. Neither he nor Christ is longer "in the midst of the golden candlesticks."

Note. The student should at this point answer the questions of the examination on Sections I. and II.

Section 3: "The Things That Shall Be." iv. 1—xxii. 21.

The historical beginning of this section, while not to be fixed in terms of years and months, is absolutely fixed relatively to other prophetic periods. It begins with the rapture of the church. 1. Thess. iv.14-18; 1 Cor, xv. 51,52; Rev. iv: 1. That the "things" of Section III. do not begin until after the "things" of Section II. are ended, is expressly affirmed in Rev. i. 19, and Rev. iv. 1, where they are called "things which must be after these things'—*i.e.*, "the things which are" or the churches. The root error of the so-called "historical" school of apocalyptic interpretation lies in the disregard of this twice repeated statement. That interpretation assumes that Rev. iv.—xxii. (or at least iv.—xviii.) runs parallel to Rev. ii.—iii., covering substantially the same period of time. Hence the endless confusion of the books professing to interpret the Apocalypse. This is inevitable, for possibly no two minds, ranging through profane history from the first to the nineteenth centuries for fulfillments of Rev. iv.—xviii., would see those fulfillments in the same incidents. Indeed, except as they obviously take from one another, there is no agreement—unless it be in calling the papacy antichrist. Doubtless the papacy is anti-Christian, but antichrist is a person, not a system, so even this is wrong.

But when we see that all beyond iv. 1 is yet future, we are compelled to the use of Peter's safe rule: "Knowing this first, that no prophecy of the Scripture is to be interpreted by itself." 2 Pet. i. 20. Instead, therefore, of seeking in profane history for something which in some respects resembles the predicted events, we seek to interpret them by searching other portions of the "sure word of prophecy," comparing spiritual things with spiritual.

Let it be at once said, that this method will not yield that minute interpretation in which curious minds delight. What it does yield is a firm and broad outline of events and their meaning. This brings apocalyptic prophecy into exact harmony with Old Testament prophecy. The student of Old Testament prophecy knew that Messiah was coming. He knew that Messiah would be divine and human. He knew that Messiah would be rejected and sacrificed; and he knew that Messiah would reunite and restore Israel, and establish in the earth the perfected society, which the prophets called the kingdom. But he did not know that those contradictory results would be accomplished by two comings instead of one; he did not know that the church would be called out in the interim, nor could he have known such details as (for example) that. Hosea xi. 1 meant that Messiah, as a babe, should be carried into Egypt and brought back again. Matt. i. 15. In a word, this great section maps out for us the general outline of the events which follow the catching away of the church; and, doubtless, holds also a multitude of predictions which, obscure to us, will be luminous with meaning to the people of God in the midst of fulfillments.

Another word of caution is most needful. Excluding the parenthetical passages (to be presently indicated), this section, speaking broadly, gives an order of events. Three great series of judgments are predicted—the seal, trumpet and vial judgments. These are successive. But beyond that order there is little which is chronological. That is, the visions go backward and forward without regard to the sequence of time. This is another way of saying that we must not read this section as a steadily progressive narrative.

What portions of the older prophetic word belong to the period covered period covered by Section III.? The answer is. that such portions of the "prophecies of the Old and New Testament as relate to the day of the Lord," the "tribulation" and the time of the beast connect with and shed light upon this section down to the end of Chapter XIX. Whatever in previous Scripture relates to the millennium and the eternal state connects with and sheds light upon Chapters XX.—XXII. Chapters IV.— XIX. bridge the tremendous chasm of the Tribulation.

Section III. falls into seven parts and three parentheses, as follow:

(Parenthesis 1. Chapters IV.—V. Scenes in Heaven after the Rapture.)

Part 1. Chapter VI. The Seal Judgments.

(Parenthesis 2. Chapter VII. The Tribulation Saints.)

Part 2. Chapters VIII.—XI. The Seven Trumpet Judgments.

Part 3. Chapters XII.—XIII. Israel and the Beasts.

(Parenthesis 3. Chapters XIV.—XV._ Visions not chronological.)

Part 4. Chapter XVI. Vial (or Bowl) Judgments.

Part 5. Chapters XVII.—XVIII. Doom of Babylon.

Part 6. Chapters XIX.—XX. Marriage of the Lamb; the Glorious Appearing of the Lord; Millennium; Great White Throne Judgment.

Part 7. Chapters XXI.—XXII. The Church in Millennial Glory and the Eternal State.

Note. The student will do well at this point to mark in his study Bible (the Bible which he uses for devotional reading should have no marks) the analysis of the Revelation.

Parenthesis 1. Scenes in Heaven after the Rapture of the Church, iv.—v.

Verse 1 indicates the rapture. In the actual visions in Patmos it indicates John's changed point of view. It was an experience like 2 Cor. xii. 1-4. Hitherto (chapters i.—iii.) John has been with Christ among the churches. Now Christ, speaking no longer among the churches, calls him to the new viewpoint. Henceforth he looks down.

"Throne'—of God. "Four and twenty thrones…four and twenty elders." These represent symbolically the church in glory. The number is symbolical of priesthood, according to the temple order (1 Chr. xxiv. 4; Luke i. 5), and the thrones of royalty. In no body of saints other than the church are these two distinctions, priesthood and royalty, united.....1. Peter ii. 9; Rev. i. 6,, v. 10. We) have, then, the enthroned church symbolized in these "elders."

"Four living creatures" or "living ones" (not "beasts') are identical with the cherubim and seraphim of the Old Testament. They have the attributes of strength (lion), patient endurance (ox), intelligence (man) and swiftness (eagle).

The seven-sealed scroll is explained by what occurs as the successive seals are opened. The breaking of the seals sets loose the first two series of the apocalyptic judgments. The trumpet judgments come out of the seventh seal. viii. 1, 2. The scroll may therefore be said to contain the mandate of God for the beginning of the judgments preparatory to the setting up of the kingdom. In reality, therefore, the scene, v. 1-7, is identical with Daniel's vision, Dan. vii. 18, 14. "In so far as Israel is concerned, the scene marks the beginning of that series of purifying judgments which, according to Old Testament prophecy, precede the restoration and conversion of Israel. See, e.g., Is. 1. 24-27, xxvi. 8, 9; Mal. iv. 1, 2; Zeph. i, 14-18, and generally the "day of the Lord" passages.

Part 1. The seal judgments. vi. 1-17. The structure is simple: when a seal is opened something occurs on earth. Symbols abound. 'The general symbol is the horse, signifying aggressive power, courage. Prov. xxi. 31; Job xxxix. 19-25: Jer. viii. 6. This general symbol is modified by colors, and these are interpreted by the context; ¢. 2, the white horse rider conquers; the red horse rider kills, etc. The series of events is as follows:—

First seal: Rise of a peaceful conqueror. An illustration (not fulfillment) might be found in the return of Napoleon from Elba. He conquered France without firing a gun.

Second seal: Universal war. Also a saturnalia of murder, '*that they should kill one another."

Third seal: Famine—the natural result of universal war and insecurity of life. Under such circumstances the fields are unsown, and commerce languishes.

Fourth seal: Pestilence, sword, famine, and wild beasts. The "four sore judgments" of Ezek. xiv. 21.

Fifth seal: This seal discloses, as it were, the results (so far as the Jewish remnant is concerned) of the terrific scenes through which the earth has been passing. The "souls under the altar" are part of the martyred remnant. See, *e.g.*, Zech. Xili. 8, and, generally, the references to the remnant in Part 4, Section II., of this Course.

Sixth seal: Here the chief symbol is an earthquake, signifying an upheaval from beneath, or anarchy. The kings and great men are first affected; but anarchy soon reacts upon the very classes which create it, so that soon "every bondman"' is also in distress. The French Revolution illustrates this. Anarchy always prepares the way for despotism. In this case the coming despot is "the man of sin," the " beast out of the sea."'

Parenthesis 2. The tribulation saints. vii. 1-17. The student will remember that this chapter is not, so to speak, part of the story. The narrative is suspended, and this chapter written to show that a mighty work of salvation is going on through this entire period, from the taking away of the church (iv. 1) to the glorious appearing of the Lord (xix. 11-21). It is the great mercy chapter of the Revelation; affording infinite relief to the heart, and removing completely that thought of the myriads of unsaved in the earth, which might make us hesitate to cry, "Come quickly, Lord Jesus." When we perceive that the saved of the tribulation will inconceivably outnumber those now finding Christ in any equal period of time, we have a powerful motive to desire His coming for us. There is, first, a definite number saved out of all Israel. This number may well be symbolic rather than literal. This primacy of Israel denotes that, the church being no longer in the earth, God takes up

again the interrupted course of His dealings with His ancient people. But more. Converted Jews are to be the preachers during the tribulation. The "two witnesses" of chapter xi. are probably Moses and Elijah (not Peter and Paul); and Zech. viii. 13, 23 is to the same purport. "And it shall come to pass that as ye were a curse among the heathen, O house of Judah and house of Israel; so I will save you, and ye shall be a blessing," etc. "In those days it shall come to pass that ten men shall take hold, out of all languages of the nations [note that expression], even shall take hold of the skirt of him that is a Jew, saying, We will go with you; for we have heard that God is with you."

This saved remnant of Rev. vii. 4-8, appears again in Rev. xiv. 1-5. Imagine the effect upon the Gentile world, of the simultaneous appearance of one hundred and forty-four thousand Pauls! We cease to wonder at what follows in verses 9, 10. Observe: (1) These are Gentiles "of all nations, and kindreds, and people, and tongues."'' (2) They are gathered out of the whole earth. "Nations" mean organized world-powers —the sense in which we use the word. But what follows: "kindreds,"' etc., includes the smallest conceivable body of persons. (3) They are not of the church, the body of Christ. This is represented by the elders. Verse 15 fixes their relative place of blessing. The church being priestly, the tribulation saints may be called heavenly Levites. (4) The earth time to which they belong is fixed by verse 14. "These are they which came out of the great tribulation." See Revised Version. It is not, as in Authorized Version, tribulation merely, but the period called by our Lord "great tribulation." Matt. xxiv. 21. And, (5) they are innumerable—"a great multitude, which no man could number."' It is easy to keep missionary statistics now. Here is one of the mighty motives to missions now. We see in Rev. vii. the full fruition of this time of seed sowing. That tremendous ingathering would probably be impossible but for the preparation of the minds of the people of the earth through present-day testimony. In other words, were the Lord to take away His church today, and the seal judgments to begin to-morrow, the translated laborers in home .and foreign lands would be transported and amazed by the results of their now so discouraging toil. This chapter gives every warrant for the belief that between the coming of the: Lord for His church, and His return to the earth with His saints, the overwhelming majority of living humanity will be saved. "Come, Lord Jesus!"

The student is reminded that in so far as chapter vii. describes the heavenly blessedness of the tribulation saints, it is anticipatory. The vision overleaps what remains of the earth life of these saints, and reveals their eternal state. Neither are we to suppose that they are saved between the sixth and seventh seals. The vision, in a timeless way; shows the redemptive work of the tribulation period. It is the fulfillment of Isaiah xxvi. 9: "When thy judgments are in the earth, the inhabitants of the world will learn righteousness."

Part 2. The trumpet judgments. vili.—xi. The student will note in these judgments that they differ from the seal judgments in one important respect. THe seal judgments are not strictly speaking supernatural. The anguish and horror of the period during which they run their awful course are the results of human ambition, hatred, cruelty, and improvidence. All that God does is to remove restraint. He takes away the church, that is to say, the "salt" which restrains the full working of leaven. 2. Thess. ii. 6;.7, R.V.; Matt. v. 13; Mark vii. 21-23. For, possibly, the first time in the history of the world, unregenerate human nature has its unhindered day. Peace is a divine quality. In the seal judgments peace is "taken from the earth." The natural man is a hero worshiper—in the first seal he gets his hero. He is a worshiper of force, of military achievement —in the second seal he gets his fill of blood. Two natural consequences follow, famine and pestilence. The natural man fancies himself competent to overturn civil government and establish a millennium by law,

and by social reorganization—in the sixth seal he is given scope for his calamitous experiment. The worst tyranny earth ever saw is not so awful as anarchy.

But when we reach the trumpet judgments the supernatural enters the scene. The "angel" of viii. 3 is Christ, the " High Priest over the house of God." In harmony with Hebrews xiii. 15, the prayers of the saints are seen ascending up " before God out of the angel's hand," and He adds His own intercessions. Then the censer is filled with fire from the altar and cast into the earth. Fire symbolizes discriminating judgment. Altar fire speaks of God's holiness. Toward sin the divine holiness is pure wrath. 'This, then, is the new element brought in with the trumpets. God is judging sin according to the altar test.)

Symbols again abound. Trees stand for human greatness; green grass, human glory and prosperity. A mountain, in biblical symbolism, means a great earth-power; the sea, the turbulent, unorganized mass of men; a great star, a conspicuous ruler. E.g., Isa. xiv. 4-12, 13.

The fifth, sixth and seventh trumpet judgments are called "woe" trumpets.

The sounding of the fifth angel affords at once an example of the non-chronological method of very much in the Revelation. The fallen star of ix. 1 is, as the context shows, Satan. But we are not to suppose that this is the moment of his fall. This had occurred before the events of Gen. iii. 1-6— how long before is not revealed. But all through Old Testament times he is seen at work, especially incarnating himself in great earthly rulers. See Isa. xiv. 4-13; Ezek. xxviii. 12-17; Luke x. 18.

The fifth trumpet introduces an element of unspeakable horror—an irruption of demons out of the abyss. For five months they are to be suffered to work. One has but to turn back to the demonology of the four Gospels to gain some slight idea of what this fifth trumpet may be. Imagine the crass ineptitude of the interpretation which sees in this the rise of Saracen power!

The "mighty angel" of x. 1 is, again, Christ. The "little book" is explained by the context. It is the scroll of the remaining unfulfilled purposes of God—sweet to the taste, because it is God's will; bitter when comprehended, because it speaks of more judgment.

The "temple"' of xi. 1 is the tribulation temple of Matt. xxiv. 15; 2 Thess. ii. 3, 4. The student will remember the testimony of the prophets concerning the restoration in unbelief of a portion of the Jews, who will, in consequence of a covenant with "the prince that shall come" (Dan. ix. 26), namely, "the beast out of the sea" of Rev. xiii. 1, resume the form of the ancient worship in Jerusalem. This covenant is broken in the midst of the " week" (of years) when the events of 2 Thess. ii. 3, 4 occur. The Jewish use of the temple, under the "beast" covenant, will continue three and one-half years. During this time the "two witnesses" (possibly Moses and Elijah, see verse 6) shall prophesy in Jerusalem to these unbelieving Jews. When the " beast" breaks his covenant with the Jews and deifies himself he will slay the witnesses. The "great tribulation," properly so called, begins with the breach of the beast covenant, the self-deification of the beast and the slaying of the witnesses. Matt. xxiv. 15,21. "When ye shall see," etc., "then shall be great tribulation," etc. In other words, the events of Rev. iv. 1—xi. 13 have occupied three and one-half years. A like period of three and one-half years remains for the events of Rev. xi. 14—xix. 21. Awful as have been the scenes which have led up to the manifestation of the man of sin, they were but introductory to what Christ describes as "great tribulation such as was not since the beginning of the world to this time, no, nor ever shall be." Matt. xxiv. 21. The present division (Part 2) closes with a scene in heaven. The manifestation of the " man of sin," the "beast," is accepted there, as it will be by the sorely tried saints on earth, as the beginning of the end. 2 Thess. ii. 8, and the order of events in Matt. xxiv., following verse 15 down to verse 30.

Part 3. Israel, Satan, and the beasts. xii.—xiii. Chapter xii. affords another illustration of the non-chronological arrangement (in part) of the Revelation. It goes back to the birth of Christ, and comes down to the midst of the tribulation.

The woman of xii. 1 is Israel. The dragon (see verse 9) is Satan. The man child is Christ. He is seen here as identified with the church of this dispensation, as in 1 Cor. xii. 12, 13; Eph. i. 23; iv. 15, 16. The ascension of Christ and the rapture of the church are seen as one event. This whole dispensation is in verse 5. Satan, instigating Herod, seeks to destroy Christ at His birth, but is defeated.

The woman (Israel) from verse 6 is seen, not in the long history from the destruction of the temple to the present time— that is passed over in silence. Verse 6 resumes the story of the woman, dropped after the ascension of Christ, at the precise point which has now been reached by the Revelation, namely, the middle of the period beginning with the rapture of the church and ending with the return of the Lord to the earth. In other words, verse 6 takes up the story of Israel in the middle of Daniel's seventieth week. The casting out of Satan in xii. 7-12 is not identical with that of ix. 1. For some unexplained reason, during the time of the working out of redemption, from the fall of Adam to Rev. xii. 9, Satan has access to heaven for purposes of accusation.. Zech. iii. 1, 2; Luke xxii. 31, 32; Rev. xii. 10, "which accused them before our God day and night." Cast finally down, Satan persecutes Israel (verses 13-16) and, when she is delivered, persecutes the believing remnant of Israel (verse 17).

The "beast out of the sea" (xiii. 1) is the " fourth beast " of Dan. vil. 7; the "fourth kingdom" of Dan. ii. 40; the "prince that shall come" of Dan. ix. 26, 27. It will be remembered that in Dan. ii. 41-43 the deterioration and division of the Roman or "fourth" kingdom was predicted, but in a dateless way; the only indication of time being the predicted destruction of the whole fabric of Gentile domination by a crushing catastrophe "in the days of these kings," i.e., the kings symbolized by the toes of the image. Dan. ii. 44, 45. Dan. vii. is more explicit. The "ten horns" of the "fourth beast" (vii. 7) are "ten kings that shall arise'? So far Dan. vii. does not go beyond Dan. ii. But verses 8 and 24-26 take up the detail. The tenfold division of the Roman Empire is not a present-day nor continuous division, necessarily. What is in view is not the course of history, but the end time. In the end time what was Rome shall be under ten kings—that is Daniel's point. Among these "horns" (kings) Daniel sees a "little horn" intrude. He takes three of the ten kingdoms (verses 8, 24), and is also remarkable for blasphemy (verse 25). So far Daniel. Rev. xiii. takes up the matter at that point. The "beast out of the sea" is the rising again of the Roman imperium—the civil power, not the papacy. The identification of the beast out of che sea with Daniel's fourth beast in ten-kingdom form is made sure by comparing Rev. xiii. 1 ("ten horns ") with Rev. xvii. 12 ("the ten horns which thou sawest are ten kings"). The student will observe that this "beast out of the sea" is both a person and a form of civil government—the revived Roman Empire. It will be observed that the Apostle, in xiii. 1, sees this last phase of Gentile world supremacy in the precise state in which Daniel saw it in vii. 8. There are "ten horns," but, since the "little horn" has acquired three of them, there are but seven heads. Verse 2 appropriates the symbolic beasts of Dan. vii. 4-6. It is the final proof of identity; proof that Daniel and John write of the same matter. Verses 2 and 3 are tv be taken together. So taken there is a significant advance iu the thought. The "head," which was "wounded to death," refers to the imperial form of government. The fragments of the ancient Roman empire never ceased to exist as civil governments; it was the empire which ceased: the head, into which the power of the whole was centralized, was wounded to death. What we see here is the revival of the imperial form of government under the "little horn" as emperor. The "beast" in verses 2 and 3 is the empire in its divided

form; the " beast" in verses 3-8 is the emperor. It isa common use of language. In the line—

"I am dying, Egypt, dying"

"Egypt" means Cleopatra, Queen of Egypt.. Gathering up, then, the teachings of Dan. ii., Dan vii., and Rev. xiii., we see foretold a future re-constitution of the Roman empire—the "legs of iron," with "feet part of iron and part of clay," of Dan. ii. ; the "fourth beast" of Dan. vii., the "beast out of the sea" of Rev. xiii. But there is a great modification of the primal Roman empire. It is that empire resolved into ten kingdoms, in which the iron of autocracy has become mingled with the brittle clay of democracy. In the earlier part of the period, beginning with the departure of the church, a personage arises who gains three of the ten kingdoms. During the tribulation proper he becomes emperor of the whole—probably a federal empire, such as that of Germany, rather than an autonomous empire such as that of Russia.

This emperor will be the beast. Daniel, Paul, and John give the outlines of his character and career. Daniel vii. 8, 24, 25; ix. 27; Matt. xxiv. 15; 2 Thess. ii. 3-10; Rev. vi. 2; xiii. 3-8. In this final head of Gentle authority Satan will be for the last time incarnate. xiii. 2, 4. From verse 11, the "beast out of the earth," the "false prophet" of xix. 20, is described. He is the head of ecclesiastical power, as the beast of xiii. 3-8 is the head of civil power. In chapter xiii. we have the "infernal trinity," in which the civil head assumes the place of God the Father, as the object of worship; the false prophet the place of the Son, as prophet and priest; while Satan, as the invisible energizing power of it all, assumes the place of the Holy Spirit. Thus linked in time they are not separated in eternity. xx. 10.

Parenthesis 3. Visions, not chronological. xiv.— xv. First vision, verses 1-5. The Jewish tribulation remnant of vii. 1-8 seen in their future millennial blessedness. Chapter vii. 9-17, it will be remembered, gave the eternal blessedness of the

Gentile tribulation saints. The present vision takes up again the one hundred and forty-four thousand. There is not the smallest ground for inventing another one hundred and forty-four thousand to fulfill this vision, while xiv. 1 distinctly identifies them with vii. 3.

Second vision. Verses 6-13. The flying angel. The encouraging and warning testimony during the time described in xiii. 5-18.

Third vision. Verses 14-20. The sickle vision. Prophetic foreview of the gathering of the beast and his armies against the Jews in Jerusalem and Palestine, which forms the closing scene of the Tribulation. The final battle occurs just outside the land, in Idumea. See Isa. xxiv. 1-8; Zech. xiv. 1-3; Isa. lxii. 1-6; 2 Thess. i. 7-10; 11. 8; Rev. xix. 11-21.

It will be seen, therefore, that the first vision gives the position in blessedness of the Jewish tribulation saints; the second vision loving warnings and encouragements for those saints, Jewish or Gentile, who may be undergoing persecution in antichrist's day, while the third vision overleaps the vial judgments and the doom of Babylon, and predicts the final overthrow of the beast and his hosts by the appearing of the Lord. Surely, the third vision will be Gnatay | comforting to the tried ones of antichrist's day.

Fourth vision, xv. 1-8. A scene in heaven. "The elements are simple. Verses 2-4 show the martyred ones of antichrist's day (the last three and a half years of the period covered by chapters iv.—xix.), as the "sixth seal" (chapter vi.) shows the martyred Jewish remnant of the earlier part of the period. Verses 5-8 give the preparation for the vial (or "bowl") judgments. This chapter is not chronological, except as it depicts a scene in heaven during the beast's reign.

Part 4. The vial (or bowl) judgments. xvi. In the trumpet judgments we saw the altar fire, symbol of God's holiness consuming the sin-laden sacrifice, cast into the earth. Now we enter upon a series of judgments which are the expression of the wrath of God. xv. 7; xvi. 1. Of this period the type and foreshadowing is found in the plagues upon Egypt. Ex. vii.— xii. Verses 14-16 fix the period of the vial judgments. They are just before the end of the three and one-half years of antichrist's full manifestation, and preparatory to the great battle of the sickle vision of chapter xiv. Accordingly there is the final warning of His coming. Verse 15. The battle of Armageddon is Messiah's battle. Zech. xiv. 3; Isa. lxiii. 1-6. It will be observed that the seventh vial is, in effect, poured upon what is here called "great Babylon." The preceding vials were filled with the " wrath of God"; this with "the cup of the wine of the fierceness of His wrath." It is accompanied by another "earthquake "—an anarchic revolt from beneath—provoked, no doubt, by the intolerable despotism of the beast, and the desperate sufferings resulting from the vial judgments. Verse 18.

Part 5. The doom of Babylon. xvii.—xviii. The word Babylon means "confusion." The details seem to leave no doubt that the symbolic word means here the whole. system: of corrupt and apostate papal Christianity, which was fully developed in the Thyatira period as to its distinctive features, but appears now in a state of mere confusion. It may well have gathered under the general headship of the papacy the apostate Protestant bodies left in Laodicea when the true, or Philadelphian, saints were caught away. " Babylon," in a word, is apostate Christendom headed up in Rome. The student will note, however, that the system is judged and destroyed as an historic whole. The accumulated sins of the past are upon the whore at the end. This is in harmony with the judgment of the end upon Gentile civil government. It is the revived Roman Empire which is destroyed, but God judges in her the "times of the Gentiles." "Then was the iron, the clay, the brass, the silver, and the gold, broken to pieces together."' Dan. ii. 35.

The marks of the papal system are evident.

1. Unchastity, or union with the world. Verses 1, 2. Witness state churches, concordats, the "patrimony of Peter," as the Roman Catholic Papal States were called.

2. Identity with Thyatira. Verse 2, with Rev. ii. 21, 22.

3. Oppression. Verse 1, "sitteth upon many waters." See verse 15.

4. She is "the mother of harlots'"—*i.e.*, of churches which have unchaste commerce with the civil governments.

5. She is "drunk with the blood of the martyrs of Jesus."

From verse 7 we have explanations. The "beast" of verse 8 is the revived Roman empire. The "seven mountains" of verse 9 have an undoubted symbolic reference to the seven hills of Rome (see verse 18), but the larger reference is to seven papal kingdoms or world powers, as e. g., Spain, France, Italy, Austria, Portugal, Belgium, Hungary—though the divisions of papal Europe in the time of the beast may be different. It should be remembered that the conditions stated in Rev. xili. 4-17 are consistent with some shadowy allegiance to Rome if we suppose a federated empire. In verse 11 the antichrist is meant. Verses 12-14 give a swift sketch (as in chapter xiii.) — again of the revived empire and its end in the battle of Armageddon.

Verses 15, 16 describe the instruments of the judgment upon Babylon. The subjects of her long tyranny, her oppression of the free spirits and bodies of men, turn upon and rend her. "These shall hate the whore, and shall make her desolate and naked, and shall eat her flesh, and burn her with fire."

Chapter xviii. goes back. It sounds the moral judgment of God upon that which is about to perish. This is clear from the warning cry of verse 4. There was no call to come out of Laodicea; but there is a call to come out of Babylon. Babylon is the system in which Thyatira and Laodicea end after the true church is caught away. There is an elevated and awful beauty in this moral judgment upon Babylon.

Part 6. The marriage and glorious appearing of the Lamb; His victory over the infernal trinity; the millennium, final apostasy and last judgment. xix.—xx.

The order here is consecutive and simple.

1. Heaven rejoices over the vindication of the faithfulness of God. xix. 1-6.

2. The marriage of the Lamb. Verses 7, 8.

3. The blessedness of the guests at the coming marriage supper. Verse 9; Luke xxii. 18; Matt. xxvi. 29; Matt. xxii. 1-14,

4. The descent of Christ in His millennial character of "King of kings and Lord of lords"; the battle and victory. Verses. 11-21—-xx. 3 Zech. xiv. 1-10.

5. The saints of the first resurrection, including the martyrs of the tribulation, associated with Christ in millennial power. xx. 4-7.

6. The final apostasy at the end of the thousand years. xx. 8-10.

Note. The student will observe that individuals are in view in Number 5, not the church as a corporate body. Church saints are here as being in the first resurrection, but, as chapter xxi. is devoted to the millennial glory of the church, it is natural that the tribulation martyrs should be more prominent here.

Note. The question is often asked: supposing a converted world, for one thousand years under the personal reign of Christ, from whence does Satan gather this new army? The question misapprehends the moral state of the millennial earth. It is nowhere said that every individual of that period will be converted. Doubtless, the general state will be one of conversion, but the entire period is one of the absolute reign of righteousness. Evil is not borne with as now. The will of God is enforced. At any given time there will be an unconverted element. To these Satan makes his final appeal. The result brings the kingdom age into harmony with the six previous dispensations—it ends in failure and judgment. Fallen man is incorrigible. Isa. i. 5,6; Mark vii. 21-23; Rom. viii. 7; 1 Cor. ii. 14.

7. The second resurrection and the judgment of the great white throne. .

Note. The student will observe that this is by no means a "general" judgment. Only those who, up to the end of the post-millennial apostasy, have been in the graves, etc., are in this scene. As "all who are Christ's" have been raised at His coming (1 Cor. xv. 22, 23; 1 Thess. iv. 14-18); and as the tribulation saints are (xx. 4) expressly included in the first resurrection, it follows that only the impenitent dead are in the great white throne judgment. The "book of life" is there, for "Many will say to me in that day, Lord, Lord, have we not prophesied in thy name? and in thy name have cast out devils? and in thy name done many wonderful works? Then, will I profess unto them, I never knew you: depart from me, ye that work iniquity." Matt. vii. 22, 23.

"Death" in verse 13 refers to the bodies of the wicked dead, as "hades" in the same verse to their souls and spirits. " Death and hades were cast into the lake of fire." That is, the contents of "death" and "hades." The "lake of fire," it will be noted, is the eternal abiding place of Satan and of the wicked. xx. 10. There are two names for this place: "the lake of fire," and "the second death." These are equivalent expressions. xxi. 8. It is not that the lake of fire produces the second death in the sense of extinction of being, or of consciousness. The beast and false prophet were cast alive into the lake of fire in xix. 20; they are still alive after one thousand years. xx. 10.

Part 7. The millennial glory of the church, and the eternal state. xxl.—xxii. The student will have noticed that the judgment of the great white throne occurs neither on the earth nor in heaven, but in space. xx. 11. At its conclusion John sees heaven and earth again, but "new." xxi. 1. During the interval the predicted purgation of the earth has occurred. 2 Pet. iii. 10-13; 'Is. li. 6. This subject is very obscure, no details being given. The statement of this fact completes, so to speak, the story of the earth. Scripture has told its history

from chaos (Gen. i. 2) to purification (Rev. xxi. 1), from creation to re-creation.

John now goes back into the millennium. xxi. 2-27. This is the uniform method of the Revelation. When, e.g., we are told in chapter vii. of salvation during the tribulation we are shown at once the tribulation saints in their eternal state. But that anticipates the history, for as a matter of fact they are still on earth, and soon to encounter the awful tyranny of the beast.

So here the prophetic foreview is completed, and then the story is resumed.

"The holy city, new Jerusalem," is the church in her millennial glory as the bride, the Lamb's wife." xxi. 2, 9, 10. John sees her descending out of heaven after her marriage. xix. 7, 8. Chronologically, it is identical with xx. 4-6. The general state of "men" (living inhabitants of earth) during the millennium is then described. xxi. 3-8. It is most blessed, but probational. Verses 6-8. Having shown this lovely picture the church in glory is described. Verses 10-23. Verses 24-27 give the relation of the church to the kingdom during the millennium. But this picture of the church in glory during the one thousand years gives, also, her eternal state. Such she is forever and ever.

Chapter xxii. 1-5 gives the general eternal state. From verse 6 to the end follows a most fitting close of this wonderful book and of our wonderful Bible. This close implies urgency. The words are "shortly," " quickly." Once more the tender appeal is made to the unsaved to "come." The church turns her eyes heavenward and sends back to Christ the same word, "Even so, come, Lord Jesus." It is the last prayer of the Bible.

Beloved student, your teacher greets you with a full heart. We have journeyed together through God's holy Word. Some precious truths are now to be gathered up, but the greater task is done. May God bless His Word to your sanctification, and make it through you a blessing to this world.

THE REVELATION

Section I

1. Into what three general divisions, or sections, does the Revelation fall?

_____

_____

_____

2. What passage gives these divisions?

_____

_____

_____

3. Of what does Section I. consist?

_____

_____

_____

4. Why do you say that the first chapter is Section I.?

_____

_____

5. Into how many parts does Section I. fall?

_____

_____

6. Is it correct to call this book " The Revelation of St. John the Divine"?

_____

_____

7. What is its inspired name?

_____

_____

8. Why did God give this revelation to Jesus Christ?

_____

_____

9. To what class of Christians is the book addressed?

_____

10. In what characters is Jesus Christ presented in Part 2, Section I.?

_____

_____

11. What aspect of the second advent is presented in verse 7?

_____

_____

12. What is meant in i. 2, 9, by "the Word of God"?

_____

_____

13. What is meant by "the testimony of Jesus Christ"?

_____

_____

14. State, in your own words, the meaning of "the seven spirits." i. 4

_____

_____

_____

15. What is meant by:
    (1) Golden candlesticks?

_____

_____

    (2) Girdle?

_____

_____

    (3) Fire?

_____

_____

    (4) Seven stars?

_____

_____

    (5) Sharp two-edged sword? Heb. iv. 12.

_____

_____

16. In what characters does Christ reveal Himself in Part 3, Section I.?

_____

_____

Section II

17. State, in your own words, why the entire Section II. is given to messages to the seven specified churches in Asia?

_____

_____

_____

_____

18. Prophetically, what period of time is covered by these messages?

_____

_____

19. Give, from memory, the reasons why you say that Section II. is prophetic.

_____

_____

_____

_____

20. What application may legitimately be made of the messages to the churches?

_____

_____

21. Of what (historically) is Ephesus a picture?

_____

_____

_____

22. What was praised in Ephesus?

_____

_____

23. What was blamed in Ephesus?

_____

_____

24. State, in your own words, the meaning of Nicolaitanism?

_____

_____

_____

_____

25. Of what (historically) is Smyrna a picture?

_____

_____

26. What period of time is covered by Smyrna?

_____

_____

27. Is verse 10 a promise of eternal life to such as are faithful until death?

_____

_____

28. Of what are crowns symbolical?

_____

_____

29. In what character does Christ reveal Himself to persecuted saints? i

_____

_____

30. Of what (historically) is Pergamos a picture?

_____

_____

31. What period of time is covered by Pergamos?

_____

_____

32. What is the moral state of Pergamos?

_____

_____

33. What symbolical language is used to denote the worldly place of the church at this period?

_____

_____

34. Where is Satan's throne?

_____

_____

_____

35. Do you know any Scripture which represents Satan as ruling in hell?

_____

_____

_____

36. What does the name Balaam signify?

_____

_____

_____

37. What is meant by the " doctrine of Balaam"?

_____

_____

38. What is the difference between the "deeds" and the "doctrine" of the Nicolaitanes?

_____

_____

_____

39. In what character does Christ come to Pergamos?

_____

_____

40. In your judgment are Balaamism and Nicolaitanism 'present day evils?

_____

_____

41. What promise is given to overcomers in such churches as Pergamos?

_____

_____

_____

42. Where does Christ appropriate manna as a type of Himself?

_____

_____

43. What, then, would "hidden manna" mean?

_____

_____

Note. The "white stone" is not, so far as I know, a biblical symbol. It is variously interpreted, but the meaning is clear: the overcomer, in the midst of worldliness and priestly assumption, will be fed through personal communion with Christ, and will know His mind and realize His promises. "The secret of the Lord is with them that fear Him."

44. Of what (historically and prophetically is Thyatira a picture?

_____

_____

45. What period of time is covered by Thyatira?

_____

_____

46. What is commended in Thyatira?

_____

_____

_____

47. In what symbolical character does Christ come to Thyatira?

_____

_____

_____

48. Who (historically) was Jezebel?

_____

_____

_____

49. Of what is Jezebel a symbol in Revelation?

_____

_____

50. What proof is here given of the presence of true believers in Thyatira?

_____

_____

_____

51. What great promises are given to the godly in Thyatira?

_____

_____

_____

52. Of what (historically) is Sardis a picture?

_____

_____

_____

53. What period of time is covered by Sardis?

_____

_____

54. Does the description iii. 1-6 apply to the beginning of the Sardis period?

_____

_____

55. What is blamed in Sardis?

_____

_____

_____

56. What especial danger is disclosed?

_____

_____

57. What aspect of our Lord's return is indicated?

_____

_____

58. Would the return of the Lord at this time surprise Sardis as a whole?

_____

_____

59. What does "Philadelphia" mean?

_____

_____

60. Does the message prefigure a period of time or a moral condition? ,

_____

_____

_____

61. Does the message prefigure an organization?

_____

_____

_____

62. In what great body of professing Christians may we expect to find Philadelphians?

_____

_____

63. Why is "Philadelphia" a good symbol for true Christians?

_____

_____

64. What three things are said in verse 8 to mark Philadelphians?

_____

_____

_____

65. What has Christ done for them?

_____

_____

_____

66. What tremendous event is referred to in iii. 10?

_____

_____

67. Will, then, true believers, whether in Thyatira (ii. 28) or Sardis (iii. 10), be in the great tribulation?

_____

_____

68. What special exhortation, in view of the Lord's return, is addressed to Philadelphians?

_____

_____

69. Is Laodicea a period of time and a distinct organization?

_____

_____

70. In what great body of professing Christians may we expect to find Laodiceans?

_____

_____

71. What is said of the temperature of Laodicea?

_____

_____

72. Can Christ use lukewarm servants?

_____

_____

_____

73. What are the outward marks of the Laodicean state?

_____

_____

_____

74. What is the real state as God sees it?

_____

_____

_____

75. What, in the midst of prevailing Laodiceanism, will be an outward sign of Christ's love?

_____

_____

_____

76. Where is Christ when Laodiceanism is the prevailing state?

_____

_____

77. What is Christ represented as doing?

_____

_____

_____

78. Should we repudiate the churches before Christ does?

_____

_____

79. What three things should we do in the midst of Laodiceanism? Rev. iii. 20; 2 Tim. ii. 20, 21.

_____

_____

_____

80. What promise is given to overcomers in Laodicea?

_____

_____

_____

81. On whose throne is Christ now?

_____

_____

82. What throne shall we share with Him?

_____

_____

83. What great event is indicated in iv. 1?

_____

_____

_____

84. What two great bodies of professing Christians go on to the end?

_____

_____

_____

85. In what two phases will Protestantism exist to the end?

_____

_____

86. What proportion of the membership of Protestant churches are known as praying, giving, working?

_____

_____

Section III

87. Into how many parts does this section fall?

_____

_____

88. Into how many parentheses?

_____

_____

89. What distinguishes a part from a parenthesis?

_____

_____

90. What great event is indicated in iv. 1?

_____

_____

_____

91. Give, in your own words, the reasons why the elders represent symbolically the church.

_____

_____

_____

92. What passages in the Old Testament help us to understand the "living creatures"?

_____

_____

_____

93. What are the "living creatures" Old Testament names?

_____

_____

94. State, in your own words, what is meant by the symbol of the seven-sealed book.

_____

_____

_____

95. Give your reasons for thus answering question 94.

_____

_____

96. In what character does Christ "prevail to open the book'?

_____

_____

97. What Old Testament passage gives light upon the action of v. 7?

_____

_____

_____

98. Give, in your own words, an account of the meaning of the first seal judgment.

_____

_____

_____

99. Give an account of the meaning of the second seal judgment.

_____

_____

_____

100. Give an account of the meaning of the third seal judgment.

_____

_____

_____

101. Give an account of the meaning of the fourth seal judgment.

_____

_____

_____

102. Give an account of the meaning of the fifth seal judgment.

_____

_____

_____

103. Give an account of the meaning of the sixth seal judgment.

_____

_____

_____

104. During what prophetic period do the events of chapter vii. occur?

_____

_____

_____

105. State the meaning of vii. 1-8.

_____

_____

_____

106. State the meaning of vii. 9-17.

_____

_____

_____

107. Are the saved of vii. 9-17 the church?

_____

108. Give reason for the last answer.

_____

_____

_____

109. Are the saved of vii. 9-17 Jews?

_____

_____

110. What proof is there that the saved are Gentiles?

_____

_____

_____

111. What proof that they are saved during the tribulation?

_____

_____

_____

112. What is the effect in heaven of the Spempe of the seventh seal?

_____

_____

113. What is the significance of altar fire?

_____

_____

114. What is the symbolic meaning of "trees"?

_____

_____

115. Give a passage to prove that.

_____

_____

116. What is the symbolic meaning of "green grass"?

_____

_____

117. What is the symbolic meaning of "great mountain"?

_____

_____

118. What is the symbolic meaning of "star"?

_____

_____

119. What occurs at the sounding of the fifth angel?

_____

_____

_____

120. Who is that "star"?

_____

_____

121. Who are the "locusts'?

_____

_____

122. Who is the "angel" of chapter x.?

_____

_____

123. What does the " little book" signify?

_____

_____

124. What "temple" is meant by xi. 1?

_____

_____

125. Why may we say that the "two witnesses" of xi, 3 are Moses and Elijah?

_____

_____

126. How long do Moses and Elijah testify?

_____

_____

127. What biblical reason have we for believing that the unconverted Jews will have a temple in Jerusalem during the tribulation?

_____

_____

_____

128. How long does the tribulation, properly so called, last?

_____

_____

_____

129. What is meant by the "woman" of xii. 1?

_____

_____

130. What is meant by the "man child'?

_____

_____

131. What historic event is meant by xii. 4?

_____

_____

132. Do xii. 9 and Luke x. 18 refer to the same event?

_____

_____

133. What was Satan allowed to do in heaven up to the time of xii. 9?

_____

_____

_____

134. Whom does Satan persecute after his final casting out?

_____

_____

135. What is the difference between the persecutions of xii. 13 and xii. 17?

_____

_____

_____

136. Define in your own words what is meant by the "beast."

_____

_____

_____

137. Who is meant by the personage of xiii. 3-8?

_____

_____

138. What other names does he bear in Scripture?

_____

_____

_____

139. How long does he endure after coming to be the head of civil power?

_____

_____

140. Into how many kingdoms will the former sphere of Roman imperial rule be divided at the end time?

_____

_____

141. What are these divisions called in Daniel?

_____

_____

_____

_____

142. What are these divisions called in Revelation?

_____

_____

_____

_____

143. What name is given to the "beast" of xiii. 10?

_____

_____

_____

144. Who are the one hundred and forty-four thousand of xiv. 1-5?

_____

_____

_____

145. If these are the "first fruits" out of Israel, where in Scripture is mention made of the church as "a kind of first fruits"?

_____

_____

_____

146. Where in Scripture is mention made of Christ as first fruits?

_____

_____

_____

147. Give in your own words the meaning of the first vision of xiv.

_____

_____

_____

_____

148. Give in your own words the meaning of the second vision.

_____

_____

149. Give in your own words the meaning of the third vision.

_____

_____

_____

150. Give in your own words the meaning of the fourth vision.

_____

_____

_____

_____

151. During what earth period will this scene occur in heaven?

_____

_____

_____

152. What distinction, on the divine side, do you find between the trumpet and the vial judgments?

_____

_____

_____

153. Explain, in your own words, the meaning of " Babylon" as used in chapters xvii. and xviii.

_____

_____

_____

154. Give the marks of papacy in chapter xvii.

_____

_____

_____

155. By what instrumentality is Babylon at last destroyed?

_____

_____

_____

_____

156. Give, in your own words, an account of the predicted transactions of chapters xix.—xx.

_____

_____

_____

_____

_____

157. Who is meant in xix. 16?

_____

_____

158. What Old Testament passages predict the scene of xix. 19-21?

_____

_____

_____

159. For how long is Satan sealed?

_____

_____

160. What occurs on earth during the one thousand years?

_____

_____

_____

_____

_____

161. Give some Old Testament passages describing this period.

_____

_____

_____

_____

_____

162. What ends the period?

_____

_____

_____

163. Where is the great white throne set?

_____

_____

164. Who are judged before the great white throne?

_____

_____

_____

165. What occurs on earth during the great white throne scene?

_____

_____

_____

166. What great symbol is given of the millennial and eternal glory of the church?

_____

_____

_____

167. Where else in the New Testament are the saved of this age said to belong to the heavenly Jerusalem?

_____

_____

_____

168. What is the last prayer of Scripture?

_____

_____

_____

169. Give, in your own words, a history of what will occur on earth from the catching away of the church to the end of human history. This should be a brief summary of the revealed order of events. In writing this, disregard the heavenly scenes. Imagine you are telling the story to an intelligent child of (say) fifteen years.

_____

_____

_____

_____

_____

_____

NUMBER IN SCRIPTURE
by E.W. Bullinger

E.W. Bullinger does it again! This wonderful expose on the beauty, order, and majesty of God's use of numbers in scripture will give you a deeper appreciation for God's word.

ISBN 1500865354

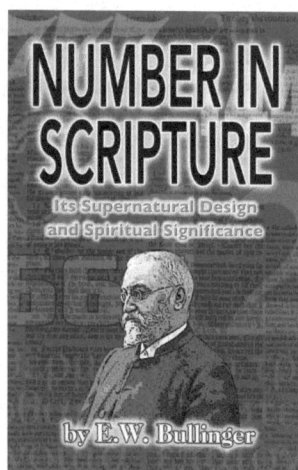

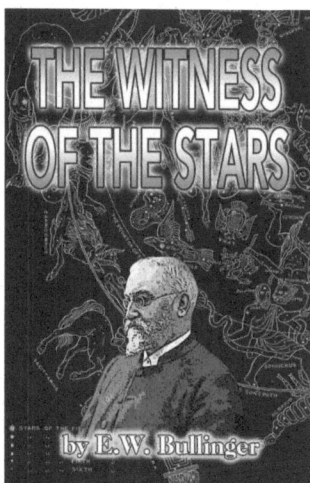

THE WITNESS OF THE STARS
by E.W. Bullinger

Long before the Mosaic law and the advent of Christ, God revealed his plan of salvation through the stars. Unfortunately, many modern Christians are unaware of this since pagan religions perverted the meaning. In this masterpiece of scholarship, E.W. Bullinger shows how the gospel is truly "written in the stars."

ISBN 1505784948

EARTH'S EARLIEST AGES
by G.H. Pember

Written in the late 19th century, G.H. Pember's *Earth's Earliest Ages* is a book that might possibly be even more relevant in the 21st century. In *Ages,* Pember presciently observes the decline of Godly fear in society that was predicted in the Bible. Pember details seven points by which Christians can discern the relentless march of prophetic events leading to the rapture of the Church, the Great Tribulation, and the return of Jesus Christ.

ISBN 1508656096

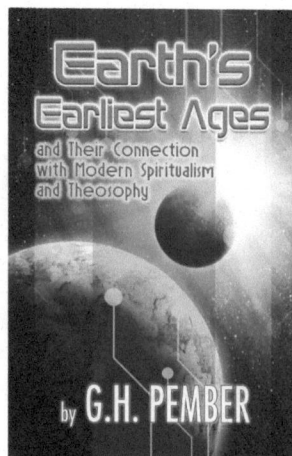

Made in United States
Troutdale, OR
03/04/2025